JOAN C. WRENN
27226 Dunbar Place, Hayward, CA 94544

PULLTROUSER SWAMP

The Texas Pan American Series

Pulltrouser Swamp

Ancient Maya Habitat, Agriculture, and Settlement in Northern Belize

Edited by B. L. TURNER II and PETER D. HARRISON

 University of Texas Press, Austin

First Edition, 1983

Requests for permission to reproduce material from this work should be sent to Permissions, University of Texas Press, Box 7819, Austin, Texas 78712.

The Texas Pan American Series is published with the assistance of a revolving publication fund established by the Pan American Sulphur Company.

Publication of this book was assisted by the National Science Foundation under grant BNS-8115720. Any opinions, findings, conclusions, or recommendations expressed in this publication are those of the editors and do not necessarily reflect the views of the National Science Foundation.

LIBRARY OF CONGRESS CATALOGING IN PUBLICATION DATA

Main entry under title:

Pulltrouser Swamp.

(Texas Pan American series)
Bibliography: p.
Includes index.
1. Mayas—Agriculture—Addresses, essays, lectures. 2. Mayas—Antiquities—Addresses, essays, lectures. 3. Pulltrouser Swamp (Belize)—Antiquities—Addresses, essays, lectures. 4. Indians of Central America—Belize—Pulltrouser Swamp—Agriculture—Addresses, essays, lectures. 5. Indians of Central America—Belize—Pulltrouser Swamp—Antiquities—Addresses, essays, lectures. 6. Land settlement patterns, Prehistoric—Belize—Pulltrouser Swamp—Addresses, essays, lectures. 7. Belize—Antiquities—Addresses, essays, lectures. I. Turner, B. L. (Billie Lee), 1945– . II. Harrison, Peter D., 1937– . III. Series.
F1435.3.A37P84   1983   972.82'6   83-5906
ISBN 0-292-75067-6

Dedicated to WILLIAM M. DENEVAN
pioneer in the study of pre-Hispanic wetland agriculture

Contents

Preface

The stimulus for this study occurred in 1973 when Peter Harrison and I independently identified ground patterns in the *bajos* Morocoy and Acatuch, Quintana Roo, as relics of Maya raised fields and canals. We subsequently learned that Alfred Siemens had photographed some of these patterns previous to 1973. The large areas covered by these patterns in the southern Quintana Roo area alone had major implications for Maya agricultural and cultural histories, and challenges concerning the proper interpretations to be given to these and other finds quickly developed. It was obvious that an interdisciplinary project was needed to solve various facets of the raised-field controversy. The Instituto Nacional de Antropología e Historia, Mexico, awarded a permit for the study. Unfortunately, by the time that funds were procured for an examination of the Quintana Roo patterns, the project was unable to meet the procedural requirements of INAH study. In addition, by 1979 much of the *bajos* Morocoy and Acatuch had been leveled as part of a large-scale agricultural project. These circumstances promoted a shift in study area to Pulltrouser Swamp, Belize.

This volume constitutes the analyses and brief interpretations of the data collected by the 1979 University of Oklahoma–National Science Foundation Pulltrouser Swamp Project. We felt that the initial Pulltrouser evidence was sufficiently significant to various issues of Maya prehistory, especially agricultural issues, to warrant more complete publication of the data beyond article summaries. In addition, during the preparation of this text we had no assurances that a second phase to the project would be funded. Fortunately, such funding was awarded by NSF through the auspices of the University of New Mexico. The results of the second phase will not be known for some time because of the large amount of data retrieved, and publication of that material is several years in the future. For these reasons, it was decided that the presentation of the first phase of the project was useful.

The 1979 Pulltrouser Swamp Project was divided into two parts. The agricultural-ecological branch was headed by myself, principal investigator and geographer. Peter Harrison, coprincipal investigator and archaeologist, headed the settlement pattern program. Despite these needed managerial and technical divisions, the principal investigators attempted to facilitate involvement of all parties of either branch with one another's work. The main effort of the 1979 season lay with the agricultural-ecological section in that the identification of the ground patterns at Pulltrouser Swamp was the principal research goal.

Because of monetary and time constraints, the coprincipal investigator was not able to be with the project from the outset of the field season. However, our move to a new and "unknown" study location necessitated an immediate search of the swamp zone for settlements. These factors placed the burden of instigating a settlement survey and limited excavation on Nancy Ettlinger and myself, without the much needed guidance of the coprincipal investigator. The catalog system (operation, suboperation, and lots) and the survey implemented are thus the responsibility of Ettlinger and myself. On arrival, Harrison began the mapping and continued the settlement survey of the Pulltrouser South zone, while Ettlinger conducted the bulk of the excavations at Kokeal. The descriptions and interpretations of these excavations are hers, although Harrison guided the placement of certain excavations and assisted in some of the stratigraphic interpretation. Obviously, the settlement section of the project would have been enhanced had Harrison been able to guide these studies from the outset, but his scheduling and the structure of the 1979 project did not allow this.

Editorially, Harrison and I have altered the original texts in order to maintain cohesiveness among cross-disciplinary works and to adhere to accepted format and terminology. However, we have not attempted to alter descriptions or interpretations and, in some instances, we do not necessarily agree with the specifics in various sections of the text. Our broader interpretations appear in the final chapter.

An interdisciplinary project of this nature owes a large measure of its success to the abilities of its specialists to communicate with one another and to share a concern for the broader issues of the project beyond their own line of study. To this end the Pulltrouser Swamp Project had an exceptional team of personnel: codirector Peter D. Harrison (Middle American Research Institute, Tulane University, and the University of New Mexico), Robert E. Fry (Purdue University), William C. Johnson (University of Kansas), Alan P. Covich (University of Oklahoma), Frederick M. Wiseman (Louisiana State University), Harry J. Shafer (Texas A&M University), Nancy Ettlinger (University of Oklahoma), Janice P. Darch (University of East Anglia, Norwich, England), Charles H. Miksicek (University of Arizona), and Alexandra C. Madeira. The project was also assisted in the field by Tanya Luhrman (Harvard University) and Charles Lincoln (Harvard University).

In addition, various laboratories and personnel assisted in several facets of the analysis, including Arturo Gómez-Pompa and the Instituto Nacional de Investigaciones sobre Recursos Bióticos (Xalapa, Mexico), B. L. Turner, C. P. Cowan, and the Plant Resources Center (University of Texas at Austin), Mary Pohl (Florida State University), V. R. Switsur of the Godwin Laboratory (Cambridge University), and Herb Haas of the Radiocarbon Laboratory (Southern Methodist University). Paul Bloom (University of Minnesota) has offered valuable criticisms of the soil work.

The project could not have progressed without the assistance of various other agencies and individuals. Norman Hammond encouraged our move to Belize, provided aerial photographs and the use of his field camp at Cuello, introduced us to various facilities and agencies in Belize, and made available the services of Charles Miksicek. John Yellen and the Anthropology Division of NSF facilitated our request to move field locations, and Elizabeth Graham Pendergast, then archaeological commissioner of Belize, and members of that office expedited the procedures to obtain permits to work in Belize. Tom Hester and Harry Shafer allowed us to utilize the University of Texas at San Antonio–Colha Project as a vehicle for lithic analysis.

The project was of such scope that the broader goals could not have been achieved without the services of various agencies and personnel who provided their services for minimal or no remuneration. Alan Covich, Frederick Wiseman, Alexandra Madeira, Tanya Luhrman, and Charles Lincoln provided field services without pay. All project staff performed laboratory analysis on their own time. Arturo Gómez-Pompa, B. L. Turner, C. P. Cowan, and Mary Pohl provided technical services without charge. In addition, the Soils Laboratory at Bedford College, University of London, and the Godwin Laboratory, Cambridge University, provided their facilities and services at reduced rates.

Foreign field projects depend on the cooperation of the host country, and the people and agencies of Belize were magnificent in this regard. Beyond those mentioned previously, Harriot Topsey, the commissioner of archaeology, and his former assistant, Mark A. Gutchen, have continued to assist the project after the completion of the 1979 field season. The Cuello brothers extended their hospitality and allowed the use of the Cuello camp after Hammond's departure. The Royal British Air Force and the Belize Sugar Industries provided aerial photographs and other services. The landowners around Pulltrouser Swamp and the workers from the village of Yo Creek assisted the project as well.

Financial support was provided by NSF, Anthropology and Geography divisions, under grant BNS 78-12537. We thank John Yellen and Patricia McWethy for their cooperative efforts to fund the project from two divisions. In addition the project was assisted by the University of Oklahoma, Office of the President, dean of the Graduate School, and Department of Geography, which provided a field vehicle, release time for the project director, and numerous secretarial and other services during and subsequent to the director's tenure there. Indeed, without the services performed by James Bohland and by the personnel of Grants and Contracts at Oklahoma, the project would have been sorely pressed. Finally, Clark University has provided various services which facilitated the preparation of project reports and this text.

During analysis of the Pulltrouser data and preparation of the text, the editors have been assisted from numerous sources. We thank Norman Hammond, Alfred Siemens, Mary Pohl, Paul Bloom, the Colha and Cuello projects' staffs, David Friedel, Vernon Scarborough, William M. Denevan, Gordon Willey, Richard Leventhal, Don Rice, and Douglas Johnson for their discussions with us.

The director owes special thanks to several people without whose assistance the 1979 project and subsequent interpretations would have been impeded. I thank Alan P. Covich and Edward S. Deevey, Jr., who taught me to be more cautious and patient. Particular appreciation is extended to Nancy Ettlinger and Janice P. Darch, who held the field camp and project together for the entire field season. At one time or another these two acted as field cooks, accountants, drivers, and counselors in addition to their research activities. Without their enormous personal efforts and their abilities to put up with the director, it is doubtful that the project could have succeeded.

Finally, I extend my deepest gratitude to codirector Peter D. Harrison, whose untiring efforts, both personally and professionally, led to the establishment of the project. He unselfishly provided his field equipment and vehicle at personal financial sacrifice.

His field efforts and guidance have been essential to the project's achievements.

Much of the manuscript was typed by the secretarial pool, Clark University, without whose assistance its production would have been difficult. Herbert Heidt and the Cartographics Laboratory, Clark University, prepared most of the preliminary figures and maps.

B. L. TURNER II
Worcester, Massachusetts

PULLTROUSER SWAMP

1. Wetlands and the Maya: An Overview of the Problem and the Pulltrouser Swamp Project

B. L. TURNER II and PETER D. HARRISON

THE PROBLEM

The agricultural base that supported the pre-Hispanic Maya civilization of the Yucatán peninsular region has become a major topic of interdisciplinary research during the past half decade (Harrison and Turner 1978). This interest has been sparked by recent research and discoveries indicating that the lowland Maya were not limited, for whatever reason, to slash-and-burn technologies of cultivation but employed a variety of agricultural techniques indicative of high input and output cultivation, such as terraces (Turner 1974a, 1979; Healy, van Waarden, and Anderson 1980), raised fields (Siemens and Puleston 1972; Belisle, Musa, and Shoman 1977; Puleston 1977a), and, possibly, irrigation (Matheny 1976). The evidence of raised fields was especially controversial because of its nature and because this form of hydraulic technology has been used as a major explanatory element of state growth elsewhere in Mesoamerica.

Raised fields are cultivation mediums created by the transfer and elevation of earth above the natural terrain (Denevan and Turner 1974). They are found in a variety of surficial forms and provide numerous functions which are largely a reflection of environmental conditions and cultivars. Thick soils may be pulverized and shaped into curvilinear or linear cambered beds to provide aeration or temperature controls for crops. Monolevel platforms or islands, in association with canals, may be created in shallow lakes, swamps, or marshes to provide a noninundated cropping surface and to stabilize the local surface hydrology. Generally, field raising is recognized as involving high labor inputs to initiate and is associated with intensive cultivation.

The chinampas of the Basin of Mexico are monolevel platform varieties of raised fields. Although the fields are mostly destroyed, vestiges of this ancient system of cultivation have continued in

production since pre-Hispanic times (Armillas 1971; Palerm 1973).
High yields have been sustained by the use of numerous cropping
procedures which include transplanting, weeding, and applying canal muck on the fields. This hydraulic agricultural system was so
important to the indigenous population of the basin that its development has been postulated as one of several agents in the formation of the early states located there (Price 1977; Sanders, Parsons,
and Stanley 1979). Furthermore, the heretofore absence of evidence
in the Maya lowlands of intensive systems of cultivation involving
a hydraulic element has been used to explain the apparent non-
development of "true" state levels of sociopolitical organization in
that tropical realm. Given this explanatory emphasis, the recent
evidence of ancient Maya raised fields in the lowlands has been the
subject of critical and cautionary responses.

Critique of the Maya raised-field data has involved the identification, distribution, and function of the features. Vestiges of raised
fields were first discovered in the Maya lowlands by Alfred Siemens in the Río Candelaria Basin of southeastern Campeche. Examination of these features confirmed his aerial identification of
about 150 to 200 hectares of fields in that riverine habitat (Siemens
and Puleston 1972). Subsequent reconnaissance by Siemens identified a larger area of relic fields in both riverine and depression
(bajo) habitats in northern Belize and southern Quintana Roo.
While Siemens (1982) projected the existence of nearly 3,200 hectares of fields in northern Belize alone, based on aerial observation
and photography, actual ground examination conducted with Dennis Puleston focused on fields in the riverine habitats in the area of
Albion Island on the Hondo River (Puleston 1977a, 1978). Other
researchers reported contiguous ground-vegetation patterns indicative of raised fields in about 246,000 hectares of depressions in
southern Quintana Roo (Harrison 1977, 1978). This figure was in
error; the correct figure is 24,600 hectares between Nicolás Bravo
and Ucum, Quintana Roo.[1] However, considering the larger area of
ground patterns in the depressions of southern Quintana Roo, we
conservatively estimate that the patterns may encompass over
40,000 hectares. Most of these features have been identified solely
by aerial reconnaissance and photography. An estimate of ground
patterns in limited contiguous sectors of northern Belize and southern Quintana Roo is about 43,000 hectares.

The area of depressions in which the presence of relic raised
fields has been projected was sufficiently large to seriously challenge the assumed dichotomies between lowland and highland
cropping systems, but verification of the lowland fields was lack-

ing. Puleston (1977a, 1978) apparently equivocated on the issue of the existence of the depression fields, ultimately arguing that Maya raised fields were limited to narrow strips of inundated lands along rivers and that the depression patterns, particularly those in the large Belize–Quintana Roo zone, were gilgai or other natural features. Gilgai are elevated surfaces, usually ridges, created by the shrinking and swelling of montmorillonite clays in a seasonally wet-dry hydrological regime (Edelman and Brinkman 1962) (chap. 2). Desiccated, the clays shrink and crack to depths of at least 50 centimeters. These cracks fill with surface debris and soil so that, when inundated, the clays swell, creating surface puffs which can be regular in formation and confused for artificial features. Many of the depression habitats in the Maya area appear to approximate the circumstances that produce gilgai elsewhere in that a seasonal precipitation regime produces inundated and desiccated conditions on montmorillonite clays. Interestingly, however, no ground patterns indicative of major gilgai activity are found in the shortgrass savanna depressions which are thought to provide the most suitable conditions for it.

The proposal that Maya raised-field technology was limited to riverine situations also has functional implications. It has been assumed that lowland raised fields were basically utilized to drain the excessive water that occurs during the rainy season, although it is possible that the same canals could have been used to provide water to the fields during the dry season. In contrast, many of the projected depression fields are found in habitats that approximate, or once approximated, shallow inundated basins with surface water characteristics not unlike those associated with the raised fields in the Basin of Mexico (Sanders, Parsons, and Stanley 1979). In such circumstances, the existence of raised fields implies control of water levels so that drainage and irrigation are facilitated. Verification of such a system of agriculture in the depression habitats of the Maya lowlands, especially in the Belize–Quintana Roo zone, would indicate the existence of a large, intensive agricultural system comparable in hydraulic technology with those systems in the Basin of Mexico and elsewhere in Mesoamerica.

Subsequent studies have expanded the proposed distribution of raised fields in the central Maya lowlands and have questioned various interpretations of the early work on the topic (Adams 1980). These studies and issues are discussed throughout the text, particularly in chapter 13.

THE PROJECT
Location.   The original project proposed to address the raised-field
controversy through an examination of the ground-vegetation patterns that had been identified in the *bajos* of southern Quintana
Roo by Siemens (1978), Turner (1974b), and Harrison (1977). This
location was selected because the projected field system was larger
than fields studied elsewhere in the Maya area, the system was
located in a depression as opposed to a riverine zone, Harrison
(1981) had surveyed the area for settlements, and Turner (1974a)
had examined upland agriculture in the area. The Instituto Nacional
de Antropología e Historia, Mexico, awarded a permit for the study,
but the project was unable to meet the other requirements associated
with the permit.[2]

The project requested permission from the Anthropology
Division, NSF, to shift the study location south across the border
into the depression environment of northern Belize. This change
was stimulated by Norman Hammond, who invited the project to
move to Belize, by John Yellen, NSF, and by Elizabeth Graham
Pendergast, then archaeological commissioner of Belize, who
facilitated the move.

An examination of aerial photographs of northern Belize
(provided by Norman Hammond) was made to find a depression
habitat that approximated the conditions that existed in the depressions of southern Quintana Roo and contained the ground
patterns. Pulltrouser Swamp, a multihabitat depression located
about 40 kilometers southeast of the original Quintana Roo study
location, met the criteria: a *bajo*-type forest and grasslands, a
nearby river, and various well-defined ground patterns. Aerial and
ground reconnaissance confirmed the observations made from
the photographs and the early reports of Siemens (1978). Also,
Pulltrouser Swamp was accessible by land.

Major Goals.   The 1979 Pulltrouser Swamp Project was a pilot study
designed principally to determine the nature and origins of the
ground patterns found there. Other important objectives involved
establishing the rudiments of the past and present characteristics
of the local environments, particularly the suitability of the various
habitats to form gilgai or other natural ground patterns, and of the
Maya settlements adjacent to the depression, especially with regard
to chronology.

Field Season.   Fieldwork commenced during the dry season in late
January and continued into early June of 1979. Initially, the northern
Belize area was examined by aerial reconnaissance to confirm our
assessments made from aerial photographs that Pulltrouser Swamp

was the most accessible depression which met our criteria. Such confirmation was followed by ground reconnaissance of the periphery of the depression for access points to the zone of ground patterns and for adjacent settlements. A surface survey grid was established along the southwest section of Pulltrouser South between the depression and the northern highway, and a preliminary survey of habitation sites was initiated.

Excavations of small habitation structures and the mounds producing the ground patterns, as well as soil-vegetation study, began in February. Settlement studies were expanded and mapping began in March. Samples from all excavations were floated for plant and gastropod remains throughout the study. Ceramic analysis began in May and was completed largely in the field. At the same time ecological studies, including those dealing with pollen and mollusks, and geomorphological studies were expanded. Fieldwork ceased in June.

Most ecological materials and lithics were forwarded to various personnel and laboratories for analysis: lithics to the University of Texas at San Antonio and Texas A&M University, gastropods to the University of Oklahoma, soils to Bedford College, University of London, pollen samples to Louisiana State University, plant remains to the University of Arizona, modern flora to the Instituto Nacional de Investigaciones sobre Recursos Bióticos, Xalapa, Mexico, and the University of Texas at Austin, fauna remains to Florida State University, and radiocarbon samples to Cambridge University and Southern Methodist University.

ORGANIZATION OF THE TEXT

The various sections of an interdisciplinary report of this kind are highly interdependent. To alleviate excessive repetition, each chapter refers minimally to the details provided in others and the reader is advised to consult the appropriate sections. The text is organized into two basic parts: environmental and ground pattern studies and settlement studies. However, each part contains material directly related to the other. For example, the analysis of gastropods taken from all excavations is reported in chapter 8, ceramic analysis in chapter 11, and so forth.

The environmental and ground pattern section, chapters 2 through 8, presents an overview of the climate and geomorphology of the study area, the vegetation patterns at Pulltrouser Swamp, the excavations of the mounds (fields and canals), and the analysis of the soils, plant remains, pollens and phytoliths, and gastropods taken from the swamp, mounds, and settlement structures. The

settlement section, chapters 9 through 12, presents an overview of
known Maya settlements near Pulltrouser and a map of the site of
Kokeal, discussion of the excavations of that site, and reports on
the ceramics and lithics retrieved from each segment of the project.
Chapter 13 provides a summary and some broader interpretations
of the finds of the project with regard to various key issues concerning Maya prehistory (also see Turner and Harrison 1981).

Several abbreviations are utilized throughout the text to reduce length and repetitiveness. These abbreviations are usually
self-explanatory in the text. Three forms of notation require clarification, however.

1. Pulltrouser Swamp has three arms (chap. 2) which are designated as Pulltrouser South, East, and West and which are noted in
the text as PS, PE, and PW, respectively.

2. Three sites were selected for major excavation of raised fields:
Raised-Field site 1 (Op. III-1, 3, 4), Raised-Field site 2 (Op. III-2),
and Raised-Field site 3 (Op. IV). These sites are referred to in the
text as RF site 1, RF site 2, and RF site 3.

3. To expedite various tables and certain discussions, project
catalog numbers are used. The catalog system for the 1979 project
differed from those utilized in other archaeological contexts because of the attempt to devise a system applicable for all segments
of the project. Operation numbers (roman numerals) were used to
designate the subject of study: Op. I—the initial surface survey and
sherd collection of the settlement study; Op. II—the excavations at
southern Kokeal; Op. III—raised-field excavations along PS; Op.
IV—raised-field excavations along PE; and Op. V—selected settlement work as guides for future study in the area, including northern Kokeal.

Suboperations refer to the particular feature(s) under study, for
example, to a specific structure, house mound or monument, or a
raised-channelized field. Suboperations at Kokeal relate to numbered (arabic numerals) structures on the site map, while those for
the fields relate to a specific field or to small sets of fields as indicated on the site maps. Lot numbers were sequential and were
never repeated throughout the study area.

Finally, radiocarbon dates are reported by the recent convention of corrected and uncorrected notations. Dates which have
been tree ring–corrected are designated by small capital letters
(B.C., A.D., B.P.). Dates which have not been corrected are reported
in lowercase letters (b.c., a.d., b.p.). In most instances the correction does not change the uncorrected date much (e.g., table 10-1).
The ceramic chronology utilized here follows that developed by

Hammond and his associates (1977, 1979); it is based on their work at Cuello and employs corrected radiocarbon dates. Use of uncorrected dates throughout this study is not inconsistent with the use of the ceramic chronology because of the small correction factor involved.

NOTES

1. The error was found by William M. Denevan (1982) during the preparation of a manuscript on aboriginal agriculture in the New World. The calculation error had occurred in two volumes (Harrison 1977, 1978) and had escaped detection by various people until that time.

2. Stephen Gliessman and B. L. Turner II were able to observe the features reported as raised fields at Bajo Morocoy in 1980, when they and students of the Colegio Superior de Agricultura Tropical, H. Cárdenas, Tabasco, Mexico, studied the ongoing rice development project at that *bajo*. The finds are briefly discussed in chapter 13; reports are forthcoming.

2. The Physical Setting: Northern Belize and Pulltrouser Swamp

WILLIAM C. JOHNSON

THE GEOGRAPHICAL SETTING

Pulltrouser Swamp is a large, Y-shaped depression situated north of Orange Walk, Belize, between the northern highway and the New River (fig. 2-1). It is bounded by 18°07' and 18°12' north latitude and by 88°32' and 88°34' west longitude. The swamp complex is part of a chain of elongated depressions located between the New and the Hondo rivers. These depressions are elements of the *bajo* (Siemens 1978) complex of the eastern periphery of the Yucatán peninsular region, which skirts the central or interior uplands from south of the New River Lagoon, south of Orange Walk, to south central Quintana Roo, Mexico.

Pulltrouser Swamp is composed of three individual depressions, collectively covering an area of approximately 8.5 square kilometers. The three major segments are Pulltrouser South (3.6 square kilometers), Pulltrouser East (2.9 square kilometers), and Pulltrouser West (2 square kilometers). The extreme southern end of PS lies within 200 meters of the New River. However, the axis of the river course in relation to the axis of the depression is such that the extreme northern ends of PE and PW are located approximately 3 kilometers and 3.5 kilometers, respectively, from the nearest segments of the river.

Climate. Studies dealing exclusively with the climate of Belize are limited. The first significant climatic summary was published in the *Atlas of British Honduras*, assembled by the British Honduras Land and Survey Department (1939) and containing mean monthly and annual rainfall maps. The Directorate of Overseas Surveys (1958) produced rainfall maps two decades later. However, the most recent and complete climatic summary of Belize has been produced by Walker (1973). In recent years limited climatic data for

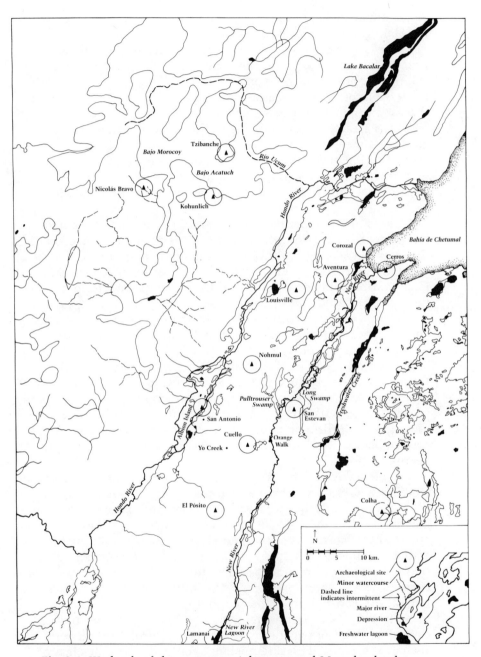

Fig. 2-1. Wetlands of the eastern periphery, central Maya lowlands.
Adapted from *Science* 213 (1981): 400, copyright © 1981 by the American
Association for the Advancement of Science.

Belize are available in the *World Weather Records,* published by
the U.S. Commerce Department.

The climate of northern Belize is a function primarily of its
tropical latitude, the prevailing winds, the adjacent ocean mass,
and the variations in land surface elevation. According to the Köp-
pen system of climatic classification, all of Belize is an *A* climate,
that is, a tropical climate, since the average temperature of every
month is greater than 18 degrees C. Further, the annual rainfall is
greater than 1,000 millimeters, which is sufficient to maintain forest vegetation and exceeds annual evaporation. Northern Belize
is an *Amw* climate; total annual rainfall is between 1,300 and 2,000
millimeters, and a pronounced dry season occurs from November
to April.

The climate of the Pulltrouser Swamp study area is characterized by the data from the stations at the town of Orange Walk,
the Orange Walk Agriculture Department Field Station, the Freshwater Creek Forest Reserve, the Yo Creek Agriculture Department
Field Station, and San Estevan. All five stations are within 15 kilometers of the study area (table 2-1).

The record from the Orange Walk station is of most use in a
consideration of local historical rainfall patterns pertinent to Pulltrouser, because it provides the longest time frame. The histogram
of mean monthly rainfall at Orange Walk (fig. 2-2) exhibits the
well-defined wet and dry seasons of the region, in addition to the
subtle bimodal distribution of the wet season rainfall. Average rainfall at Orange Walk ranges from a minimum of 31 millimeters in
March to 231 millimeters in June, the wettest month; a similar
pattern persists, with minor variations, in the records of the other
nearby stations.

Appreciable variability in rainfall is evident at stations near the
study area (table 2-2). There is minimal temporal overlap among
the station records, but where it does occur the stations are generally in phase (fig. 2-3). The level of year-to-year variations in total
rainfall has changed from one period to another, as indicated by the
statistics (table 2-2). Rainfall at Orange Walk has a standard devia-
tion of 502.45 millimeters, based on forty-eight years of nearly continuous data. A range of nearly 1,005 millimeters in the annual
rainfall totals over only 68 percent of the years of record and a
mean of only 1,531.41 millimeters indicate a high degree of variation in rainfall from year to year, especially during certain periods
such as the 1930s. This circumstance contrasts with the classic
notion of rainfall constancy in the tropical lowlands. The fact that
such variation in rainfall exists today suggests that during the ten-

Table 2-1. Mean Rainfall of the Pulltrouser Swamp Area (in Millimeters)

Station	J	F	M	A	M	J	J	A	S	O	N	D	Annual
Orange Walk													
Period of record: 1906, 1910–12, 1917–60 (48 years)	86	46	31	38	126	185	231	174	222	192	93	90	1,514
Orange Walk Agriculture Department Field Station													
Period of record: 1943–48, 1956–65 (16 years)	67	54	24	27	77	208	190	151	222	157	92	81	1,350
Freshwater Creek Forest Reserve													
Period of record: 1935–61 (27 years)	116	68	36	41	175	282	263	199	319	223	150	121	1,993
Yo Creek Agriculture Department Field Station													
Period of record: 1965–70 (6 years)	75	45	11	45	134	234	161	145	269	184	73	91	1,467
San Estevan													
Period of record: 1949–54 (6 years)	90	33	27	39	139	199	182	168	296	311	101	109	1,694

Source: Walker 1973.

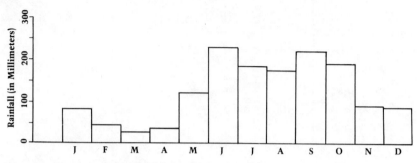

Fig. 2-2. Mean monthly rainfall at Orange Walk.

ure of the pre-Hispanic Maya the Pulltrouser Swamp area may have experienced a similar level of year-to-year and decade-to-decade variation in rainfall.

Air temperatures in the area show little annual variation in accordance with temperature data from other areas of Belize. However, temperature data available for the Orange Walk area are sparse, limited to the nearby station at Yo Creek (table 2-3). The average maximum monthly and average minimum monthly temperatures vary only by 4.5 and 9.1 degrees C., respectively.

Geology.   The geology of northern Belize has been mapped by several researchers, including Sapper (1899), Ower (1927, 1928, 1929), Flores (1952), Dixon (1956), Wright and colleagues (1959), and Buterlin and Bonet (1963). Others, however, have considered the geology of northern Belize in broader contexts (Waddell 1938; Murray and Weidie 1965; West 1964; Furley 1968; Furley and Crosbie 1974). Northern Belize is underlain by Tertiary and Cretaceous carbonates (primarily limestone), with a discontinuous or localized mantle of Quaternary river alluvium (fig. 2-4). Specifically, Flores (1952) mapped Upper Cretaceous, Paleocene–Lower Eocene, Middle Eocene, and Miocene-Pleistocene strata, in addition to Quaternary alluvium. Earlier, Ower (1928) had reported Oligocene deposits in the region as well. Using paleontological evidence, Flores (1952) refutes Ower's report of beds of Oligocene age.

The Cenozoic geologic history of the Yucatán area, which includes Belize, has been dominated by the deposition of marine beds (limestones), by the subsequent emergence of the peninsula in the Oligocene-Miocene epoch (Flores 1952), by further emergence and tilting in a westward and northwestward direction during the Pleistocene (West 1964), and by postemergence erosion.

Table 2-2. Mean Rainfall Statistics of the Pulltrouser Swamp Area

Station	Years	Sum	Maximum Recorded Value (Mm.)	Minimum Recorded Value (Mm.)	Annual Mean	Standard Deviation	Variance
Orange Walk	43	64,319	3,583	840	1,531.41	502.45	252,281.19
Orange Walk Agriculture Department Field Station	12	16,358	1,853	811	1,363.17	291.00	77,622.14
Freshwater Creek Forest Reserve	20	41,404	3,202	1,032	2,070.20	498.27	235,855.26
Yo Creek Agriculture Department Field Station	6	8,742	1,760	987	1,457.00	294.18	72,118.33
San Estevan	5	9,317	2,754	1,323	1,863.40	570.05	259,965.04

Source: Walker 1973.
Note: Years with one or more months of missing data are not utilized.

Table 2-3. Air Temperature at Yo Creek, 1965–1970 (in Degrees Centigrade)

Temperature	J	F	M	A	M	J	J	A	S	O	N	D	Annual Range	Annual Mean
Highest maximum	32.8	36.7	37.2	36.7	37.2	36.1	35.0	36.7	37.2	35.0	33.3	35.0		
Average maximum	28.6	29.7	31.4	32.8	33.1	30.9	31.8	31.7	31.8	30.9	29.9	28.6	4.5	31.1
Average minimum	13.6	18.3	18.9	20.6	22.7	21.0	19.7	19.3	20.0	18.8	12.8	15.6	9.1	18.1
Lowest minimum	10.6	10.6	14.4	7.8	17.2	12.8	13.3	10.0	10.0	10.0	4.4	11.1		

Source: Walker 1973.

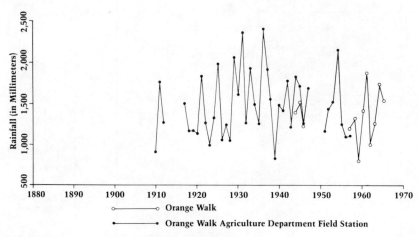

Note: Years with missing data are not plotted.

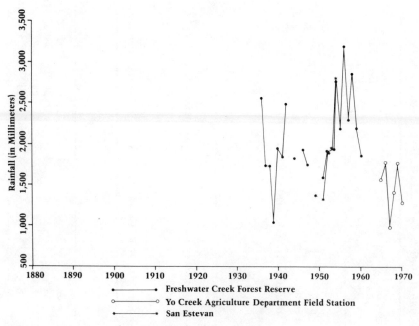

Fig. 2-3. Rainfall of the Pulltrouser Swamp area.

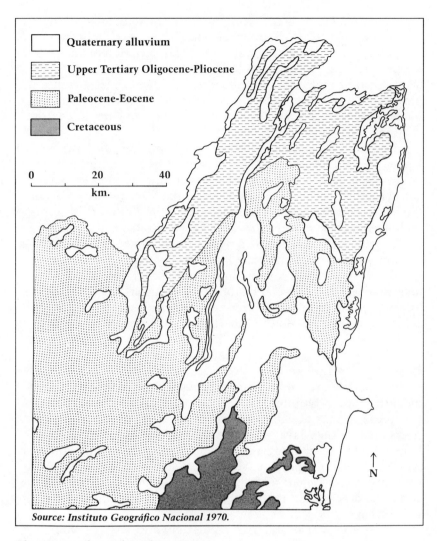

Quaternary alluvium

Upper Tertiary Oligocene-Pliocene

Paleocene-Eocene

Cretaceous

0   20   40
             km.

N

Source: Instituto Geográfico Nacional 1970.

Fig. 2-4. Geology of northern Belize.

Northern Belize is no exception from the remainder of the Yucatán in that it has experienced and is experiencing limestone solution, that is, the creation of karst. The initiation of karst likely began in the Late Miocene as broad-scale emergence first occurred (MacDonald 1979). Karst development is, however, less intense in northern Belize than in other areas of the peninsula. Recently, Siemens (1978) has discussed the various features of karst in context with the prehistoric Maya.

Bedrock geology of the Pulltrouser Swamp area is comprised of Upper Tertiary Oligocene-Pliocene strata (fig. 2-4; Buterlin and Bonet 1963). It should be noted, however, that if Flores (1952) is correct in his interpretations the age of the beds may be Miocene-Pliocene. The bedrock has been referred to by a number of terms, including sascab, sahcab, and marl. The last term is the primary one utilized by geologists who have worked in northern Belize, for example, Cayo marls and New River chalky marls (Ower 1927, 1928). Confusion over terminology and the character of the bedrock may be due to several factors, including variation in the composition of the limestone, differing weathering processes, varying degrees of drainage, and the experience of the field investigator (Darch 1981).

The white to yellow soft, chalky limestone common to the Pulltrouser Swamp area is called sascab (chap. 5). It has reportedly been a major source of building material for the pre-Hispanic and modern Maya in Quintana Roo (Folan 1978). A survey of the literature presents four possible origins of sascab: (1) silt deposited by rivers eroding the Maya Mountains, (2) sediments eroded from the Maya Mountains creating a coastal fan that subsequently emerged, (3) shallow water deposition along the coast, and (4) deeply weathered limestone. Recent research in the field and laboratory has suggested no other origin than that of deep weathering of the limestone (Darch 1981).

The terms sascab and marl are used in a variety of contexts. Although an old term possessing a considerable range of uses, marl technically refers to freshwater calcareous clay. We are not certain at this time if materials at Pulltrouser are freshwater or marine. To avoid implications, all unconsolidated limestone material is herein termed sascab until further work can produce a more accurate term or classification.

Regional fault systems which trend northeast-southwest have influenced the study area so that a series of scarps and intervening swampy swales has evolved. The Hondo and New rivers, which flow north past Pulltrouser Swamp to the west and east, respectively, are flowing in fault-guided valleys. Albion Island, an elevated landmass bounded by the main channel and a secondary channel of the Hondo, has likely been isolated by faulting. Although folding has not been reported in the area, an anticlinal fold was observed in a quarry on the crest of Albion Island.[1]

GEOMORPHOLOGY OF PULLTROUSER SWAMP
Regionally, Pulltrouser Swamp is located in an area of low rolling to hilly limestone terrain. At least three geomorphic surfaces have been identified: an upland surface, an intermediate bench, and the depression or *bajo* basin proper. The swamp complex is bounded on the west by a low, east-facing escarpment which extends south of the swamp into the Kokeal–Yo Tumben area. The stairsteplike features in the scarp face immediately north of Kokeal illustrate these surfaces because the intermediate surface is of limited breadth. These may be fault-related, wave-cut surfaces created during still-stands of the Pleistocene emergence, solution (bedrock) features, or lake-swamp shores of a possible ancestral Pulltrouser system. The land situated between the swamp complex and the New River is only slightly higher in elevation than the mean level of the New River.

The Pulltrouser complex seems to adhere to the criteria of low-level *bajos* in the central Maya lowlands, as described by Siemens (1978). Topographic symmetry is apparent in the depression. PW—its north end in particular—is higher than the other two arms. The explanation of this circumstance involves either the nature of solution or erosion of the limestone (sascab) or the dip of the bedrock (likely not regional but local due to faulting).

Unlike the northern Yucatán, northern Belize is characterized by surface, as well as subsurface, drainage. Surface water and groundwater are inextricably connected in the Pulltrouser depression complex. During rainfall, water either infiltrates directly into the groundwater reservoir or flows as surface runoff into the few stream channels that exist or directly into Pulltrouser Swamp. Although the former mode of water movement dominates, the role of surface channel flow must not be ignored, particularly for PW.

Net gain (storage) of groundwater occurs in the wet season (May to October), whereas net loss (depletion) occurs in the dry season (November to April). Loss is due to the nearly imperceptible draw of groundwater by the New River and by evaporation. Both sources of depletion are likely of comparable importance. Annual fluctuation in the groundwater level of the depression complex is minimized by the slow rate of flow (and low discharge) of the New

River, by the large volume of water stored in the complex, in the swamp basins proper and probably in bedrock cavities, and by the existence of upstream sources of water for the New River during the dry season.

Although these depressions are noted for their relatively stable water regime, some fluctuation in the water level of the swamp occurs. The fluctuation is small, perhaps on the order of less than 50 centimeters in PE and PS. PW, however, experiences annual variations in water level which can approximate 1.5 meters; during the course of the dry season, evaporation and flow to PS transform an area inundated by approximately 50 centimeters or more of water into a dry savanna in which the water table is situated 1 meter or more below the surface. Such fluctuation in PW is attributable to its elevation above the other segments of the swamp complex and to the relatively large slope imposed upon it by the higher surface immediately to its west.

The characteristic stability of the groundwater level is related to the usually small annual variation in the water level (less than or equal to 1 meter) of the New River (Siemens 1978; local testimony). The New River is not prone to frequent or excessive flooding because of the buffering effect created by the groundwater reservoir; the swamp and groundwater zones act as a sink for excessive rainfall, thereby attenuating the response of the river. Further, there is no evidence to date that the New River overflows its banks into PS, at least on an annual basis or for prolonged periods of time. A peculiarity of the New River is its almost imperceptible flow during a large part of the year—floating on the river is like being on a long, narrow lake rather than on a river. Low velocities are often associated with river systems dominated by groundwater flow and with the extremely low gradient that is characteristic of the river. The influence of the Bahía de Chetumal may be evidenced by the growth of mangroves, normally an indicator of brackish waters. Water chemistry will be considered in subsequent studies.

The important role of groundwater in the Pulltrouser Swamp area is a function of the karst development that has occurred, possibly since the Late Miocene (MacDonald 1979). Although not the tower karst of the Maya Mountains region, some karst has developed in the study area because the limestone bedrock readily dissolves, the groundwater flows, and fluctuations occur in the water table. Evidence of subterranean flow in the Pulltrouser Swamp area was noted in several excavations that were placed across a wide, shallow surface channel which holds water only during the wet season. The north-south channel is located several hundred meters

west and south of the southern terminus of PS (chap. 9). The excavations in the channel bed penetrated a water-filled cavity. The
cavity, situated approximately 1.5 meters below the channel bed,
was approximately 1.6 meters in depth and apparently elongated
with the axis of the surface channel. No attempt was made to trace
the cavity for great distances up- or downstream. Connection with
the surface was implied by the presence of frogs and crayfish in the
subterranean water. The subsurface channel, if in fact it is such, is
probably related to flow in and development of the surface channel.
Similar subterranean features were not encountered in excavations,
although other surface channels away from the swamp areas were
not excavated.

Recent analyses of the sediments in several of the proposed
wetland fields at Albion Island by soil scientists (Antoine, Skarie,
and Bloom 1982) have suggested that the proposed raised fields immediately adjacent to the river are a product of natural sedimentation which occurred in response to a rise in sea level beginning
circa 3500 B.P. (1500 B.C.). and ending circa 2500 B.P. (500 B.C.).
Research by High (1975) identified widespread deposition along
northern coastal Belize during the same period of time that deposition was proposed by Antoine and others at the Albion Island site.
A rise in mean sea level could possibly have had an effect on river
water levels because of low river gradients. Such an event could
affect low-lying areas adjacent to rivers where fields are located.
The chemical and physical evidence for natural deposition, rather
than for human construction, offered by the soil scientists for the
Albion Island fields appears to be a viable alternative to the raised-
field model. Antoine and colleagues do indicate, however, that the
canals may be human artifacts. The raised fields described by Puleston (1978) may in fact be equivalent to the channelized fields found
at Pulltrouser (chap. 4).

The stratigraphy described at San Antonio by Antoine and
others has not yet been found in the Pulltrouser Swamp complex.
Such a sequence of deposition may have occurred in the low-lying
areas along the New River and may have spilled over into portions
of PS. Fields located within PS nearest to the river have not been
excavated, however. Those fields examined to date are clearly of
cultural origins (chaps. 4, 5, and 13) and do not appear to be constructed in or of deposition related to the sea-level changes discussed.

On the basis of the initial geomorphic survey, there is little
reason to suspect that Pulltrouser Swamp has changed significantly
in morphology since Maya occupation of the zone. Pulltrouser has
probably been a swamplike habitat with relatively permanent water

since Maya tenure there, although there are indications that earlier conditions in the depression differed (Darch 1981) (chap. 5). Any change in the surface water that may have occurred from Maya tenure onward, other than that created by Maya use of the depression, is uncertain, as are the precise levels of waters that were once present (chap. 8). However, the postglacial rise in sea level which dwindled about 2,500 years ago (Emery 1969; Bloom 1971) suggests that the hydrological regime of the depression should have stabilized.

The soil data lend support to this interpretation. Pristine soils in the swamp complex buried during Maya construction activities are characteristic of those which develop under the present climate and hydrological regime. In addition, the character of the soil in the savanna of PW indicates that a fluctuating water table has existed there for at least several hundred years, given the limited knowledge of the rates of soil horizon development in the area. Finally, excavations into the fields have not yet yielded any sediments which might be construed as lakeshore or beach deposit. The small rise in sea level mentioned may have slightly increased the water level in the lower portions of the swamp complex. However, the sum of the geomorphic indicators does not suggest that the depression was a major, open body of water during Maya use, although this interpretation is tentative.

NOTE

1. The existence of anticlinal folding in the limestone quarry on Albion Island was noted during our fieldwork and is discussed in an unpublished report by Roy C. MacDonald to the Corozal Project.

3. Vegetation Associations at Pulltrouser Swamp

JANICE P. DARCH

Minimal attention has been given to the details of *bajo* or depression vegetation in the central Maya lowlands. Wright and colleagues (1959), Miranda (1959), and Pennington and Sarukhan (1968) treat the topic, but for the most part details have not been advanced much beyond the early works of Standley and Record (1936) and Lundell (1934, 1937, 1940). These works relate plant associations to the broad patterns of depression hydrologies and soils. However, the nuances of *bajo*-type vegetation (*akalche, aguada*, marsh, and so forth) are difficult to establish on the basis of vegetation associations alone. Here, the rudiments of the vegetation associations at Pulltrouser Swamp are described and related to the basic soil moisture zones in which they occur (for the association relationship with soil types, see chap. 5).

The data were collected principally along two transects at PS, a 67-meter transect perpendicular to the depression-mainland border extending from the interior edges of the field at RF site 1 (fig. 4-6; chap. 4) and a seventeen-meter transect across a field at that site. Identifications and collections were also made at PW and the southwest side of PE. Unfortunately, few species were found in flower or fruit during the field season, hindering identification (table 3-1). The project and I are indebted to the efforts of Arturo Gómez-Pompa and his staff at the Instituto Nacional de Investigaciones sobre Recursos Bióticos, Xalapa, Mexico, who graciously labored to identify specimens. Subsequent field identifications by C. P. Cowan and project personnel confirmed the presence of the principal species identified in the original collection.

VEGETATION ASSOCIATIONS

At least four vegetation associations occur at Pulltrouser Swamp, each associated with particular water regimes (fig. 3-1). These asso-

Table 3-1. *Species Identified at Pulltrouser Swamp*

Family	Species	Common Name
Anacardiaceae	*Metopium brownei* (Jacq.) Urban	Chechem, poisonwood
	Spondias sp.	Jocote, hog plum
Annonaceae	*Annona glabra* L.	Custard apple
Apocynaceae	*Tabernaemontana* sp.	*Cojone de caballo*
	Thevetia plumeriaefolia Benth.[a]	*Cojeton*
Araceae	*Philodendron* sp.	
Asteraceae	*Melampodium divaricatum* DC	*Flor amarilla*
	Melanthera nivea[b]	*Botoncillo*
	Neurolaena lobata (L.) R.Br.	*Mano de lagarto*
	Neurolaena triloba[b]	*Mano de lagarto*
Bombacaceae	*Ceiba* cf. *pentandra* (L.) Gaertn.	Kapok
	Hampea sp.	*Moho*
Bromeliaceae	*Aechmea* sp.	Bromeliad
	Tillandsia sp.	Ball moss
Burseraceae	*Bursera simaruba* Sarg.	Gumbo-limbo
Celastraceae	*Rhacoma* sp.	
Ceratophyllaceae	*Ceratophyllum* sp.	
Combretaceae	*Bucida buceras* L.	Bully tree, bullet tree
	Terminalia amazonica	*Nargusta*
Cyperaceae	*Cyperus* sp.	Sedge
	Rhynchospora sp.	Sedge
Euphorbiaceae	*Euphorbia heterophylla* L.[6]	Wild poinsettia
Flacourtiaceae	*Casearia* sp.	Wild sage
Gramineae	*Andropogon* sp.	Bluestem grass
	Lasiacis sp.	Bamboo muhly
	Panicum sp.	Panic grass
Leguminosae	*Acacia cornigera* (L.) Willd.	Bullthorn acacia, cockspur
	Acacia sp.	Acacia
	Bauhinia sp.	Bull hoof
	Desmodium sp.	
	Inga vera	*Bribri*, turtlebone
	Lonchocarpus latifolius HBK.	*Balche*, cabbage bark
	Pithecellobium sp.	
Malpighiaceae	*Bunchosia* sp.(?)	
Moraceae	*Chlorophora tinctoria* (L.) Guad. (?)	Mora
	Ficus sp.	Wild fig
Nymphaeaceae	*Nymphaea ampla* DC	Water lily
Palmae	*Acoelorraphe* sp.	Palmetto
	Bactris sp.	Poknoby, javacte palm
	Chamaedorea sp.	Bamboo palm
	Crysophila argentea Bartl.	Escoba palm, give-and-take palm
	Roystonea sp.	Royal palm
	Sabal sp.	Botan palm
Passifloraceae	*Passiflora* sp.	Passion fruit
Polygonaceae	*Coccoloba* sp.	Bobwood, wild grape

Table 3-1, *cont'd.*

Family	Species	Common Name
Rhizophoraceae	*Rhizophora mangle* L.	Red mangrove
Rubiaceae	*Hamelia* cf. *patens* Jacq.[b]	Redhead, *corallilo*
Salviniaceae	*Salvinia* sp.	
Sapotaceae	*Chrysophyllum mexicanum*	Star apple, caimito
	Manilkara zapota	Sapote, sapodilla
Solanaceae	*Solanum* sp.	Nightshade
Sterculiaceae	*Guazuma ulmifolia* Lam.	Wild bay cedar
Theophrastaceae	*Jacquinia* sp.	Knock-me-back, tkansik
Typhaceae	*Typha dominguensis* Pers.	Cattail
Verbenaceae	*Lantana* sp.	Lantana
Vittariaceae	*Vittaria* sp.	

Note: Voucher specimens are on file at the Plant Resources Center, University of Texas at Austin, and the Instituto Nacional de Investigaciones sobre Recursos Bióticos, Xalapa. Common names are provided by Charles Miksicek and Frederick Wiseman.

[a]*T. plumeriaefolia* has not been reported previously in northern Belize. *T. ahouai* (L.) DC is the common species for the area.

[b]Successional herb identified along the forest-sugarcane border one year after the excavation of RF site 1.

ciations include the botan forest, escoba forest, saw grass community, and grass savanna. The existence of these associations appears to be related to the spatial variability of local fluctuations of water. In this regard, Pulltrouser Swamp provides several of the biotypes that characterize other depressions in the northern Belize–southern Quintana Roo region.

The surveyed sections of PE and PS display a common pattern of vegetation associations. Both arms contain a saw grass association in the central and wetter part of the depression. The saw grass zone is surrounded by a forest zone where well-defined ground patterns are visible, although well-defined fields with palmettos or small palms (in this case *Acoelorraphe* species) commonly extend into the saw grass zone. The forest appears to be that designated by Standley and Record (1936) and Lundell (1937) as Intermediate Forest Canopy of the Sabal–Give and Take association. Examinations at PS indicate that the forest can be divided into a wetter escoba association and a drier botan association. The escobal occurs adjacent to the saw grass association and is dominated by the palm

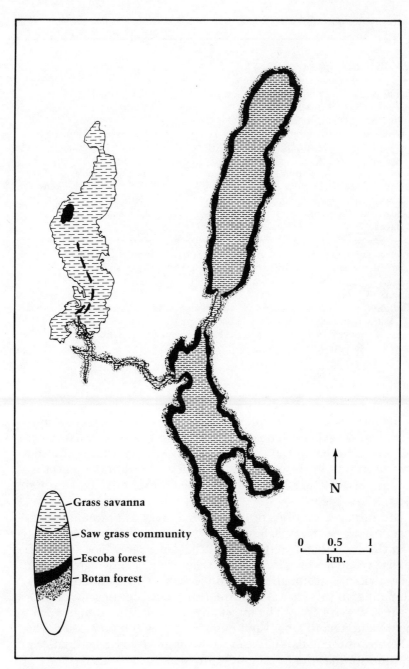

Fig. 3-1. Pattern of vegetation associations at Pulltrouser Swamp.

Crysophila argentea Bartl.; the botanal is adjacent to the mainland and is dominated by a species of palm belonging to the genus *Sabal*. Both forest types occur only on the relic surfaces of the fields and on unaltered segments of the mainland border. Previous to the establishment of sugarcane fields near the swamp, the botan forest may have extended further inland in association with particular soil moisture qualities. A transect across the escoba and botan forests shows that the escoba forest is associated with fields in the depression proper where soils remain at or near field capacity throughout the year. The botan forest is concentric about the escoba zone, growing on the mainland edge, and the fields cut into it where a dry season soil moisture deficit occurs. In addition, an aquatic community is found in the water-filled but silting canals between the fields.

PW is largely a grass savanna studded with small trees, although an apparent escoba or botan forest occurs on relic fields which are situated in the center of the western arm (chap. 4). Most of the western arm is marked by severe fluctuations of the water regime (chap. 2) which apparently give rise to conditions amenable to grass savanna, as may be found elsewhere in the region. It is not certain whether the savanna was initially created by burning for livestock grazing; informants stated that large segments of PW have always been a seasonally inundated savanna.

Saw Grass.   This plant community is dominated by dense stands of grasses and sedges of the tussock variety, including *Cyperus* species and *Rhynchospora* species, and the cattail *Typha dominguensis* Pers. Bluestem grass, *Andropogon* species, also occurs in drier niches. *Acoelorraphe* species occurs where drainage conditions permit, especially on the relic fields which extend into the interior of the depression (chap. 4). Near the escoba forest zone, the grasses may reach heights of approximately 2 meters. Although the saw grass community is fully exposed to the sun, dense ground cover impedes excess evapotranspiration; the soil remained saturated throughout the dry season of 1979.

Escoba Forest.   This association along the first transect is characterized by the dominance of leguminous trees and shrubs (fig. 3-2), including *Pithecellobium* species, *Lonchocarpus latifolius* HBK., *Bauhinia* species, *Inga vera*, and *Acacia cornigera* (L.) Willd., and of palms, especially *Crysophila argentea* Bartl., from which this forest type receives its name (Lundell 1937). Palms not only dominate the shrub layer but form emergents 17 meters high. Other species include *Rhacoma* species, *Bucida buceras* L., *Coccoloba* species, and *Thevetia plumeriaefolia* Benth.

Fig. 3-2. Escoba forest of field zone, Pulltrouser Swamp.

Along the second transect, 40 meters from the first transect, the following plants were observed: *Manilkara zapota* (common), *Rhacoma* species, *Pithecellobium* species, and *Bursera simaruba* Sarg. *Metopium brownei* (Jacq.) Urban (chechem) and various native figs (*Ficus* species) were also present. Epiphytic species belonging to the genus *Tillandsia* were also common.

Three distinct vegetation layers are recognized in the escoba association. An upper tree layer, reaching to 15 meters with emergents at 17 meters, consists primarily of broadleaf trees. A second layer of palms, *Acacia cornigera* (L.) Willd., and sapling broadleaf trees occurs at 8 to 10 meters. The third is a weakly developed herb layer 1 to 3 meters in height.

The trees in the escoba forest are slender, with an average diameter at breast height of 10.47 centimeters. The diameter at breast height ranges from 2.6 centimeters to 55 centimeters with a majority of the trees measured having a diameter of between 1 centimeter and 10 centimeters (fig. 3-3). The density in this assemblage is 0.243 trees per square meter, as sampled in a 300-meter-square plot.

Botan Forest.   This association has a physiognomy and structure similar to the escoba forest, and many species are common to both associations, such as *Bucida buceras* L., *Bactris* species, *Coccoloba* species, and *Lonchocarpus latifolius* HBK. *Crysophila argentea* Bartl. is absent here, but *Sabal* species, *Chrysophyllum mexica-num*, *Tabernaemontana* species, *Guazuma ulmifolia* Lam., *Neuro-laena lobata* (L.) R.Br., *Hamelia* cf. *patens* Jacq., and *Solanum* sub-species occur. In the outer 10 meters of the botan forest, adjacent to croplands, several herbs associated with clearing and cultivating have invaded, including *Desmodium* species, *Melanthera nivea*, and *Euphorbia heterophylla* L.

The botan forest has almost twice the number of trees as does the escoba forest (fig. 3-3): 0.44 trees per square meter compared with 0.243 trees per square meter. Also, the botan forest has a sub-stantially larger range of tree size than does the escoba forest as

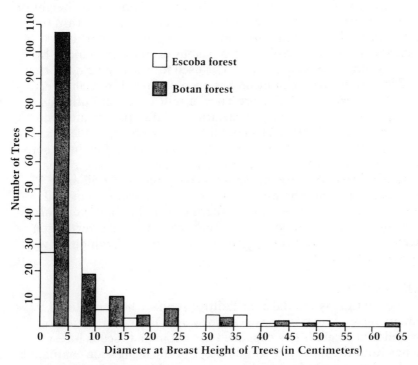

Fig. 3-3. Escoba and botan forests: diameter at breast height.

judged by the diameter at breast height, 1.59 centimeters to 60.48 centimeters, and its average diameter at breast height is smaller than that of the escoba forest, 8.05 centimeters compared with 10.47 centimeters.

The two forest associations are apparently associated with soil moisture differences between the depression proper and the marsh-land edge. The soils within the depression on which the escoba forest occurs apparently remain at or near field capacity throughout the year, as indicated by Bouyoucos Blocks (chap. 5). Similar tests on the mainland border and the fields that occur there indicated that in the dry season a moisture deficit is common. During the latter stages of the dry season, in late April and occasionally early May, the water content drops in this area, in some cases, to the permanent wilting point. These conditions are associated with the botan forest.

Grass Savanna.   The area of grass savanna is confined to PW. This association consists of an herb cover of grasses, mostly *Panicum* species and *Andropogon* species, and sedges. Scattered savanna trees, particularly *Curatella americana*, provide a savannalike physiognomy. The moisture regime is extreme, and at the height of the dry season the vegetation becomes parched. Areas within the savanna with less extreme soil moisture regimes support low, wooded communities which form islands of trees surrounded by grass savanna. The savanna of PW is used for cattle grazing during the dry season, so its condition has been disturbed in recent years.

Open-Water Habitat.   The presence of relic canals at Pulltrouser Swamp creates an additional vegetation habitat, that of the open water in canals. Many canals contain water for most of the year, although since field abandonment the canals have silted in to some extent and have been reduced in depth. Many of the larger canals contain at least 60 to 100 centimeters of water. A sample from PS indicated that approximately 70 percent of the water is covered with *Salvinia* species. At the southern edge of PE, however, *Salvinia* species is absent, and the water is free of surface vegetation except for some water lilies, *Nymphaea ampla* DC, which grow in the shallower areas.

COMMENTS

The vegetation assemblages at Pulltrouser have been modified by human activity in at least two major ways. The construction of the fields and canals has expanded the botan and escoba forest niches from the narrow, natural border of the depression-mainland to a band that extends into the depression. Presumably the forest invaded the fields on their abandonment and has helped preserve the features.

The logging of selective woody species has also modified the vegetation of the depression. Logging has been an important activity in the greater area for almost three hundred years (Benya 1979a, 1979b). Wetlands, such as Pulltrouser, have been disturbed for logwood (or tintal, *Haematoxylum campechianum*), mahogany (*Swietenia carapa*), Santa Maria (*Calophyllum brasiliense*), rosewood (*Dalbergia stevensonii*), and siricote (*Cordia dodecandra*). Remains of mahogany and siricote have been found in archaeological contexts at Kokeal and at PS (chap. 6). Informants indicated that logwood was once taken from the depression, and remains of the species were found in the excavations at Kokeal. Wright and colleagues (1959) classify the depression as suitable for sustained logging. It seems likely that past logging has removed most of the breeding population of the species in question.

Finally, Pulltrouser displays at least four of the more common vegetation associations characteristic of wetland depressions in the central Maya lowlands. If these associations largely coincide with varying hydrological conditions, which they appear to do, then the Pulltrouser evidence may be interpreted as indicating that relic fields in wetlands occur in both depression forests and forest-saw grass borders. They may not occur in grass savanna zones (chap. 13).

ACKNOWLEDGMENTS

I thank B. L. Turner, director of the Plant Resources Center, University of Texas at Austin, and C. P. Cowan for reviewing this work.

4. The Excavations of Raised and Channelized Fields at Pulltrouser Swamp

B. L. TURNER II

The wetlands—depressions and riverine zones—of northern Belize display numerous ground patterns (Siemens 1982), most of which appear as quadrilateral platforms or mounds surrounded by ditches. At least four types of patterns are prevalent: short-row, long-row, irregular, and amorphous. Short rows (fig. 4-1) tend to occur along wetland edges or in small depressions. Long rows (fig. 4-2), reminiscent of the patterns identified in southern Quintana Roo (chap. 1), cross some depressions. Irregular or sectional patterns (fig. 4-3) are associated with curvilinear wetland edges, while amorphous patterns occur in the interior of larger depressions.

This chapter presents the survey and excavation results of the mounds and ditches producing ground patterns at Pulltrouser Swamp and marshals the evidence which indicates that most of the mounds with row or sectional patterns are Maya-made agricultural features. Specific information on soils, paleoecological materials, ceramics, and so forth is presented in the various chapters that follow.

THE SURVEY

Ground patterns are ubiquitous throughout much of Pulltrouser Swamp as first reported by Siemens (1978: figs. 6 and 7) (fig. 4-4). Aerially, these patterns include the row, irregular, and amorphous types. The row and irregular varieties occur along the edges of PS and PE and the interior of PW and are marked by their well-defined angularity. These patterns, many of which underlie the peripheral escoba-botan forests, cover 3.118 square kilometers (311.8 hectares) of the Pulltrouser depression: PS, 1.542 square kilometers (154.2 hectares); PE, 1.351 square kilometers (135.1 hectares); and PW, 0.225 square kilometer (22.5 hectares). The amorphous patterns occupy portions of the marshy interior of PS and PE, contiguously covering an additional area of 3.575 square kilometers (357.5 hec-

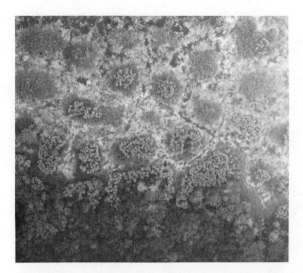

Fig. 4-1. Short-row patterns of fields at Pulltrouser South. The sides of the fields range from 10 to 30 meters in length. Photograph provided by the Royal British Air Force.

Fig. 4-2. Long-row patterns of fields at Long Swamp. Long Swamp lies about 10 kilometers east and across the New River from Pulltrouser Swamp. The sides of the fields range from 10 to 30 meters in length.

Fig. 4-3. Irregular patterns of fields at Pulltrouser East, north end. The sides of the fields range from 10 to 30 meters in length. Reprinted from *Science* 213 (1981): 401, copyright © 1981 by the American Association for the Advancement of Science.

tares): 2.039 square kilometers (203.9 hectares) in the southern arm and 1.536 square kilometers (153.6 hectares) in the eastern arm.

A ground reconnaissance initiated along the western edge of PS, the southwestern edge of PE, and a portion of the interior of PW established that mounds and ditches occurred almost continuously along the edges of the southern and eastern arms of the depression, although portions of this distribution were not readily detectable by aerial photography. Aerial reconnaissance and examination of aerial photographs also confirmed the broader distribution as described above. The band of patterns extends through the escoba-botan forests into the saw grass marsh, where the patterns are marked by stands of palmettos (chap. 3; fig. 4-5).

This distribution of the patterns within the depression is associated with the local hydrology. Those areas that seasonally desiccate in a major way, such as the exterior segments of PW, show no

signs of surficial patterns. Those areas which have rather permanent high-water levels, including the interiors of PS and PE, maintain poorly defined, amorphous patterns. The well-defined row and
sectional patterns occur in those zones where water levels fluctuate seasonally but where desiccation is not prevalent.

The reconnaissance revealed two basic surficial shapes of the
well-defined ground patterns: (1) angular but multisided and (2) quadrilateral. Both shapes occur along the depression edge, apparently
in association with the linearity of the mainland-depression border.
The multisided shape is less frequent in the depression and tends
to be associated with the curvilinear segments of the border. The
quadrilateral shape is dominant away from the depression-mainland
edge, although erosion of the mounds has apparently rounded or
smoothed various corners.

The associated ditches vary considerably in length and width.
Spaced at seemingly regular intervals on the border of the marsh
and forest are short but wide (8 to 10 meters or more) ditches that
lead into the interior of the depression. Long but narrower (about 3
to 5 meters) ditches tend to follow the mainland-depression edge,
especially where that edge is linear. Between these two ditch types
are a variety of others that create a network of waterways through
the ground patterns. Occasionally small ditches, about 1 meter in
width, cross a large ground pattern or penetrate about 10 meters
into the mainland.

The survey also revealed the presence of at least two major
ditches leading from PS to the New River. The first such ditch was
found on a reconnaissance around the south end of PS. Foot passage was blocked by a ditch 5 meters to 8 meters wide that ran
southward for about 120 meters from the depression, curved south-
westerly for nearly 50 meters, and turned southward for another 40
meters to the river. Such ditches are extremely difficult to observe
from the river, and we were able to identify the confluence of the
first ditch with the river only by marking a tall, nearby tree. The
second ditch was found on a river reconnaissance about 1 kilometer (linear distance) downstream from the first. This ditch was a bit
smaller than the first one; its length is estimated at about 100 meters. It too had a peculiar bend in its course as it approached the
river.

EXCAVATIONS

Three sites were selected for excavation of the mounds and ditches,
based on accessibility, shapes, and location. RF sites 1 and 2 were
located along the southern and central segments of the western

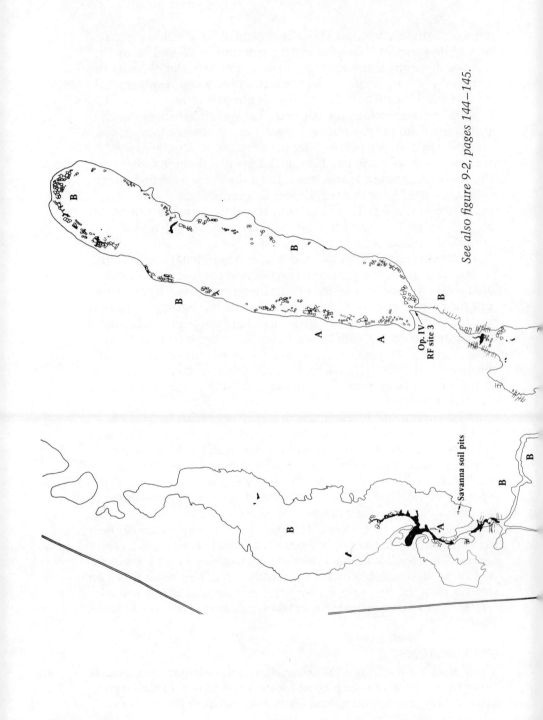

See also figure 9-2, pages 144–145.

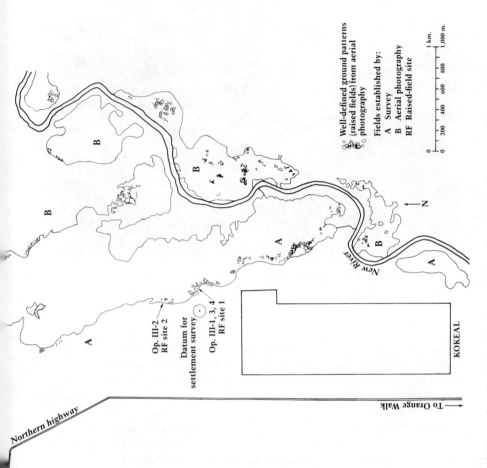

Fig. 4-4. Distribution of well-defined fields at Pulltrouser Swamp and immediate environs.

Fig. 4-5. Palmettos (*Acoelorraphe* species) on raised fields in the interior marsh zone. Palmettos occur on the higher ground of the fields.

edge of PS (fig. 4-5; table 4-1). RF site 1 excavations focused on the quadrilateral mounds in the depression proper, although one multi-sided mound was examined. This site was the subject of the most extensive study because of its proximity, immediately north of Kokeal, to the main settlement work. RF site 2 centered on a quadrilateral mound apparently located on the mainland edge of the depression. RF site 3 was located at the extreme southern edge of PE where it drains into PS (fig. 4-4; table 4-1). This site had both shapes of mounds.[1] As shall be demonstrated, the mounds and ditches are remnants of ancient fields and canals. To avoid confusion in the discussion that follows, the features will be referred to as fields and canals.

RF Site 1 (Operation III, Suboperation 1, Units 1 to 9; Suboperation 3, Units 1 to 5; and Suboperation 4, Units 1 to 4).   Suboperation 1 was comprised of a series of pits transecting two fields and a small canal that separated them (fig. 4-6). In conjunction with this transect, four of the five soil data pits were treated as excavation units (soil pit 1 was unit 6; pit 2 was unit 7; pit 4 was unit 8; and pit 5 was unit 9). Units 1 to 5 were evenly spaced from the mainland edge of field 1 to the depression-facing edge of field 2. All units

Table 4-1. Field and Canal Dimensions at RF Sites 1 to 3

Location		Type	Shape	Maximum Length (M.)	Maximum Width (M.)	Depth (M.)	Area (M.²)	Volume (M.³)
RF site 1								
Field	2	Raised	Multisided	26.5	24.6	1.0	472.2[a]	472.2
	3	Raised	Quadrilateral	28.6	24.0	1.5	538.5[b]	807.8
	4	Raised	Quadrilateral	25.6	19.0	1.5	455.6[b]	683.4
	5	Raised	Quadrilateral	12.0	8.0	1.5[a]	82.2[b]	123.3
	6	Raised	Quadrilateral	12.0	7.5	1.5[a]	83.0[b]	124.5
Canal	1	Border		16.5	1.0		16.5	
	2	Depression		21.0	7.2	1.0[c]	119.8[b]	119.8
	3	Depression		67.0	4.0	1.0[c]	261.4[b]	261.4
	4	Depression		73.0	4.5	1.0[c]	342.0[b]	342.0
	5	Depression		29.0	4.4	1.0[c]	143.8[b]	143.8
RF site 2								
Field	1	Channelized-raised	Quadrilateral	29.5	23.5	0.6[c]	693.2	415.9
Canal	1	Border		12.0	1.0	0.8	12.0	9.6
	2	Border		9.0	1.0	0.8[a]	9.0	7.2
RF site 3								
Field	1	Channelized-raised	Multisided	37.5	20.0	1.0[c]	750.0[a]	750.0
	2	Raised	Multisided	29.6[d]	17.0	0.8[c]	503.2	402.6
Canal	1	Border		19.5	4.0	0.7	78.0	54.6
	2	Depression		28.0	8.5	1.0[c]	238.0	238.0
	3	Depression		16.0	4.8	1.0[a]	76.8	76.8
	4	Depression		8.0	0.8		6.4	

Note: Complete dimensions for field 1 at RF site 1 are lacking because it extended into a plot of sugarcane, prohibiting accurate surveying and calculations of area and volume. Also, due to the merger of various canals with one another, such as at RF site 3, segments of the features were measured to produce these calculations.

[a] Estimated figure.

[b] Figure established by averaging three planimeter readings (L-40 digital). The area estimated by length-width distance may vary.

[c] Average figure for feature.

[d] Excludes panhandle portion of field.

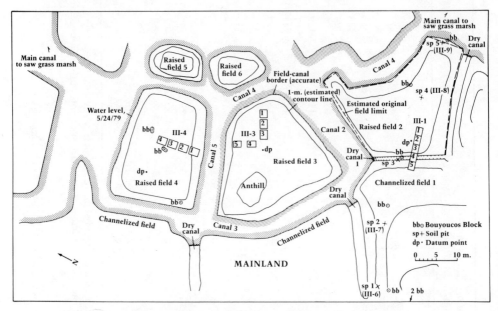

Fig. 4-6. Raised-Field site 1, operation III, suboperations 1, 3, and 4. The numbered rectangles are excavation units. Adapted from *Science* 213 (1981): 403, copyright © 1981 by the American Association for the Advancement of Science.

of this suboperation were shallow because the excavations were begun early in the dry season, when water tables were high. Time did not permit continued excavations at the end of the dry season, although subexcavation material was obtained by the use of a bucket auger. Suboperation 3 was an L-shaped transect in the northeast quadrant of field 3. Units 4 and 5 faced field 4, where the transect was continued as suboperation 4.

Field 1 is peripheral to the excavations and was not totally cleared for mapping. Field 2 is a multisided but angular-shaped feature. Its maximum dimensions are 26.5 meters by 24.6 meters (approximate area of 472.2 square meters). Field 3 is quadrilateral in shape with maximum dimensions of 28.6 meters by 24 meters (538.5 square meters, planimeter calculation). Field 4 is rectangular with dimensions of 25.6 meters by 19 meters (455.6 square meters, planimeter calculation). Fields 5 and 6, which were not excavated, have approximate areas of 82.2 and 83 square meters respectively (planimeter calculation).

Unit excavations and sampling with a bucket auger at field 1 revealed that a solum (A and B horizons) rests directly on white-gray sascab (unconsolidated limestone, C horizon) at a depth of 30 to 40 centimeters. Toward the small canal (1), the boundary between the solum and the sascab was difficult to define because of the high water table (app. 5-1, soil pits 1 to 3). Field 2 demonstrated characteristics of the depression fields elsewhere in that a thick, mottled fill was situated between the topsoil and the underlying sascab (chap. 5; fig. 5-3); sascab was found at depths ranging to 130 centimeters from the surface (see the sascab definition in chap. 2) (app. 5-1, soil pits 4 and 5).

Fields 3 and 4 provided good profiles in that the fields were well preserved. The various units on the fields proper displayed similar profiles. A humus-topsoil zone 15 to 35 centimeters thick gave way to a zone 90 to 130 centimeters thick of mottled fill. The water table was encountered at 75 to 80 centimeters below the surface; profile information below this depth was obtained by the use of a bucket auger throughout the units. At 250 to 300 centimeters below the surface a buried soil of light black to black clay, peppered with molluscan remains (shells), was found. This soil, about 40 centimeters thick, apparently was the old depression soil that had been covered by the mottled fill material. It lay immediately on top of sascab, which was found at a depth of 330 centimeters.

Bucket auger samples taken across the canals surrounding fields 3 and 4 revealed a profile different from that of the fields. At the edges of the fields the gray clay of the solum and the mottled zone dipped at sharp angles to the sascab. The canals, then, were composed of infilled materials resting directly on the sascab at depths of 75 centimeters near their edges and 125 centimeters in their centers. The canals were large, commonly exceeding 4 meters in width, shallow, U-shaped cuts into the sascab from which the original soils had been removed and replaced by erosional and depositional materials.

Plant remains (chap. 6) of interest taken from the excavations included remains from the mahogany family in unit 9, field 2 (31 centimeters), and in unit 1, field 4 (50 centimeters). The latter find, a small intact trunk and roots, was in a vertical position on the edge of the field. Radiocarbon analysis of a sample produced a date of 124 ± 53 b.p. or a.d. 1826 (table 4-2). Also identified were carbon remains of *Ficus* species in unit 4, field 1 (40 to 50 centimeters), and seeds of *Bucida buceras* in units 1 and 3, field 3 (38 and 50 centimeters), and of *Solanum* species in unit 1, field 3 (38 centimeters). Siricote (*Cordia* species) samples were found as well in units

Table 4-2. Radiocarbon Dates of Materials from Raised-Channelized Fields

RF Site	Provenience	Material	Tree Ring– Corrected Date	Uncorrected Date (Libby Half-Life)	Laboratory & Sample No.
1	50 cm. below surface, in fill material	Wood: trunk	43 ± 53 B.P. (A.D. 1907)	124 ± 53 b.p. (a.d. 1826)	SMU[a] 842
2	75 cm. below surface, on contact of fill material & sascab	Carbon		1800 ± 150 b.p. (a.d. 150 ± 150)	Cambridge[b] Q-3117
3	34 cm. below surface, on contact of solum with fill material	Carbon	417 B.P. (A.D. 1533)	365 ± 78 b.p. (a.d. 1585)	SMU 839

[a]Radiocarbon Laboratory, Southern Methodist University, by Herb Haas. The dates here have been recalculated by the laboratory and differ slightly from those initially reported (Turner and Harrison 1981).
[b]Godwin Laboratory, Cambridge University, by V. R. Switsur.

7 and 9 of field 2 and the adjacent channelized field at depths of 24 and 26 centimeters, respectively.

Ceramics were retrieved from each field excavation and from the small canal between fields 1 and 2. The ceramics were stratigraphically mixed, with most units showing Cocos Chicanel, Nuevo Tzakol, and Santana Tepeu. The dominant ceramics were Nuevo Tzakol.

RF Site 2 (Operation III, Suboperation 2, Units 1 to 4).   These excavations included three pits placed across the length of a field on the edge of the mainland and one pit on the south central side of the field where it dips into an adjacent canal (fig. 4-7). This field is rectangular with dimensions of 29.5 meters by 23.5 meters (693.2 square meters). It has no western side proper as the mainland simply dips gradually toward the depression. Its northern and southern sides are established by canals that penetrate the mainland. These canals average about 12 meters by 1 meter (12 square meters) and 9 meters by 1 meter (9 square meters). A series of probable raised fields extend east of this channelized feature (fig. 4-7).

Excavations in units 1 to 3 revealed soil profiles similar to those of the field excavation at RF site 1. Solum ranged to 40 centimeters in depth, where it merged along an irregular boundary with white-gray sascab. Apparently a perched water table occurred about 1 meter from the surface. Slightly higher levels in the units closer to the depression or canals were found. Soil samples taken in units 1 and 2 to depths of 3.65 meters below the surface of the field encountered dry sascab with numerous marine clams and large gypsum crystals (for unit 1 see app. 5-1, soil pit 6). Unit 3 displayed a sascab profile with a 40 degree dip into the canal. The canal side of this dip was infilled with material from the field above. The water table here was at 40 centimeters. Unit 4 had characteristics of fields 3 and 4 at RF site 1 (app. 5-1, soil pit 8).[2] Here the solum was interrupted at 35 centimeters by an apparent mottled zone beneath which the sascab was situated at 70 centimeters below the field surface, as measured from the southwest corner of the unit.

Several botanical materials were retrieved from relatively deep levels in the solum. These include *Solanum* species at 20 centimeters in unit 1, avocado and sapodilla at 30 to 40 centimeters and 35 centimeters, respectively, in unit 3, and a carbonized maize stem at 35 centimeters in unit 2. Radiocarbon analysis of a charcoal sample taken from unit 1 at 75 centimeters produced a date of 1800 ± 150 b.p. or a.d. 150 ± 150 (table 4-2).

Artifactual materials included an intact, highly polished oval biface pick found in the mottled fill of unit 4, 85 centimeters from

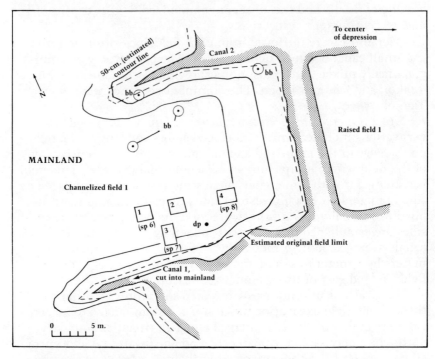

Fig. 4-7. Raised-Field site 2, operation III, suboperation 2. The numbered rectangles are excavation units.

the southwest corner of the unit and 70 centimeters from the surface (fig. 12-3j). Ceramics found above the mottled zone of this unit were definitely Nuevo Tzakol and Santana Tepeu types. Unit 2 ceramics may be Cocos Chicanel or López Mamom.

RF Site 3 (Operation IV, Suboperation 1, Units 1 to 11).   These excavations included a long transect (units 1 to 8) that began on the mainland, crossed a large but high canal and an irregularly shaped field, and ended on a quadrilaterally shaped field with a panhandle-like extension (fig. 4-8). Field 1 contained several tree falls which produced large cavities in the solum.

Field 1, amorphously shaped, is approximately 750 square meters in area with a maximum length and width of 37.5 meters and 20 meters, respectively. This field is segmented from the mainland by a shallow and elevated canal (1) that dried before the other canals at the site. The canal's dimensions are 19.5 meters by 4 meters (78 square meters). Field 2 is multisided, but with the exclusion of

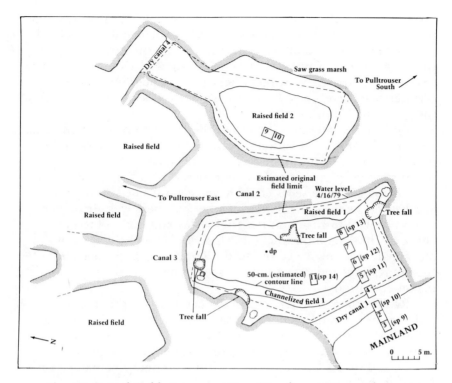

Fig. 4-8. Raised-Field site 3, operation IV, suboperation 1. The numbered rectangles are excavation units.

a panhandle-shaped extension on its north side the bulk of the field is quadrilateral. Excluding the panhandle, the field's dimensions are 29.6 meters by 17 meters (503.2 square meters). Fields 1 and 2 are separated by a large canal (2) with dimensions of 28 meters by 8.5 meters (238 square meters).

The excavations showed that the elevated canal (1) is an elongated depression with a steep mainland side. The solum rests directly on top of white-gray sascab. The canal profile differs from the mainland profile in that the solum is thicker. Interestingly, the western portion of field 1 displays a profile similar to that of the mainland up to the western edge of unit 6, where the sascab makes a sharp decline at what appears to be the natural edge of the depression. The surface of the field does not dip with the sascab. A thick, gray, mottled fill maintains the surface plane, similar to the extension of the field at RF site 2. This mottled zone extends some 6 meters onward from the sascab dip before it merges into a large, water-filled canal (2). Soil samples from the canal demonstrate that it is infilled by erosional materials from the field and by litter fall. The infilling, about 1 meter in depth, rests on the sascab. Continuation of the excavations onto field 2 showed a situation similar to that of the eastern portion of field 1. The underlying sascab was at differential levels below the surface but was separated from it by the gray mottled fill.

Biological materials taken from the excavations revealed seeds and carbon samples of various species common to depression habitats. Interestingly, uncarbonized seeds of *Bucida buceras* were found at 50 centimeters and 55 centimeters in the mottled zone of units 8 and 9. These seeds could have been intruded during the excavations as the species grew nearby, and there was virtually no way to control intrusion in the sticky clay and water of the pits. However, in several instances, fresh pick cuts into the floor of the pits apparently uncovered the seeds. Remains of gastropods from the excavations indicate a suite of species associated with swamp-marsh conditions.

Radiocarbon analysis of charcoal taken at a depth of 34 centimeters from unit 6 produced a date of a.d. 1585 or 365 ± 78 b.p. (table 4-2). Ceramics were found from depths of about 20 centimeters to 40 centimeters. Units 5 to 8 on field 1 contained Nuevo Tzakol and Cocos Chicanel types. Unit 9 on field 2 contained Cocos Chicanel types.

INTERPRETATIONS
Fields and canals creating ground patterns are ubiquitous throughout the escoba-botan forests and marsh edges of PS and PE and are less prevalent in the south central portion of PW. In only a few instances are the two features discontinuous along the edges of PS and PE. The longitudinal dimensions of the area of patterns vary from about 30 to 40 meters to 150 meters. The area of well-defined fields covers over 3 square kilometers in the three segments of the depression.

The cross-sectional profiles of the mounds and ditches revealed by excavation transects, combined with other data, indicate that (1) the features are of cultural, not natural, origins, (2) their construction is that of fields and canals, (3) two types of fields, channelized and raised, are present, and (4) the raised-field type is a monolevel platform variety (Denevan and Turner 1974).

Channelized fields occur on the edge of the natural mainland-depression border. They are usually rectangular in shape but can be multisided where the border of the depression has a nonlinear configuration. The landward sides of the fields are created by the extension of canals into the mainland, typically cut to about 200 centimeters below the natural surface of the terrain (fig. 4-9). The profile of the field created between the canals is that of the mainland, a 30-to-50-centimeter solum resting directly on white-gray sascab (chap. 5). No major elevation of the solum has taken place. As the field approaches the depression, the sascab either abruptly or gradually dips. Some channelized fields may be extended into the depression by the removal of the solum and the addition of a mottled fill over the sascab. Here the solum has been raised and, as such, channelized fields can display raised-field characteristics.

Raised fields occur in the depression, generally in a linear arrangement which extends from a channelized field, through the escoba-botan forests, into the saw grass zone. They usually are quadrilaterally shaped but can be multisided where incongruities in the depression border occur. These fields have been raised artificially in that the solum has been elevated above the natural surface of the depression and, presumably, above the water level of the de-

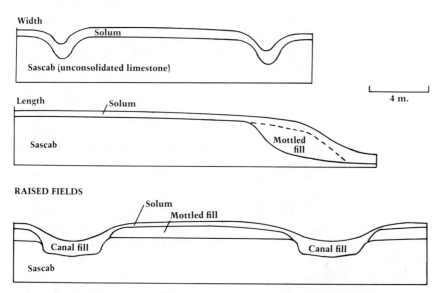

Fig. 4-9. Typical construction of field types. Adapted from *Science* 213 (1981): 404, copyright © 1981 by the American Association for the Advancement of Science.

pression (fig. 4-9). They are distinguished by a 30-to-50-centimeter solum which rests on a thick, 100-to-150-centimeter fill of mottled gray silt, clay, and sand. The fill lies on white-gray sascab and/or on a black soil above the sascab.

Raised fields are surrounded on all sides by canals or, on the extreme interior sides, by the saw grass marsh. These canals have been cut about 60 centimeters into the sascab zone and are infilled by as much as 120 centimeters of materials from the fields and from litter fall. The maximum vertical distance from the floor of the canals to the field tops seems to have exceeded 250 centimeters in some instances. The canals vary in size and, presumably, function. The wide canals leading into the interior of the depression are of such size as to suggest that they could handle canoes. The small canals running across some fields and into the mainland may have served principally as drainage and/or irrigation devices. All canals apparently provided water for raised-field cultivation.

The average size of the fields surveyed by alidade is 447.2 square meters. The six raised fields averaged 355.8 square meters, and the two channelized fields averaged 721.6 square meters. These averages may be misleading, given the sample size. For example, most raised fields appear to range from 400 to 500 square meters, but our sample included two small fields at RF site 1 that lowered the average considerably. The surveyed sites suggest that the ratio between the surface areas of fields and of canals is about 3 : 1 or that approximately 75 percent of the zone of raised fields and canals is covered by field surfaces. This figure suggests that about 2.338 square kilometers (233.8 hectares) of field surfaces cover the 3.118 square kilometers (311.8 hectares) where well-defined raised and channelized fields occur in Pulltrouser Swamp. This estimate may be slightly biased because it is based on fields and canals near the edge of the depression. Observation of aerial photographs suggests that detailed mapping of the fields nearer the interior of the depression may result in an average field surface estimate of 60 to 65 percent of the field-canal zone.

The profiles and other information from bucket augers indicate the manner in which the raised fields were constructed. In most cases much of the original depression muck was removed and the underlying sascab was exposed. Canals were excavated and a fill was dumped into the space designated for the field. Most of this fill was probably composed of materials taken from the excavation of the canals, but other materials may have been mixed with it. Finally topsoil was placed over the fill; perhaps this soil included the excavated depression soils. The discovery of the buried soil of the original depression surface in a few instances confirms that such a surface was once present. Also, in at least two cases, channelized fields were extended into the depression by the procedures described here.

The overall construction procedure and the layout of canals and fields suggest rather sophisticated planning. The linearity and complexity of the canals and the procedure of stripping the original topsoil from the depression suggest that entire segments of fields and canals were planned before construction. The labor required to construct the fields and canals at Pulltrouser is discussed elsewhere (chap. 13), but we suggest that the system took from 710 to 3,266 workyears to construct.

An alternative interpretation of the patterns is that the mottled fill is natural and that its failure to occur in canals indicates that only the canals are Maya-made features. Several lines of evidence argue against this interpretation. (1) Soil analysis indicates that the mottled zone is a product of mixing and dumping and not an *in situ* development (chap. 5).[3] (2) The find of the apparent remnants of the original depression soils in a buried context indicates that the fields were constructed over the old depression floor. (3) The artifactual distribution demonstrates that cultural disturbance generally stops a few centimeters above or below the fill material. (4) The paleoecological data found at depths in the mottled zone indicate that it was once exposed to surface cultivation or composed of surface materials during Maya occupation of the area (chaps. 6 and 7).

The biface pick found 70 centimeters into the fill extension of the field at RF site 2 is interesting. It apparently was a tool which could have been used to cut trees, hoe local soils, or excavate sascab. Its wear patterns indicate its use for soil preparation or excavation (chap. 12). Its location in the fill toward the end of a channelized field suggests that it may have been lost during the creation of the fill material or in the excavation of the adjacent canal. Regardless of the activity with which it was associated, the pick is firm proof that the fill zone of this field was penetrated to depths for some reason by the Maya and attests to the culturally disturbed state of that zone.

The possibility that the well-defined fields are natural formations is inconsistent with the evidence presented here. In addition, the soil studies at Pulltrouser (chap. 5) and at Albion Island (Antoine, Skarie, and Bloom 1982) indicate that gilgai or other such natural ground swells of the size of the fields do not form in the local habitat.

The cultigens associated with the fields remain uncertain, and few crops can be eliminated as possibilities. The strongest evidence is that for maize (*Zea mays*). Fossil pollen of maize was found in small amounts from various layers of the fields, and a carbonized maize stem was found at 35 centimeters in a channelized field at RF site 2. The maize pollen could have been introduced into the fields during their construction or during the use of maize stubble as a mulch, or it may have washed in from the mainland (chap. 7). The antiquity of the carbonized maize fragment is uncertain. Maize has been grown within 10 meters of the excavation in which the fragment was found. However, modern cultivation is done with the use of tractors, and tractors do not penetrate the channelized fields because of the deep side canals which create them. In addition, the excavation was within the escoba forest, and the local landowner could not recall planting in the immediate area of the pit. Concentrations of soluble salts in the fields would seem to inhibit maize growth at this time (Paul Bloom, personal communication), but techniques such as mulching and soil flushing could have been used to counter the problem if it existed during field use.

Possible pollens of cotton, amaranth, and a root crop were also taken from the fields. These pollens have not been positively identified as those of the domesticated species, and there is a strong possibility that the finds are associated with wild flora (chap. 7). Examination of plant remains from the fields has not provided conclusive evidence of cultigens other than maize. Most seeds were uncarbonized and were found in zones that were penetrated by roots and other disturbance phenomena, making their antiquity suspect. Tree fall cavities as well as root and burrow holes in the solum could explain the presence of some of the plant remains (chap. 6). Remains of woody species typical of the swamp forest were found in the fill, but these remains could have been introduced during field construction. Two remains, both small stumps, of a mahogany species were taken from the sides of fields, suggesting their use to anchor or stabilize the sides of the fields. However, the radiocarbon date of one of the trunks proved it to be recent (table 4-2).

In summary, the best evidence for cultigens on the fields is that for maize. Other crops cannot be discounted, but the combined evidence (chaps. 6 and 7) from the fields and the adjacent settlement of Kokeal does not lend support to the cacao or other specialty crop theses (chap. 13).

The paleoecological data also indicate a possible procedure utilized to sustain cultivation on the fields. Remnants of *Nymphaea* (water lily) were found throughout the lower solum and fill of the fields (chap. 7). These remains may have been introduced in the fill and solum during construction of the fields. But the solum provenience also suggests that the species was used as a mulch on the fields and/or that muck from the canals was periodically collected and deposited on the field surfaces (chap. 7). Both procedures, use of aquatic mulches and use of muck, are associated with raised-field cultivation elsewhere (e.g., Wilken n.d.a, n.d.b). Recent experiments in Tabasco, Mexico, by the Colegio Superior de Agricultura Tropical indicate *Nymphaea* to be a good mulch on raised fields there (Stephen Gliessman, personal communication).

Finally, the paleoecological remains from the fields suggest that at the time of field construction the escoba-botan forests were not present but that the saw grass association was dominant (chaps. 3 and 7). This preliminary evidence suggests that the construction of the field system came after much of the marshland was opened (chap. 7) and that the system expanded the escoba-botan niches after abandonment. The gastropod evidence suggests that water has been present in the depression during its recent geological history and that the canals probably retained water throughout the dry season.

The distribution of the fields indicates that locations suitable or chosen for field usage in the depression included the edges of PE and PS and the more interior sections of PW. The common hydrological characteristic of these zones is rather permanent but seasonally fluctuating surface water. Amorphous patterns of unknown origin occur in the deeper-inundated, interior sections of PE and PS. No patterns occur in those sections of PW where soil moisture falls to the wilting point and water levels drop to at least 1 meter below the surface.

The two long ditches connecting PS with the New River are major finds with regard to hydraulic regulation in the depression. They are canals that may represent the vestiges of a water transportation system and/or a means of water regulation. The data are not adequate to provide definitive answers, but it appears feasible that the canals could have been used to channel water into or out of the depression, particularly the latter. Severe inundation of the fields could have been regulated by opening the canals and allowing excessive water to drain into the river. If incubation of soils on the fields by inundation were desired, the procedure could be controlled by impeding the flow of water through the canals.

A caveat is warranted with regard to these two canals. Informants suggest that past logging activity included the removal of the logs out of the south end of PS, presumably through the canal in question. It is not certain if the canal was constructed by the loggers or only cleared by them. The peculiar bend in the canal seems puzzling with regard to mere log floating. Also, informants verified that loggers had only cleared existing channels for floating elsewhere. It seems likely that the canal is a relic Maya feature which was utilized in historic times. Indeed, the lucrative logwood operations in the eastern periphery zone may have been enhanced by the large number of Maya waterways found there.

The ground pattern study provided a wealth of data applicable to interpreting the past use of the depression and the issues of Maya raised-field cultivation. Although continued work will undoubtedly change some specifics and clarify other issues, the information strongly points to the existence at Pulltrouser some time between the Late Preclassic and Terminal Classic periods of a raised and channelized field and canal system, not dissimilar to that in the Basin of Mexico or on Frederik Hendrik Island (Serpenti 1965). Monolevel platforms in conjunction with canals controlled planting surfaces in relation to water levels in the canals. Drainage was apparently not the sole function of the system; rather, the subtle manipulation of the seasonal fluctuations in water was possible. Multiple harvests were feasible with a stabilized water source. Some evidence suggests that at least maize was cultivated by hoeing and mucking. Canoes could be maneuvered through the system and, apparently, to the New River and beyond. The potential for major crop production and trade from the depression may have been significant (chap. 13).

ACKNOWLEDGMENTS

The survey and excavations of the fields and canals at Pulltrouser Swamp would have been impeded had it not been for the unselfish assistance of several project members. Nancy Ettlinger helped survey the peripheries of PS, and Janice Darch helped survey and excavate the features as time allowed. Major excavation attention was provided by Tanya Luhrman and Charles Lincoln, who were project volunteers. The number of excavations would have been severely limited without the assistance of these individuals. Their efforts are deeply appreciated.

NOTES

1. Originally, a mound in the center of PW was selected for study. It was abandoned after several fer-de-lance were discovered on it. Other mounds were surrounded by too much water to allow adequate access to them until late in the field season. Sampling by

bucket auger in these features revealed a profile which appeared to be similar to that on the excavated raised fields.

2. Unit 4 was placed on that portion of the field that dipped toward the depression and a canal. Depths were recorded from a datum point in the southwest (highest) corner of the unit. The associated soil data were retrieved from the east (lowest) wall of the unit, and following convention depths were recorded from the immediate surface. As a result, the depths and thicknesses of the mottled zone differ in the two measures. The excavation records this zone as between 35 to 70 centimeters at the datum point; the soil pit reports it at 16 to 35 centimeters at the low end of the unit.

3. During the editing of this work, we were presented with new information from Paul Bloom (University of Minnesota) concerning the problems of soil analysis in a gypsiferous environment (n. 2, chap. 5). He argues that the "mottled zone" appears to be much more like natural swamp material than we contend and that much of the "mottling" may be gypsum, created in a seasonal, wet-dry circumstance. This information has been most helpful and is being used as a guide to analysis of the materials taken from the fields in 1981. However, the multiple lines of evidence presented here—the variability of the composition of the mottled zone from field to field, the botanical remains found in the zone, and the artifactual materials (including stone picks) that are so abruptly absent below the mottled zone—lead us to maintain that the zone has been altered substantially by human activity. Bloom's evidence does indicate that the bulk of the material comprising the mottled zone apparently was derived from the excavation of the canals in the swamp. Subsequent discussions with him have led us to propose that the high gypsum level in the mottled zone is a product of the creation of the fields and canals. Such a system provides the correct physical conditions for gypsum to form as water levels fluctuate in the base of the fields. Evidence to support this position involves the apparent absence of the mottled zone in those parts of the depression where fields and canals were not found, such as the savanna zone of PW.

5. The Soils of Pulltrouser Swamp: Classification and Characteristics

JANICE P. DARCH

Studies by the British Land Use Survey (Wright et al. 1959) and by Olson (1974; 1975; 1977) indicate that many of the soils in northern Belize are mollisols (formerly called rendzinas). The character of the poorly drained depression soils is less well understood than that of the upland soils. Olson (1977) categorizes some of them as vertisols, while Stevens (1964) suggests that the lowland hydromorphic soils include groundwater podzols (spodosols) and groundwater laterites (oxisols and ultisols). The British Land Use Survey classified depression soils in northern Belize as suite 58b, non-saline, organic soils, referred to as Sibal peaty clay, which include the Turner and Kinlock soils described by Charter (1941).

Data on the nature of depression soils elsewhere in the peninsular region are conflicting. Bajo de Santa Fe, adjacent to Tikal, Guatemala, is reported to be composed of sticky, black, infertile clay, locally referred to as Yalock soil (Cowgill and Hutchinson 1963; Laws 1961). Similarly, analysis of soils from the Aguada de Santa Ana Vieja, 34 kilometers southeast of Tikal, indicates a comparatively infertile environment, with a clay content consisting primarily of halloysite (Cowgill and Hutchinson 1966). In contrast, a brief examination of several depression soils by Turner (1978) in southern Campeche and Quintana Roo, Mexico, indicates a relatively fertile environment, with soils categorized as mollisols, mostly of the haplaquoll variety.

These studies may be interpreted in several ways. They may indicate that an assortment of specific soil types with varying qualities are found within depressions of the central Maya lowlands, despite the rather uniform but broad types of vegetation patterns that occur in them. They may also reflect different study methodologies and terminology. And they may reflect the degree of past or present human impact on particular depressions. For example, it is doubtful that the massive alteration of the landscape associated with the occupation of Tikal did not affect the soils of Bajo de Santa Fe in a major way. Interpretations of depression soils have probably been influenced by each of these factors.

This chapter examines the physical and chemical characteristics of the soils of Pulltrouser Swamp, emphasizing those soils associated with raised and channelized fields. Attention is given to soil qualities and classification and to the present pedological environment. Reference is also made to the characteristics of the unconsolidated limestone, or sascab, that underlies the depression.

PARENT MATERIAL
The parent material of the soils of northern Belize is derived from Cretaceous and Eocene limestones (Dixon 1956) which are mantled with a Miocene chalky marl (Ower 1928). Dixon describes the white marl as "unconsolidated calcareous material together with some white clays and white quartz sand beds" (1956:26). Similar deposits have been described from various parts of the Yucatán peninsular area. Wilson (n.d.) refers to the chalky marl of the region as a soft, usually friable weathering product of limestone which is almost pure calcium carbonate. Folan (1978) labels such deposits in northern Quintana Roo as calcareous sand. In this study the soft chalklike limestones of the Pulltrouser depression zone are referred to as sascab, a local term used throughout the Maya region to refer to various gradations of unconsolidated limestone (Darch 1981).

METHODS OF STUDY
Four sites in the depression were chosen for study. Three of these sites were in the relic-field zone: RF sites 1 and 3 on raised and channelized fields and RF site 2 on a channelized-raised field. Fifteen soil units were excavated in the fields and canals from which fifty-eight samples were collected for analysis (figs. 4-6 to 4-8). At RF site 1, five 1-meter-by-1-meter pits were dug across two fields which were separated by an infilled canal with a width of 1 meter. The soil pits were oriented along a west-east transect line which commenced at the edge of a large water-filled canal that bordered the saw grass association and extended 60 meters in a westerly direction toward the edge of the escoba-botan forests. The soil units at this site were situated on a channelized and a raised field. At RF site 2, soil samples were extracted from three excavation units on a channelized-raised field. Two of the pits occurred on the flat surface of the fields, and a third was dug to intersect the break in slope of the field as it dipped into a canal. At RF site 3, five sets of soil

samples were collected from units that transected an infilled canal and a field that displayed both raised- and channelized-field segments. Additional sets of soil samples were collected from the summits of two raised fields at that site.

The fourth site was in the seasonally inundated grass savanna at PW where surface field-canal patterns do not occur. Three pits were used to investigate the soils away from the immediate vicinity of the patterns in an effort to understand their absence in that type of depression habitat and to provide information on gilgai or other natural ground pattern formations. The latter analysis included a visual survey of soil microrelief and physical and chemical analyses to assess soil clay mineralogy, sodium content, and pH-pertinent factors in gilgai formation. Also, comparisons of the sascab in PW and that of the raised-field zones were used to determine whether the Maya used grassland savannas as sources of sascab to construct the base of their raised fields and/or to acquire topsoil to be used as additional A horizon material for their fields.

DESCRIPTION OF FIELD EXPERIMENTS

Various field experiments, including the installation and monitoring of Bouyoucos Blocks, the determination of infiltration rates and soil color, and measurements of pH and calcium carbonate content, were conducted. Twenty Bouyoucos Blocks, to measure the changes in soil moisture in the dry season, were installed at RF sites 1 and 2. The blocks were placed at depths ranging from 5 centimeters to 80 centimeters in the mounds and the underlying sascab to monitor the moisture conditions at various depths within the plant rooting zone. On the average, three sets of readings were taken each week throughout the field season, although the blocks in the deepest locations could not be installed until the end of April because of the high level of the water table. Bouyoucos Block measurements were compared with daily rainfall readings made at the field camp at Cuello, located 15 kilometers away.

Twenty-three soil infiltration experiments were conducted to estimate the rate of drainage of water into the soil. Twenty-one of these experiments were performed on the present field surfaces, and two sets of measurements were taken on the sascablike base of the mounds which had been exposed by excavations. The equipment was designed following instructions presented by Hills (1970: 6–7). It was composed of two cans open at both ends and a 10-liter polythene bottle. The smaller can had a diameter of 10 centimeters, the larger one a diameter of 15 centimeters. These were inserted into the soil to the same depth, taking care not to disturb the soil structure. The outer can was filled with water to act as a buffer against lateral flow from the central can, in which the infiltration capacity was to be measured.

Two holes, each 1.5 centimeters in diameter, were cut in the lid of the polythene bottle, and tubing 1.5 centimeters in diameter was cemented into each of them. One piece of tubing projected 1 centimeter further from the top of the polythene bottle than the other. The bottle was filled with water to act as a reservoir for the equipment. A wooden stand was constructed to support the bottle so that the feeder tubes could penetrate the inner cylinder and supply water without pressure from the heavy bottle disturbing the soil structure and causing settling of the equipment. A scale, graduated in centimeters and liters, was marked on the side of the bottle. Readings were taken at five-minute intervals during the first two or three hours of the experiment, depending on the rate of infiltration at the particular site, and at fifteen-minute intervals for the remainder of the experiment. Infiltration rates were recorded over a five-hour period. A variation of the experiment, whereby the surface organic matter was loosened and mixed with the A horizon to simulate a cultivated surface, was also used.

The measurement of soil pH was undertaken in the field using pH indicator papers to establish if variations in the soil reaction occurred at the various field sites; pH is one of the many criteria used in statements of the availability of cations in soils. Field estimates of the calcium carbonate content of the soils were made using the dilute hydrochloric acid test, which yields qualitative data on the amount of calcium carbonate present by comparing the effervescence of a sample in contact with hydrochloric acid to a predetermined effervescence scale. Soil structure, texture, plasticity, and stickiness were established by simple field tests (USDA 1975) as an estimate of the physical characteristics of the soil, and soil color was determined by comparing moist soil samples with a Munsell color chart.

DESCRIPTION OF LABORATORY TESTS

Soil laboratory tests were conducted by the investigator at Bedford College, University of London. Tests included loss on ignition, particle size analysis, the determination of the exchangeable bases calcium, magnesium, sodium, and potassium, exchangeable iron and copper, total nitrogen, phosphorus, organic carbon, calcium carbonate, cation exchange capacities, and x-ray diffraction. Loss on ignition was calculated after heating 5 grams of soil at 600 degrees C. for eight hours in a muffle furnace to oxidize the organic matter and calcium carbonate. Particle size analysis was carried out using the pipette method to determine the texture of the soils and sascab. The exchangeable bases calcium, magnesium, sodium, and potassium as well as iron and copper were determined by atomic absorption spectrophotometry after digestion with dilute nitric acid. Available phosphorus was determined in dilute ammonium-fluoride with hydrochloric acid. Organic carbon was determined by the Walkley-Black method; total nitrogen by semimicro Kjeldahl; calcium carbonate after Richards (1954); and cation exchange capacities by a sodium saturation method recommended by Black (1965) for use on calcareous soils. X-ray diffraction, on powder samples, was carried out on twenty-three samples to determine their mineralogy.

RESULTS

A comparison of soil horizons in the various field profiles reveals that the same patterns are not repeated at each site and that pedogenesis has not continued long enough to create a distinct B horizon at all sites. Here the A horizon is defined as the rich humic surface soil, and the B horizon refers to a soil zone distinct from the A horizon and the underlying C horizon, either sascab or fill. The A and B horizons are referred to as solum (USDA 1962).

At the three field sites a distinct A horizon exists and varies in thickness between 6 centimeters and 26 centimeters, the mean depth being 20.3 centimeters (app. 5-1). In contrast, the savanna section of PW has an A horizon of 46 centimeters. B horizons were not always distinguishable at RF site 3, but at RF sites 1 and 2 definite B horizons were found. In many cases the depth of the B horizon could be determined only by probing below the water table with a bucket auger. At RF site 1 the maximum depth of the B horizon is 150 centimeters, while at RF site 2 it is much shallower, never extending below 45 centimeters.

In all cases the boundaries between the A and B horizons are difficult to distinguish, especially when the soils are damp. After exposure of the profiles for several days, however, the boundaries became more distinct. The A horizons dry and crack while the B horizons retain their massive structure (fig. 5-1). The B-C horizon boundaries are clear at RF site 2, where the gray B horizon rests on gray sascab. The other soil pits demonstrate distinct B-C horizon boundaries, but they are not as clear as those at RF site 2.

The A horizons at each site could easily be distinguished by soil color. At RF site 1 the A horizons are black, and at RF sites 2 and 3 their color ranges from black to dark gray (app. 5-1). Where B

Fig. 5-1. Depth of desiccation in solum of fields. Desiccation sufficient to cause cracking in the solum occurs when fields are stripped of vegetation or the soil is exposed during the dry season. Cracking does not extend into the fill zone.

horizons occur they are gray. At RF site 2 (pits 6 and 7) and at RF site 1 (pit 1) the sascab is white (fig. 5-2), although with depth it tends toward a yellow color which may result from the precipitation of iron in association with fluctuations of the watertable, causing the alternation of oxidizing and reducing conditions. However, once disturbed the yellow lenses blend with the surrounding sascab to produce a gray color rating on the Munsell system. Lenses of gypsum are also found in the sascab, usually occurring at least 100 centimeters into the horizon.[1] A sascablike material is found in the other pits at RF site 1 and at RF site 3. It is light gray and displays puddling and mottling (fig. 5-3). The mottles, although easily distinguishable, are amorphously shaped and irregularly distributed; they sometimes consist of small limestone fragments, carbonate casts, and perhaps gypsum, as suggested by Paul Bloom (personal communication). Below this material is sascab.

Fig. 5-2. Soil profile, channelized field, Raised-Field site 2. Note the absence of a "horizon" between the dark solum and the white sascab. No evidence of disturbance in the solum is apparent.

At each site the soil structure is massive when the soil is wet, but drying produces cracking of the exposed A horizons into clods with vertical and horizontal dimensions of 10 centimeters or more. Consistency varies between slightly sticky and very sticky and slightly plastic to very plastic. In general, plasticity tends to decrease with depth but stickiness demonstrates no vertical trends. Inspecting for texture, defined in the field by examining a moist-hand specimen of soil between the fingers, revealed that many specimens have a definite gritty texture. The greatest textural variations occur in the sascab, particularly at RF sites 1 and 2, where coarse gypsum crystal layers alternate with heavy clays and silts. *Bouyoucos Blocks.*   The installation of Bouyoucos Blocks was affected by the very high water table at RF sites 1 and 2. At soil pit 1, bordering a sugarcane field, the water table was at 49 centimeters on February 19, and by the beginning of March it had dropped only to 55 centimeters. This pit was on the edge of the botan forest; the

Fig. 5-3. Soil profile, raised field, Raised-Field site 1. Note the mottled fill zone below the dark and cracked solum. The mottling is created by limestone fragments in various stages of decomposition, carbonate casts, and perhaps gypsum.

soil pits located deeper in the escoba forest had even higher water tables. For this reason Bouyoucos Blocks could be installed only at very shallow depths between January and April without placing them in saturated conditions. At the end of April, blocks were placed in the soil to a maximum depth of 80 centimeters at RF site 1. Only one Bouyoucos Block placed below a depth of 10 centimeters ever registered less than 100 percent available moisture (i.e., the soil remained at or above field capacity throughout the dry season). The one exception was block 10, placed at 40 centimeters in the B horizon at RF site 1 in a position on the edge of a channelized field, near the boundary of the escoba forest and the sugarcane plantation (fig. 4-6). Six of the ten blocks located within the top 10 centimeters of soil indicated less than 100 percent available water in May and June. Block 1, placed adjacent to block 10 at the edge of the escoba forest, began recording some water loss on March 13. Eventually this block indicated a complete water deficit or no available water. Other blocks reached 24.5, 38, 54, and 97.5 percent available water. Within twelve hours of a rainshower the Bouyoucos Block readings equilibrated with the additional water penetrating the soil. Considering the high temperatures, exceeding 37° C. at noon, which persisted throughout May and early June as well as the dense vegetation covering the raised fields, transpiration was thought to be rapid and great demand for soil water existed at this time of year. Rarely, however, did a water deficit occur.

Infiltration Capacity.   Experiments to measure the infiltration capacity of the soils of the fields were conducted for four and one-half weeks at the end of the dry season when the soils were at their driest. At many of the sites where infiltration experiments were conducted, the soils registered over 100 percent available moisture on the adjacent Bouyoucos Blocks at the height of the dry season. Infiltration rates were measured on soils with the humus layer intact and with the humus layer removed. The humus at some sites is thick (ca. 9 centimeters), which tends to promote high rates of infiltration. For example, a rate of 291.53 cubic centimeters per hour during the first hour of the experiment was recorded at RF site 3. Such rates are indicative of the present infiltration capacities. When the fields were under cultivation, however, the thick humus layer probably did not exist but was mixed with the A horizon. To approximate the infiltration capacities of the fields when under cultivation, the surface soil and the humus were combined. At sites 1 and 3 a number of infiltration experiments were conducted, and the results have been computed to give the average infiltration rate per hour as well as for each hour during the experiment (table 5-1). Measurements were taken over five-hour periods. A rapid drop in the initial infiltration rate occurred after the first hour of the experiment, and the rate continued to drop as the soil became saturated.

One set of experiments was performed in the dry feeder canals (table 5-1). This showed that the sascab base of the canals had low infiltration rates but that they were no lower than those of the fill or base of those fields surrounded by water-filled canals. Two infiltration experiments were conducted on top of sascablike fill exposed at the base of soil pit 1 and soil pit 9. At pit 9 no drainage from the infiltrometer occurred, while at pit 1 a rate of 3.96 cubic centimeters per hour was recorded.

Particle Size Analysis.   Soil textural distributions rather different from those obtained in the field are demonstrated by particle size analysis. This circumstance is due to laboratory treatment of the samples with dilute hydrochloric acid, which dissolved the small fragments of calcite that gave the field specimens such a gritty texture. Such problems pervade the analysis of calcareous soils. There-

Table 5-1. *Average Rates of Infiltration (in Cubic Centimeters per Hour)*

Raised-Field Site	Location	Mean Rate	1st Hour	2nd Hour	3rd Hour	4th Hour	5th Hour
3	Channelized-raised field, composite of three runs with humus removed	103.32	157.10	108.00	98.86	86.70	65.93
3	Channelized-raised field, composite of three runs with humus intact	122.72	291.53	114.40	78.23	73.15	56.30
1	Raised field, composite of four runs with humus removed	9.54	22.15	7.64	7.81	7.55	2.57
1	Raised field, composite of three runs with humus intact	112.61	177.62	132.55	151.92	87.15	13.80
1	Dry feeder canals, composite of six runs with humus removed	17.87	31.75	19.51	16.59	13.55	7.96
3	Sascab			0.0 throughout 5 hours			
1	Sascab	3.96	7.96	4.65	3.37	2.71	1.13

fore, the laboratory-determined texture is less gritty than the actual field specimens. Mineral recoveries from the grain size analysis are rather low because of the high organic matter and calcium carbonate contents of the soils.

The data (fig. 5-4; table 5-2) indicate textural similarities and differences between the soils at the sites. The figures are constructed to show the dominant textural classes—sand, silt, or clay fractions—at each site in a 20-gram sample of soil. It is apparent from these diagrams (fig. 5-4) that the textural distributions tend toward a dominance of silt (e.g., RF site 1, B horizon), but exceptions occur.

Comparisons of sites indicate a preponderance of silt in the A horizons of the fields at RF sites 1 and 3. The clay contents of the A horizon soils at the two sites are variable. Sand contents in the A horizons at RF site 1 cluster around 20 to 30 percent; at RF site 3, they cluster around 15 to 20 percent. In general, samples with large silt fractions have very little clay and a moderate sand content. The textural characteristics of the A horizons at RF site 2 are dissimilar to those at RF sites 1 and 3. Some of these samples show a dominance of silt, while the clay contents vary from pit to pit.

Silt is the major constituent of the B horizon soils at RF site 1. Sand contents at this site are between 9 and 31 percent, while little clay is present. In contrast, at RF site 2 the B horizons are clayey, pits 6 and 7 having over 55 percent clay. At RF site 3 no B horizon is apparent in four of the pits, but in two pits, where a B horizon exists, the trend is toward a dominance of silt.

An examination of the textures of the C horizons shows some similarities between the sites. The C horizon of soil pit 1 at RF site 1 is the only sample to indicate a dominance of clay. Other samples from RF site 1 are silty with variable sand contents. At RF site 2 silt dominates in the C horizon at pit 8, but at pits 6 and 7 the sand content is sometimes higher than the silt content. Clay contents in the C horizons at RF sites 2 and 3 vary between 0 and 10 percent. At RF site 3 the sand and silt contents are almost equal. Fine sands (50 to 250 microns) dominate the sand fraction at all sites, giving many samples a silty, fine texture.

The textural comparisons of the three sites show general similarities between RF sites 1 and 3 and provide contrasts with soils at RF site 2. The channelized-field section at RF site 2 is distinguished by a sharp textural break between the solum and the sascab, the change being from clayey A and B horizons to clay-poor C horizons.

Pits crossing infilled canals at RF sites 1 and 2 exposed only the top 50 centimeters of the profile because of the high level of the water table, but at RF site 2 deeper samples were also obtained by bucket auger. The canal soil at RF site 1, soil pit 3, has the highest clay content and the lowest silt content of any of the A horizon soils collected at that site. At RF sites 2 and 3 the A horizon soil from the infilled canals has textural distributions similar to those of the soils from the raised fields. The B horizon soil collected from the canal at RF site 2, however, has a very high clay content and less sand and silt than the field samples at that site. The C horizon material from the same pit shows little textural variation compared to that of the field samples.

At the sites sascab was collected from various depths to investigate whether or not it possessed a uniform texture throughout. The data show that at soil pit 1, RF site 1, the texture of the sascab at 160 centimeters and 260 centimeters is clay-dominated and silt-dominated, respectively. In contrast, the samples from soil pit 4 display a uniform silty texture in the sascab between 173 centimeters and 236 centimeters. At RF site 2, samples collected between 126 centimeters and 311 centimeters at soil pit 6 indicate a low clay content, but sand and silt contents vary at different depths, although no particular trend is related to depth.

Organic Matter.   As mentioned previously, the soils have high organic matter contents as manifested by a weight loss of 24.151 percent in the A horizon at soil pit 2, RF site 1, following loss on ignition experiments (table 5-3). In general, the levels of organic matter tend to decrease with depth, although a considerable quantity of root material is preserved at depth due to the reducing conditions which persist for much of the year. Additionally, the high temperature associated with loss on ignition causes the decomposition of carbonates in the limestone so that the high organic matter contents at depth are to some extent associated with the carbonates, particularly as the calcium carbonate content also increases with depth. Some of the A horizons are not calcareous.

Organic Carbon and Total Nitrogen.   Organic carbon contents of the raised and channelized field soils range from 3.189 percent in the A horizon of pit 2 to 0.252 percent in the B horizon of pit 1, RF site 1 (table 5-3). A decline in the organic carbon content occurs with depth. Total nitrogen was determined only on five samples, and the results indicate that nitrogen contents are low. The carbon-nitrogen ratio is consequently high, for example, 48:1 at RF site 1.

Available Phosphorus.   Everywhere the available phosphorus content is under 10 parts per million, yet phosphorus values are moderate to good (table 5-3). Some variations in the phosphorus content are associated with depth, but no regular pattern occurs.

The pH.   The pH values range from 6 to 8, which is from a slightly

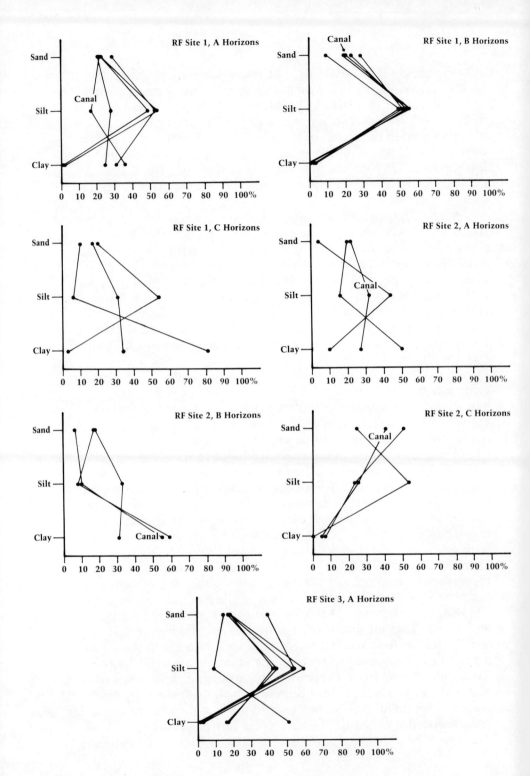

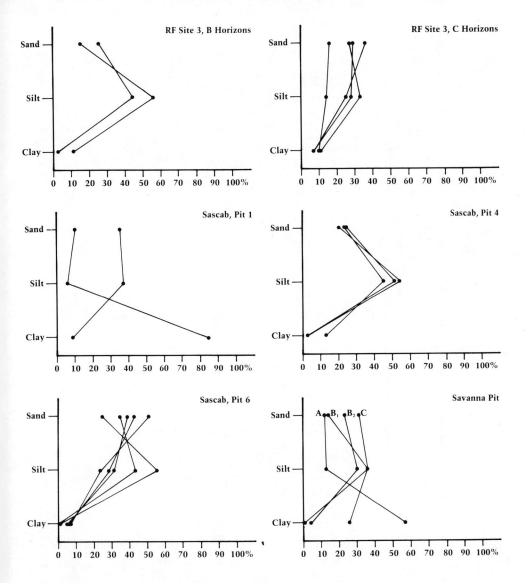

Fig. 5-4. Soil textural diagrams.

Table 5-2. Soil Textural Data

Horizon	Depth (Cm.)	Total Sand (%)	Coarse Sand (%) (2 Cm.–500 μ)	Medium Sand (%) (500–250 μ)	Fine Sand (%) (250–50 μ)	Silt (%) (50–2 μ)	Clay (%) (2 μ)	Total Mineral Recovery (%)
Pit 1								
A	0–24	29.340	2.310	4.700	22.330	53.375	30.882	113.597
B_1	24–40	27.600	1.045	4.475	22.080	50.500	1.737	79.837
B_2	40–54	24.600	1.535	3.635	19.430	47.750	8.570	80.920
C	160	10.128	0.688	0.780	8.660	5.927	84.537	100.592
C	260	35.346	9.608	4.085	21.653	37.375	9.250	81.971
Pit 2								
A	0–16	21.250	1.020	2.845	17.385	28.000	25.430	74.680
B	16–52	23.410	1.530	4.965	16.915	52.500	2.950	78.860
B	110	26.330	2.010	2.870	21.450	44.260	15.890	86.480
B	138–150	30.685	12.285	6.005	12.395	26.783	21.755	79.223
C	190	17.474	3.795	2.703	10.976	31.250	33.599	82.323
Pit 3								
A	4–15	21.608	2.770	3.240	15.598	17.250	36.360	75.218
B	15–43	20.310	1.495	2.685	16.130	54.750	0.570	75.630
Pit 4								
A	0–15	22.645	1.375	2.405	18.865	54.225	2.200	79.070
B	15–60	19.413	2.215	4.160	13.038	54.500	0.010	73.923
B	100	18.685	1.050	2.625	15.010	27.002	42.270	87.957
C	163–173	19.995	2.325	3.770	13.900	53.750	2.570	76.315
C	236	22.610	2.305	4.210	16.095	44.875	13.125	80.610
C	296	24.163	0.975	3.728	19.460	50.500	3.380	78.043
Pit 5								
A	5–20	22.745	2.515	3.695	16.535	48.875	1.105	72.725
B	20–35	9.200	1.070	2.205	5.925	48.750	3.010	60.960

Pit 6								
A	0–20	19.643	1.095	2.025	16.523	15.500	49.982	85.125
B	20–45	17.365	1.595	2.830	12.940	8.000	58.715	84.080
C	45–126	49.586	8.515	7.858	33.213	22.625	7.180	79.391
C	180–217	24.253	0.680	2.165	21.408	54.700	0.825	79.778
C	250	33.668	0.930	3.725	29.013	43.040	0.000	76.708
C	275–295	37.560	21.285	7.620	8.655	30.500	4.560	72.620
C	311	41.505	30.210	6.245	5.050	28.000	6.213	75.718
Pit 7								
A	0–6	21.495	2.395	2.625	16.475	32.000	27.315	80.810
B	6–43	6.467	2.455	2.625	1.387	10.250	55.270	71.987
C	43–83	39.743	3.570	8.060	28.113	25.250	5.335	70.328
Pit 8								
A	7–16	5.161	1.095	2.315	1.751	44.000	9.459	58.620
B	16–35	17.945	0.700	2.215	15.030	32.750	31.330	82.025
C	35–70	23.913	2.713	4.915	16.285	53.210	0.000	77.123
Pit 9								
A	0–16	17.505	1.960	4.070	11.475	59.000	3.375	79.880
C	37	29.183	0.895	1.680	26.608	28.250	6.964	64.397
Pit 10								
A	4–30	18.430	2.705	2.925	12.800	52.750	0.260	71.440
Pit 11								
A	4–23	38.505	1.095	2.080	35.330	53.500	1.410	93.415
C	23–120	15.973	1.198	1.090	13.685	14.250	10.101	40.324
Pit 12								
A	9–34	17.235	1.100	2.735	13.400	44.000	16.140	77.375
C	34–120	35.565	1.200	4.045	30.320	25.000	6.890	67.455
Pit 13								
A	5–23	18.323	1.505	2.243	14.575	41.500	16.755	76.578
B_1	23–69	24.920	0.515	1.415	22.990	44.000	2.405	71.325
B_2	69–83	21.375	2.200	5.190	13.985	37.500	4.100	62.975

Table 5-2, cont'd.

Horizon	Depth (Cm.)	Total Sand (%)	Coarse Sand (%) (2 Cm.–500 μ)	Medium Sand (%) (500–250 μ)	Fine Sand (%) (250–50 μ)	Silt (%) (50–2 μ)	Clay (%) (2 μ)	Total Mineral Recovery (%)
Pit 14								
A	6–20	14.259	1.355	2.468	10.436	8.750	50.579	73.588
B₁	20–45	15.224	1.478	2.263	11.483	55.750	10.570	81.544
C	71–141	27.159	2.313	5.493	19.353	33.000	10.950	71.109
Pit 15								
A	0–46	12.349	1.323	1.968	9.058	13.375	57.015	82.739
B₁	46–74	14.309	0.378	1.573	12.358	36.375	25.455	76.139
B₂	74–107	22.619	0.143	4.123	18.353	30.000	4.350	56.969
C	55–125	30.544	0.538	3.613	26.393	35.575	0.725	66.844

Table 5-3. Soil Chemical Analysis Data

Horizon	Ca (Ppm)	Mg (Ppm)	Na (Ppm)	K (Ppm)	Fe (Ppm)	Cu (Ppm)	P (%)	N (%)	C (%)	C:N	CaCo$_3$ (%)	CEC (Meq./100 G.)	Base Saturation (%)	Organic Matter (%)
Pit 1														
A	1,825	3,100	300	330	4,400	105.0	8.9250	0.00000	2.350		11.552			17.521
B$_1$	25,000	2,700	650	450	4,250	10.0	8.9250	0.02800	0.843	30.107	13.808			13.200
B$_2$	12,500	2,300	500	1,100	4,075	0.0	6.0900	0.00525	0.252	48.000	27.290			13.406
C	25,000	2,200	1,900	530	1,900	30.0					>50.000			7.158
C	375,000	2,100	2,300	90	1,350	105.0					>50.000			2.862
C	125,000	1,600	1,550	300	3,500	5.0					>50.000			5.477
C	157,500	1,500	2,025	90	900	5.0					>50.000			1.848
C	12,500	1,800	1,825	90	2,500	5.0					>50.000			3.025
C	25,000	1,700	1,600	140	1,600	5.0					>50.000			4.420
Pit 2														
A	6,250	2,700	400	400	5,100	5.0	5.2500		3.189		0.000	258.281	11.4030	24.151
B	30,000	2,800	600	390	4,350	5.0	4.9880		2.540		37.616	120.984	74.2610	14.492
B	77,500	4,250	800	2,330	4,600	20.0	6.9560		0.843		23.600			21.853
B	95,000	3,200	2,000	900	1,500	5.0	5.2500		1.034		49.856			7.783
C	200,000	2,500	1,600	300	1,650	5.0	3.4650		1.053		49.904			5.947
Pit 3														
A	18,000	3,100	550	330	5,000	20.0	6.0900		3.110		18.224			23.034
B	175,000	2,650	710	300	3,050	5.0	6.9560		0.619		41.306			12.960
Pit 4														
A	125,000	9,000	4,000	500	6,350	20.0	6.0380		2.483		18.518	28.547	1,285.6340	21.827
B	72,500	3,200	1,430	300	4,200	5.0	4.9880		0.824		33.854	159.047	126.1880	14.314
B	4,650	1,700	550	600	4,700	5.0	7.8750		0.462		17.936			14.548

Table 5-3, cont'd.

Horizon	Ca (Ppm)	Mg (Ppm)	Na (Ppm)	K (Ppm)	Fe (Ppm)	Cu (Ppm)	P (%)	N (%)	C (%)	C:N	CaCo$_3$ (%)	CEC (Meq./100 G.)	Base Saturation (%)	Organic Matter (%)
C	125,000	2,800	1,700	600	5,900	5.0					>50.000			10.998
C	94,500	4,000	990	1,900	2,600	5.0					48.272			15.121
C	112,500	2,700	1,000	2,100	3,200	0.5					>50.000			11.555
C	160,000	2,500	1,500	900	2,750	5.0					>50.000			8.223
C	40,000	2,100	900	800	2,750	5.0					>50.000			8.821
C	2,500	2,100	800	800	3,200	20.0					42.818			11.567
Pit 5														
A	7,500	3,500	2,000	300	4,450	5.0	3.3360		2.769		39.723			23.701
B	71,250	2,700	1,700	330	3,250	5.0	6.9560		2.178		47.084			14.181
Pit 6														
A	750	1,500	300	175	4,250	5.0	7.0880		1.186		0.000	394.171	2.4860	14.785
B	7,500	3,200	700	330	3,900	5.0	5.5125		0.691		9.500	138.656	25.9696	14.978
C	20,000	600	1,150	100	400	0.0					23.168			18.318
C	52,500	2,100	1,200	330	1,500	5.0					45.626			9.958
C	22,500	1,750	900	300	1,350	5.0					37.203			6.722
C	7,500	470	740	100	1,050	0.0					7.424			18.409
C	7,000	700	760	90	1,800	0.0					9.776			18.391
Pit 7														
A	4,000	3,850	1,400	300	4,250	20.0	5.2500				10.904			21.240
B	3,200	4,500	1,900	200	4,100	15.0	7.0880				6.260			16.788
C	62,500	1,100	900	200	1,000	10.0					13.808			18.185
Pit 8														
A	11,000	4,800	3,200	300	3,900	20.0	7.8750	0.00049	2.369	4,834.700	16.898			5.469
B	7,250	3,900	2,150	200	3,900	10.0	5.2500	0.00000	0.633		9.284			16.388
C	55,000	2,100	1,700	540	1,050	10.0					6.800			16.250

A	13,500	4,100	1,200	1,300	5,400	20.0	6.9560	2.634	21.110	112.828	52.3410	23.864
C	95,000	3,800	2,300	1,200	1,700	10.0			>50.000	146.813	180.6810	14.406
C	175,000	2,600	2,500	920	1,700	20.0			35.096			18.878
Pit 10												
A	34,500	3,600	900	750	3,500	20.0	8.9250	1.968	34.772			17.827
Pit 11												
A	7,500	4,000	3,700	750	3,600	20.0	5.2500	2.788	24.134			20.852
C	151,250	900	1,790	400	550	20.0			16.358			18.526
Pit 12												
A	11,250	3,900	4,000	600	4,000	22.0	6.9560	1.568	15.170			16.941
C	92,500	2,000	2,000	600	1,250	22.0	5.2500	0.843	17.936			19.416
Pit 13												
A	7,250	4,400	4,100	750	4,200	22.0	4.4630	2.254	9.338	516.563	10.8290	21.841
B_1	25,000	2,900	1,900	700	2,100	5.0	5.2500	0.538	14.252	126.422	66.6460	14.252
B_2	66,600	2,150	1,400	800	1,500	5.0	3.4650	0.450	35.690			14.425
Pit 14												
A	7,500	3,700	1,350	1,350	4,300	6.0	7.0880	2.483	18.572	159.047	27.1920	19.807
B	1,250	7,000	3,800	800	2,900	65.0	3.4650	1.625	40.604	140.016	36.0890	15.522
C	85,000	3,700	2,450	800	1,450	10.0			>50.000			17.307
Pit 15												
A	400	2,700	3,150	600	3,200	22.0	7.0880	1.911	0.000			21.064
B_1	9,500	7,000	4,100	800	2,250	15.0	6.9560	0.080	0.000			17.123
B_2	57,500	3,200	4,000	500	850	20.0	6.0900	0.538	0.000			19.490
C	33,200	5,500	4,400	900	1,200	10.0			0.000			17.513

acid reaction to a slightly alkaline reaction (app. 5-1). The lower values tend to occur in the surface soils.

Exchangeable Bases.   Calcium dominates the exchange complex in all horizons (table 5-3). The calcium content is lowest in the A horizons and increases with depth. Everywhere the magnesium uptake could be blocked by the high calcium levels. Sodium contents are also rather high. Potassium is the least prevalent base, but no shortage of this base occurs. The data (table 5-4) indicate the average ratio values of the exchangeable bases for each horizon; they demonstrate a marked relationship between the soils at RF sites 1 and 3.

Iron and Copper.   Iron values are high considering the near-neutral pH values, and the iron content declines with depth (table 5-3). Copper contents range from 5 to 105 parts per million in the A horizons of most soil pits. This element also declines in content with depth. At RF site 1 copper values of 105 parts per million are recorded, which is high, and it is possible that toxicity symptoms in some places could arise.

Cation Exchange Capacities.   These vary between 28.547 and 516.563 milliequivalents per 100 grams in the A horizons and 120.984 and 159.047 milliequivalents per 100 grams in the B horizons (table 5-3). There is a consistency in the cation exchange ca-

Table 5-4. *Average Ratios of the Exchangeable Bases*

Horizon	Calcium	Magnesium	Sodium	Potassium
RF site 1				
A	70.142	13.968	3.650	1
B	137.369	5.684	2.133	1
C	658.931	8.446	8.196	1
RF site 2				
A	18.100	11.357	5.683	1
B	24.993	20.466	7.457	1
C	128.944	6.716	6.058	1
RF site 3				
A	17.530	4.733	3.838	1
B	32.113	4.850	2.765	1
C	181.588	3.243	3.104	1
Savanna pit				
A	0.670	4.500	5.250	1
B	63.440	7.575	6.563	1
C	36.890	6.110	4.890	1

pacities of the B horizons. The only measurement on C horizon material, at pit 9, RF site 3, yielded a cation exchange capacity of 146.813 milliequivalents per 100 grams. The degree of base saturation of the exchange complex is high, except in the A horizon at soil pit 6, RF site 2, where a saturation of only 2.486 percent occurs. Some soils show a base saturation that exceeds the cation exchange capacity because of the decomposition of mineral elements, especially calcium, during analysis. This problem pervades the analysis of calcareous soils.

Comparisons of the soil chemistry of the fields with soil from the savanna show similarities in pH, organic matter content, phosphorus, and iron and copper values. The savanna soils are not calcareous; no reaction was recorded with 2N hydrochloric acid. This circumstance is puzzling given the prevalence of the usually calcareous parent material in the area. The calcium contents are lower than those of the field soils while the magnesium levels are comparable. Sodium and potassium levels show strong affinities to those of RF site 2.

X-Ray Diffraction.   Data indicate the presence of 2 : 1 silicate lattice clays (calcium montmorillonite, chlorite montmorillonite, illite montmorillonite, magnesium vermiculite, and saponite) and 1 : 1 silicate lattice clays (kaolinite, dickite, and both hydrated and dehydrated halloysite) (table 5-5). Gibbsite and monticellite also occur in some samples. Quartz, calcite, and gypsum are the dominant minerals present, and biotite, aragonite, and dolomite also occur. Possible identifications of a number of other peaks are also present (table 5-5). The powder samples were run through the diffractometer with the aim of rapidly assessing their mineralogical composition. Prepared standards were not used and, hence, the data cannot be used to make quantitative deductions of the occurrence of the minerals indicated.

DISCUSSION

The results of the analyses suggest that the soils of the Pulltrouser field zones can be classified as mollisols, belonging to the suborder aquoll of the haplaquoll great group within the subgroup cumulic haplaquoll (USDA 1975). In this regard, the soils are similar to those identified in the drier depressions of southern Quintana Roo (Turner 1978). The field soils at Pulltrouser conform to the characteristics of mollisols, except that the base saturation averages only 48.2 percent compared with a minimum of 50 percent established by the USDA (1975). This slightly lower figure occurs because the base saturation percentage was not calculated from exchangeable

Table 5-5. *X-Ray Diffraction Data*

Horizon	Mineral Identified	Possible Identification
Pit 2		
B	Regular illite montmorillonite	Hardystonite
	Hydrated halloysite	Zellerite
	Kaolinite	
	Aragonite	
	Calcite	
	Quartz	
Pit 4		
A	Calcium montmorillonite	Anthrophyllite
	Dickite	Navajoite
	Calcite	
	Quartz	
	Gypsum	
B	Dehydrated halloysite	Wairakite
	Kaolinite	Hoernesite
	Calcium montmorillonite	
	Quartz	
	Gypsum	
	Biotite	
C	Regular illite montmorillonite	Navajoite
	Calcium montmorillonite	Larnite
	Kaolinite	Hardystonite
	Dickite	
C	Quartz	
	Calcite	
	Aragonite	
	Biotite	
C	Hydrated halloysite	Plombierite
	Dickite	Milarite
	Aragonite	
	Quartz	
C	Regular illite montmorillonite	
	Calcium montmorillonite	
	Kaolinite	
	Monticellite	
	Calcite	
	Aragonite	
	Biotite	
	Quartz	
C	Gypsum	Englishite
		Rhodonite
		Wairakite
		Zeuente
		Marialite
		Sudoite
		Schertelite

Table 5-5, *cont'd.*

Horizon	Mineral Identified	Possible Identification
Pit 6		
A	Calcium montmorillonite	Englishite
	Magnesium vermiculite	
	Chlorite montmorillonite	
A	Kaolinite	
	Dickite	
	Gypsum	
	Biotite	
B	Calcium montmorillonite	
	Quartz	
C	Calcium montmorillonite	Hardystonite
	Illite	Englishite
	Kaolinite	Ankerite
	Gibbsite	Prehnite
	Monticellite	Thuringite
	Gypsum	Xonotlite
	Calcite	Chlorite
		Triphylite
C	Dickite	Englishite
	Kaolinite	Afwillite
	Hydrated halloysite	Cordierite
	Gibbsite	Bemenice
	Quartz	Navajoite
	Biotite	Erhihmanite
		Phlogopite
C	Illite	Navajoite
	Kaolinite	Piedmontite
	Quartz	Faujasite
	Gypsum	
C	Illite	Afwillite
	Montmorillonite	Wollastonite
	Dickite	Prehnite
	Kaolinite	Ankerite
	Gibbsite	Plombierite
C	Quartz	Schertelite
	Biotite	Becquerellite
	Dolomite	Faujasite
Pit 13		
A	Dickite	Navajoite
	Kaolinite	Mordenite
	Calcite	Rosenharrite
	Quartz	Englishite
	Gypsum	
B_1	Kaolinite	Larnite
	Gypsum	Indialite
	Quartz	Afwillite

Table 5-5, *cont'd.*

Horizon	Mineral Identified	Possible Identification
		Englishite
		Hydroboracite
B₂	Chlorite montmorillonite	Nontronite
	Illite montmorillonite	Rhodonite
C	Calcium montmorillonite	Thuringite
	Kaolinite	Bertrandite
	Biotite	Kämmererite
	Quartz	
	Gypsum	
Pit 14		
C	Kaolinite	Becquerellite
	Quartz	Calcium uranyl hydroxide
	Calcite	
Pit 15		
A	Chlorite montmorillonite	Larnite
	Kaolinite	Plombierite
	Gibbsite	Osumilite
	Biotite	
	Quartz	
B	Calcium montmorillonite	Navajoite
	Monticellite	Larnite
	Calcite	
	Gypsum	
	Saponite	
	Quartz	
	Hydrated halloysite	
	Illite	
	Gibbsite	
C	Magnesium vermiculite	Ankerite
	Saponite	Nontronite
	Monticellite	Zellente
	Quartz	Schertelite
	Calcite	Chlorite
	Gypsum	

Note: There were no data for pits 1, 3, 5, 7, 8, 9, 10, 11, and 12 and for the A and C horizons, pit 2, and the A and B horizons, pit 14.

bases extracted by the ammonium acetate method used by the USDA and because of the calcareous nature of the soils. Other features which lead to the categorization of the soils as mollisols are the presence of montmorillonite (a 2 : 1 silicate lattice clay which imparts a high cation exchange capacity to the soil), the calcareous parent material (which results in a horizon within 1 meter of the surface having more than 40 percent calcium carbonate equivalent), dark, often black soil colors, and an organic carbon content which declines regularly with depth. No evidence of gilgai, slickensides, or wedge-shaped aggregates was found within the field zone, refuting any claim that the soils are vertisols. Permanent wetness further classes the soils as aquolls. The closed depression environment with interior drainage, together with a mollic epipedon resting directly upon the C horizon, defines the great group haplaquoll. Further, the subgroup cumulic haplaquoll indicates that the soils receive occasional additions of fresh sediment during inundation in the wet season. The soils in the savanna portion of PW differ only in that they are vertic haplaquolls, which is demonstrated because during the dry season the soil moisture regime falls below field capacity, resulting in shrinking and cracking of the solum.

An important feature of the soils of the Pulltrouser depression is their silty nature. Studies in Bajo de Santa Fe (Cowgill and Hutchinson 1963) and the depressions of southern Campeche and Quintana Roo (Turner 1978) describe *bajo* soils as predominantly clayey. Such is not the case in the Pulltrouser depression. Here the soils are silty, with some fine sand. The clay content is generally quite low. When wet, the depression soils are sticky. This circumstance is attributable more to the type of clay in the *bajo* soils, montmorillonite, than to the quantity of clay present.

The soil study indicates that the proposed field categories, channelized and raised (chap. 4), can be distinguished by soil textural variations and by the presence and distribution of mottling in the fill (figs. 5-2 and 5-3). The major factors that distinguish the channelized segment of the field at RF site 2 are abrupt textural contrasts between clay-rich A and B horizons and clay-poor C or sascab horizons. This pattern of distinction between the solum and the sascab is also found in PW, where no surface patterns occur. Such a textural contrast is not found in association either with the raised fields at RF sites 1 and 3 or at RF site 2 where the fill zone has been added to the depression end of the field (chap. 4). Parallels in textural distributions between the channelized fields and the savanna zone of PW, combined with an examination of the methods of construction of the channelized fields, indicate that neither has a mottled zone and that both are associated with an underlying sascab which has not been disturbed in a major way. Alternately, the textural similarities between the solum and the mottled material on the raised fields indicate a different pedogenic environment which may be attributed to the mixing or dumping of materials to create a base for the fields. During the construction of this base, it was probably enriched with clay and other materials. In most cases the fill lies directly on sascab at depth; only a few buried A horizons were found. The boundary between the dumped material and the *in situ* sascab is gradual due to the disruptive effects of solum removal and the building of the base of the raised fields.

The distribution of mottling in the fill material also distinguishes the raised fields from the interior sections of the channelized fields. The sascab below the channelized fields is white; the only staining that occurs is in association with precipitation of iron along root channels or gypsum layers (fig. 5-2). In contrast, the fill underlying the raised fields is gray, with very irregularly distributed mottling. The mottle shapes are amorphous and appear to result from the occurrence of small limestone fragments, carbonate casts, and perhaps gypsum, as suggested by Paul Bloom. I suggest that the mottling of the fill material at RF sites 1 and 3 and the exterior section at RF site 2 owes its origins to the nature of field construction.

No evidence exists to either support or refute the supposition that the source of the fill for the raised fields is sascab from savanna grassland. X-ray diffraction data do not indicate any particular mineralogical similarities between the sascab underlying that zone and the mottled fill of the raised fields.

It has been suggested (Puleston 1977a) that the sascab (or marl) base of Maya raised fields facilitated drainage, provided support, and acted as a source of nutrients for crops. The infiltration experiments tested the drainage hypothesis and indicated little or no water movement through the basal material. The dense nature of the fill distinguished at each soil pit, combined with fine-textured sediments, hydrated montmorillonite clays, and an already saturated profile, contributed to the slow rate of drainage recorded on the sascab. Therefore, subfield drainage was probably not a function of the fill platform. In fact, excavations at RF site 3 indicated rounded channels approximately 10 centimeters in diameter occurring at the solum-fill interface. The channels slope from the fields into the canal, suggesting lateral drainage along this boundary. The origins of the channels are unknown. Nutrient analysis indicates some degree of fertility for cultivation of the fill, but it would seem that if the fill were used as a fertilizer it would have been combined with the topsoil rather than utilized in the base of the fields. The most logical function of the fill was as a material for raising the topsoil above the base level of the swamp.

No evidence that the soils of the Pulltrouser depression are prone to gilgai formation which could create the pattern of raised fields and canals was found. Much of the work on gilgai is dated, but the descriptions of this type of soil microrelief yield several similarities that can be used as guidelines to environments where gilgai formation is possible. Jensen (1911), Prescott (1931), Hallsworth, Robinson, and Gibson (1955), Stephen, Bellis, and Muir (1956), and Edelman and Brinkman (1962) state that gilgai are created by cracking of the soil to various depths, producing a patterned ground of puffs and shelves. They state that the prerequisites for gilgai formation are high montmorillonite clay contents, high sodium values, and a wet-dry climatic regime which produces alternating inundation and desiccation of the soils. Such hydrological circumstances promote the alternate expansion and contraction of the montmorillonite clays. Jensen (1911) and Prescott (1931) also report that a neutral to alkaline reaction is found in gilgai soils examined by them.

The soil analysis shows that the Pulltrouser depression soils currently conform to most of the characteristics that can give rise to gilgai, with the exception of one critical factor: moisture content. The dry season in northern Belize today is apparently not sufficiently intense to desiccate the soils in many of the depressions, except for a period of hours or days between rainshowers when only the top 10 centimeters of soil is affected. During the 1979 dry season, only the top 10 centimeters of soil registered a larger water deficit on the Bouyoucos Blocks; the montmorillonite clays remained in an expanded state throughout the dry season. No evidence of even small surface desiccation cracks was seen, and no heaving of vegetation, associated with shrinking and swelling of the soils, was visible on the raised fields.

Climatic data from the area support the field inferences that the depression soils rarely desiccate. The mean monthly rainfall at the height of the dry season in April exceeds 25 millimeters (chap. 2), and the depression captures and retains much of this precipitation as runoff from the surrounding area. Project paleoecological studies (chaps. 6 to 8) did not provide evidence that major environmental changes have taken place in the depression during Maya use. Minor climatic fluctuations have possibly influenced the area, but overall the climate has most likely remained unsuitable for gilgai formation throughout and after the term of Maya occupation of the area.

Additional evidence that the raised-field soils are not subject to gilgai formation comes from the savanna portion of PW, where the topsoils are similar to those of the raised fields. Soil conditions here are suitable for gilgai formation because a severe alternating moisture regime exists in an open grassland. Water table fluctuations of over 1 meter cause this section of the depression to become completely inundated to depths exceeding 50 centimeters in the wet season, while in the dry season the water table drops by more than 1 meter. The clay soils dehydrate and contract, producing cracking of the soil surface. Nevertheless, this section of the depression remains flat and maintains no sign of gilgai or any other ground pattern formation, although wedge-shaped structures occur within the soil profile. This evidence strongly implies that soils in the vicinity of the Pulltrouser depression are not prone to gilgai formation. As environmental circumstances in the past were probably similar to those of today, it is unlikely that gilgai have occurred in the depression during the Maya occupation or in post-Maya times.

The nutrient levels of the raised-field soils are moderate to good for cultivation, but an excess of calcium and sodium in the exchange complex, together with low magnesium levels, may lead to some fertility problems. The high sodium levels may, in part, be a response to the increasing disrepair of the fields and canals after abandonment, so that the fields may now occasionally flood. Submergence of the soil increases the sodium content and causes a decline in potassium because sodium is held more strongly by the exchange complex than potassium (Pasricha and Ponnamperuma 1977).

Boyer (1972) suggests that exchangeable potassium must equal at least 2 percent of the sum of all the other exchangeable bases to satisfy normal plant nutritional requirements, while under intensive cultivation potassium in the soil should equal 4 percent of the exchangeable bases. Calculations of potassium as a percentage of the total available bases (table 5-6) implies that only six A horizon soils have a potassium content exceeding 4 percent. In fact, the potassium contents in many cases do not equal 2 percent of the sum of the available bases. Martini (1977) indicates, however, that for soils in a similar climatic zone in southern Brazil levels of potassium above 180 parts per million are high when plant height is used as an indicator of soil fertility. The potassium levels of the Pulltrouser soils exceed this figure.

Table 5-6. *Potassium as a Percentage of the Major Bases*

Soil Pit & Horizon	Potassium (%)	Soil Pit & Horizon	Potassium (%)
1A	5.940	8A	1.639
1B	1.560	8B	1.481
2A	4.103	9A	6.468
2B	1.154	10A	1.887
3A	1.505	11A	4.702
3B	0.168	12A	1.750
4A	0.361	13A	4.545
4B	0.378	13B	3.415
5A	2.260	14A	0.968
5B	0.434	14B$_1$	6.226
6A	9.700	14B$_2$	7.090
6B	2.560	15A	8.759
7A	3.140	15B$_1$	3.738
7B	2.470	15B$_2$	0.767

The low potassium values may be accounted for by inflated calcium levels caused by the extraction of mineral calcium as well as exchangeable calcium. Easily digestible mineral calcium is a problem associated with the analysis of exchangeable bases in calcareous soil. The high calcium values accentuate the levels of available calcium in the soil, and any calculations including the calcium data, such as the computing of percentage values of the available bases, will show falsely low percentages for all bases except calcium. Calcium contents of soils are normally expected to be in excess of those of potassium by a multiple of ten, while potassium and calcium combined should be a hundred times more concentrated than phosphorus (Nemeth, Mengel, and Grimmeh 1970).

The phosphorus levels of the soils are favorable, and it would be possible to create further increases in plant-available phosphorus by incubating the soils. This situation can be achieved by using a cover of saturated muck dredged from the canals or by flooding the soils, as organic phosphorus can be mineralized to the available form in this way (Gasser and Bloomfield 1955). When the fields were under cultivation, periodic mucking and waterlogging may have been practiced to increase the phosphorus levels. Much the same process enhances the rate of nitrification in soils. Experiments by Reddy and Patrick (1979) indicate that flooding incubates the soil and increases the level of nitrates therein. Their study suggested that the highest rates of nitrification occurred when a high carbon-nitrogen mulch of plant material was added to the flooded soil surface. Blue-green algae in the surface soils and floodwater fixed 0.57 microgram of nitrates per square centimeter per day in the hottest part of the year. This type of system is used to increase the available phosphorus and nitrate content in lowland rice paddies. Additions of canal muck to the raised fields would have made possible the same type of practice and would have led to the enhancement of what today are low nitrogen levels in the soil. Some increase in sodium and a decline in potassium contents associated with waterlogging would have resulted.

At present the soil carbon-nitrogen ratio and the soil structure are not particularly favorable to agriculture, but the act of cultivation would soon promote better fertility levels by improving the soil structure and increasing soil aeration. Increased oxygen in the profile, as a result of cultivation, would promote oxidation of organic matter and reduce the carbon-nitrogen ratio.

The soils are wet throughout the year without becoming waterlogged. Evidence from the Bouyoucos Block experiments demonstrates that the raised fields are well supplied with water and that water shortages were probably rarely a problem to cultivators, although the high water table recorded in the early part of the field season may have proven bothersome. The infiltration studies indicate that soil drainage is no problem, although drainage is to a shallow water table. Waterlogging, by capillary rise from the water table into the rooting zone, is more likely to be a problem as it is on raised fields elsewhere (Wilken n.d.b). Therefore, the height of the raised fields above the groundwater level is critical to avoid such a problem.

The soils examined are confined to the escoba-botan forests and their peripheries bordering the saw grass association. Excavations in the savanna of PW did not reveal the presence of raised fields, although the surface soils are comparable to those of the raised fields (fig. 5-5). The absence of raised fields in the savanna of PW may be due to an unfavorable water regime compared to other parts of the swamp, as the area is on slightly higher ground than the raised fields. Observations indicate that water table fluctuations at PW are much greater than in the raised-field zones. In the former, the surface is inundated to more than 50 centimeters in the wet season, while a situation of physiological water stress occurs in the dry season.

The present soil conditions at Pulltrouser exhibit low nitrogen levels, high carbon-nitrogen ratios, high calcium levels, and heavy, wet soils. Without modification these conditions would restrict the agricultural usefulness of the soils. Pulverization of the soils, a key raised-field function (Denevan and Turner 1974), would reduce

Fig. 5-5. Soil profile, savanna, Pulltrouser West. Note the absence of major cracking in the solum despite the desiccated condition of the savanna.

some of these problems. A system of mucking and flooding could be used for the natural incubation of the soils and the promotion of mineralization of phosphorus and nitrates, enhancing soil fertility. Increased nitrogen and phosphorus levels, combined with the moderate inherent fertility of the soils, near-neutral pH values, and adequate soil drainage, would provide an environment suitable for the growth of a variety of crops.

NOTE

1. The origins of the sascab in the area and the interpretation of the lenses of gypsum are discussed in detail elsewhere (Darch 1981). The gypsum found at depth in the sascab that underlies the channelized field and the base of the raised fields is probably a substitution product associated with drier conditions in the past. The depth of the gypsum, typically 1 meter or deeper into the sascab zone, suggests that it was formed prior to Maya use of the depression. We have recently been informed by Paul Bloom that high levels of gypsum are apparent in the mottled zone at RF site 1 and that, without the removal of the gypsum previous to analysis, the clay content of that zone is muted. As a result of this information, the levels of clay reported here may be lower than those found if the gypsum had been removed before analysis. For the implications of this information, see note 3, chapter 4.

APPENDIX 5-1. SOIL PROFILE DESCRIPTIONS

Soil Pit 1. RF Site 1

Description: situated in botan forest at the edge of a sugarcane plantation on a channelized field at 60 meters on the west-east transect line. Field 1.

Horizon:

A
0–24 centimeters. A-B boundary gradual. Structure massive. Slightly plastic. Slightly sticky. Color 10YR 2/1 black. pH 6. Reaction to HCl 1.

B_1
24–40 centimeters. B_1-B_2 boundary diffuse. Root depth 40 centimeters. Structure massive. Very plastic. Slightly sticky. Color 5Y 6/1 gray. Clayey. pH 7.5. Reaction to HCl 3.

B_2
40–54 centimeters. B-C boundary clear. Structure massive. Very plastic. Slightly sticky. Color 5Y 7/1 light gray. Clayey. pH 7.5. Reaction to HCl 3.

C
54–64 centimeters. Structure massive. Plastic. Slightly sticky. Color 5Y 8/2 white. Gritty clay. pH 7.5. Reaction to HCl 3.

auger of C
110–123 centimeters. Structure massive. Slightly plastic. Nonsticky. Color 2.5Y 8/4 pale yellow. Gritty coarse sand. pH 7.75. Reaction to HCl 3.

auger of C
160 centimeters. Structure massive. Nonplastic. Sticky. Color 2.5Y 7/6 yellow. Gritty clay. pH 7.5. Reaction to HCl 3.

auger of C
195 centimeters. Structure massive. Nonplastic. Slightly sticky. Color 5Y 8/3 pale yellow. Gritty clay. pH 7.25. Reaction to HCl 3.

auger of C
207–230 centimeters. Structure massive. Very plastic. Nonsticky. Color 10YR 7/8 yellow. Silty. pH 7.5. Reaction to HCl 3.

auger of C
260 centimeters. Structure massive. Nonplastic. Sticky. Color 10YR 8/8 yellow. Gritty silt. pH 8. Reaction to HCl 3.

Soil Pit 2. RF Site 1

Description: situated in escoba forest on a channelized field at 45 meters on the west-east transect line. Field 1.

Horizon:

A
0–16 centimeters. A-B boundary gradual.

Structure massive. Nonplastic. Nonsticky. Color
5Y 2.5/1 black. Silty. pH 6. Reaction to HCl 0.

B   16–52 centimeters. Root depth 22 centimeters.
Structure massive. Plastic. Sticky. Color 10YR
4/1 dark gray. pH 7. Reaction to HCl 3.

auger of B   110 centimeters. Structure massive. Very plastic.
Nonsticky. Color 7.5YR 7/0 dark gray. Gritty
clay. pH 6.5. Reaction to HCl 2.

auger of B   138–150 centimeters. Structure massive. Slightly
plastic. Sticky. Color 10YR 7/1 light gray. Gritty
clay. pH 8. Reaction to HCl 3.

auger of C   190 centimeters. Structure massive. Plastic.
Slightly sticky. Color 5Y 8/4 pale yellow.
Mottled. Slightly gritty clay. pH 7.5. Reaction to
HCl 3.

Soil Pit 3. RF Site 1

Description: situated in escoba forest in an infilled canal at 30
meters on the west-east transect line.

Horizon:

O   0–4 centimeters. O-A boundary gradual.

A   4–15 centimeters. A-B boundary merging. Structure massive. Plastic. Nonsticky. Color 5Y 2.5/1
black. Clayey. pH 7. Reaction to HCl 2.

B   15–43 centimeters. Root depth 43 centimeters.
Structure massive. Plastic. Sticky. Color 10YR
4/1 dark gray. Gritty clay. pH 7.5. Reaction to
HCl 3.

Soil Pit 4. RF Site 1

Description: situated in escoba forest on a raised field at 15 meters
on the west-east transect line. Field 2.

Horizon:

A   0–15 centimeters. A-B boundary gradual. Structure
massive. Very plastic. Sticky. Color 10YR 2/1
black with white specks. Coarse sandy clay.
pH 7. Reaction to HCl 1.

B   15–60 centimeters. Root depth 60 centimeters.
Structure massive. Very plastic. Nonsticky.
Color 10YR 4/1 dark gray. Slighty gritty clay.
pH 7. Reaction to HCl 3.

auger of B   100 centimeters. Structure massive. Plastic.

	Slightly sticky. Color 10YR 4/1 dark gray. Very slightly gritty clay. pH 7. Reaction to HCl 2.
auger of C	148 centimeters. Structure massive. Plastic. Slightly sticky. Color 2.5Y 6/4 light yellowish brown. Clayey. pH 8. Reaction to HCl 3.
auger of C	163–173 centimeters. Structure massive. Plastic. Slightly sticky. Color 10YR 4/1 dark gray. Clayey. pH 8. Reaction to HCl 3.
auger of C	192 centimeters. Structure massive. Plastic. Slightly sticky. Color 5Y 5/2 olive gray. Clayey. pH 7.5. Reaction to HCl 3.
auger of C	236 centimeters. Structure massive. Plastic. Very sticky. Color 5Y 7/1 light gray. Clayey. pH 8. Reaction to HCl 3.
auger of C	250 centimeters. Structure massive. Slightly plastic. Sticky. Color 5Y 7/2 light gray. Clayey. pH 7.75. Reaction to HCl 3.
auger of C	296 centimeters. Structure massive. Nonplastic. Sticky. Color 5Y 7/1 light gray. Clayey. pH 8. Reaction to HCl 3.

Soil Pit 5. RF Site 1

Description: situated in escoba forest on the edge of a raised field bordering a water-filled canal at 0 meters on the west-east transect line. Field 2.

Horizon:

O	0–5 centimeters. O-A boundary gradual.
A	5–20 centimeters. A-B boundary gradual. Root depth 20 centimeters. Structure massive. Plastic. Nonsticky. Color 5Y 2.5/1 black with white specks. Gritty clay. pH 7. Reaction to HCl 2.
B	20–35 centimeters. Structure massive. Slightly plastic. Sticky. Color 5Y 4/1 dark gray with white specks. Coarse sandy clay. pH 7. Reaction to HCl 3.

Soil Pit 6. RF Site 2

Description: situated in escoba forest on the channelized segment of the field. Op. III-2-1.

Horizon:

| A | 0–20 centimeters. A-B boundary gradual. Structure massive. Plastic. Slightly sticky. Color 5Y 2.5/1 |

black. Clayey. pH 6.5. Reaction to HCl 0.

B   20–45 centimeters. B-C boundary abrupt. Structure massive. Plastic. Slightly sticky. Color 10YR 4/1 dark gray. Slightly gritty clay. pH 7.25. Reaction to HCl 2.

C   45–126 centimeters. Structure massive. Plastic. Nonsticky. Color 5Y 8/2 white. Very sandy silt. pH 7. Reaction to HCl 2.

auger of C   180–217 centimeters. Structure massive. Very plastic. Nonsticky. Color 2.5Y 8/0 white. Gritty clay. pH 7.75. Reaction to HCl 3.

auger of C   250 centimeters. Structure massive. Slightly plastic. Sticky. Color 5Y 7/2 light gray. Gritty clay. pH 7.5. Reaction to HCl 3.

auger of C   275–295 centimeters. Structure massive. Slightly plastic. Sticky. Color 2.5Y 7/8 yellow. Gritty clay. pH 7. Reaction to HCl 2.

auger of C   311 centimeters. Structure massive. Slightly plastic. Sticky. Color 2.5Y 7/8 yellow. Gritty clay. pH 6.75. Reaction to HCl 2.

Soil Pit 7. RF Site 2

Description: situated in escoba forest on the channelized segment of the field at its juncture with infilled canal. Op. III-2-3.

Horizon:

A   0–6 centimeters. A-B boundary gradual. Structure massive. Slightly plastic. Slightly sticky. Color 10YR 2/1 black. Clayey. pH 7.75. Reaction to HCl 1.

B   6–43 centimeters. B-C boundary abrupt. Structure massive. Very plastic. Nonsticky. Color 10YR 3/1 very dark gray. Gritty clay. pH 7.25. Reaction to HCl 1.

C   43–83 centimeters. Root depth 83 centimeters. Structure massive. Nonplastic. Slightly sticky. Color 5Y 8/1 white. Sandy clay. pH 7. Reaction to HCl 2.

Soil Pit 8. RF Site 2

Description: situated in escoba forest on the raised segment of the field. Op. III-2-4.

Horizon:

O   0–7 centimeters. O-A boundary gradual.

A   7–16 centimeters. A-B boundary gradual. Structure massive. Very plastic. Nonsticky. Color 5Y 2.5/1 black. Clayey. pH 7.75. Reaction to HCl 1.

B   16–35 centimeters. B-C boundary abrupt. Structure massive. Very plastic. Slightly sticky. Color 10YR 3/1 very dark gray. Slightly gritty clay. pH 7. Reaction to HCl 1.

C   35–70 centimeters. Root depth 70 centimeters. Structure massive. Plastic. Nonsticky. Color 5Y 6/1 gray. Slightly gritty clay. pH 7. Reaction to HCl 2.

Soil Pit 9. RF Site 3

Description: situated in escoba forest on a channelized-raised field.

Horizon:

A   0–16 centimeters. A-C boundary gradual. Root depth 5 centimeters. Structure massive. Slightly plastic. Slightly sticky. Color 10YR 3/1 very dark gray. Slightly sandy clay. pH 7.25. Reaction to HCl 2.

C   16–37 centimeters. Structure massive. Plastic. Nonsticky. Color 5Y 8/2 white. Clayey. pH 7.5. Reaction to HCl 3.

C   37 centimeters. Structure massive. Slightly plastic. Sticky. Color 5Y 8/2 white. Fine sandy clay. pH 7.5. Reaction to HCl 3.

Soil Pit 10. RF Site 3

Description: situated in escoba forest in an infilled canal.

Horizon:

O   0–4 centimeters. O-A boundary gradual.

A   4–30 centimeters. Root depth 30 centimeters. Structure massive. Plastic. Slightly sticky. Color 5Y 4/1 dark gray. Slightly gritty clay. pH 7. Reaction to HCl 3.

Soil Pit 11. RF Site 3

Description: situated in escoba forest on the bank of a channelized-raised field.

Horizon:

O   0−4 centimeters. O-A boundary gradual.

A   4−23 centimeters. A-C boundary diffuse. Structure massive. Plastic. Sticky. Color 10YR 4/1 dark gray. Gritty clay. pH 7. Reaction to HCl 3.

C   23−120 centimeters. Root depth 94 centimeters. Structure massive. Slightly plastic. Slightly sticky. Color 5Y 8/2 light gray. Gritty fine sand. pH 7.5. Reaction to HCl 7.5.

Soil Pit 12. RF Site 3

Description: situated in escoba forest on the upper bank of a chan-nelized-raised field.

Horizon:

O   0−9 centimeters. O-A boundary gradual.

A   9−34 centimeters. A-B boundary gradual. Structure massive. Plastic. Slightly sticky. Color 10YR 3/1 very dark gray. Slightly sandy clay. pH 7. Reaction to HCl 2.

C   34−120 centimeters. Structure massive. Slightly plastic. Slightly sticky. Color 5Y 6/1 gray. Sandy clay. pH 7. Reaction to HCl 3.

Soil Pit 13. RF Site 3

Description: situated in escoba forest on a channelized-raised field.

Horizon:

O   0−5 centimeters. O-A boundary gradual.

A   5−23 centimeters. A-B_1 boundary clear. Structure massive. Very plastic. Slightly sticky. Color 5Y 2.5/1 black. Slightly gritty clay. pH 7.5. Reaction to HCl 1.

B_1 23−69 centimeters. B_1-B_2 boundary gradual. Root depth 58 centimeters. Structure massive. Plastic. Sticky. Color 10YR 4/2 dark grayish brown. Gritty clay. pH 7. Reaction to HCl 2.

B_2 69−83 centimeters. Structure massive. Slightly plastic. Sticky. Color 10YR 5/1 gray. Fine sandy clay. pH 7.25. Reaction to HCl 3.

Soil Pit 14. RF Site 3

Description: situated in escoba forest on a channelized-raised field.

Horizon:

O   0–6 centimeters. O-A boundary gradual.

A   6–20 centimeters. A-B_1 boundary gradual. Root depth 19 centimeters. Structure blocky. Plastic. Sticky. Color 10YR 3/1 very dark gray. Slightly gritty clay. pH 7. Reaction to HCl 3.

B_1 20–45 centimeters. B_1-B_2 boundary gradual. Structure massive. Plastic. Sticky. Color 10YR 4/1 dark gray. Sandy clay. pH 7.5. Reaction to HCl 3.

B_2 45–71 centimeters. B_2-C boundary clear. Structure massive. Very plastic. Nonsticky. Color 10YR 3/1 very dark gray. Clayey. pH 6.5. Reaction to HCl 3.

C   71–141 centimeters. Structure massive. Plastic. Slightly sticky. Color 5Y 7/1 light gray. Slightly fine sandy clay. pH 6.5. Reaction to HCl 3.

Soil Pit 15. One Kilometer from RF Site 3

Description: situated in seasonally inundated grassland savanna.

Horizon:

A   0–46 centimeters. A-B_1 boundary gradual. Structure blocky. Very plastic. Sticky. Color 5Y 2.5/1 black. Slightly gritty clay. pH 7. Reaction to HCl 0.

B_1 46–74 centimeters. B_1-B_2 boundary diffuse, disturbed by humans. Structure massive. Plastic. Slightly sticky. Color 5Y 5/1 gray. Slightly gritty clay. pH 7. Reaction to HCl 0.

B_2 74–107 centimeters extending from 46–107 centimeters in places. B_2-C boundary clear. Structure massive. Slightly plastic. Sticky. Color 10YR 3/1 very dark gray. Slightly gritty fine sandy clay. pH 6. Reaction to HCl 0.

C   55–125 centimeters due to uneven boundary. Structure massive. Slightly plastic. Sticky. Color 5Y 7/1 light gray. Slightly gritty fine sandy clay. pH 6. Reaction to HCl 0.

Further Comments on Soils and Raised Fields

William C. Johnson

The soil work by Darch and other facets of the project research leave little doubt that the ground patterns found at Pulltrouser Swamp are anthropogenic in origin and that at least two principal field types occur. Pedogenesis has created relatively abrupt boundaries between sascab and solum on the channelized fields, while this boundary is absent on the raised fields, indicating that deep mixing and other disturbance have occurred. The zone of mixing has a mottled appearance. The use of the term mottled is not intended here in its strict pedologic sense; it does not indicate the presence of a feature created by groundwater fluctuation. Here, the term describes the speckled appearance of the zone in question (figs. 5-2 and 5-3). The mottles are small, angular pieces of limestone, carbonate casts, and possibly gypsum which have been mixed into a matrix, thereby creating not a soil horizon but a stratigraphic (depositional) unit, as suggested by Darch. This stratum does not necessarily correspond to the contemporary zone of annual groundwater fluctuation and varies in thickness from one raised field to another. Angularity of the particles of sascab suggests, first, a cutting or chopping of the material from a relatively well indurated parent mass and, second, a relatively recent origin of the particles; that is, rather limited weathering has occurred. Water-lily remains and aquatic snails found within the zone suggest that some of the material comprising the fields was dredged from the adjacent standing water and mixed with the sascab and other material being piled on the intended field structure (chap. 7). The mottled zone further contains artifacts. For example, the biface pick that was found at a mottled fill–sascab contact could not have been transported to such depth by natural soil processes. The sascab yielded no artifacts in any of the excavations (chap. 4).

Although the soil-geomorphic evidence leaves little doubt about the origin of the fields, other possible origins must be considered. Two other factors could reasonably be considered for the formation of these features: joints in the bedrock (sascab) or gilgai formation. Since reconnaissance mapping of the geology has indicated the presence of faulting, it is not unreasonable to suggest that joints or fractures have occurred to create a regular lattice or polygonal pattern at the water-land interface. Joints are often enlarged by solution or weathering. It can be postulated that the canals are solutionally enlarged joints. However, excavating and augering within canals produced no evidence of such fracture zones. Infiltration tests by Darch also indicated no fracturing in the canal bottoms. Such joints would likely have been enlarged, at least to some degree, in locations other than those within a precisely defined hydrological zone. Also, the well-defined and regularly cross-sectioned morphology of the excavated canals does not exhibit the variation anticipated in the weathering of a joint pattern.

Puleston (1978) suggested that at least some of the possible field patterns observed from the air or on aerial photographs may be a result of gilgai formation (chap. 1). Gilgai is an Australian term which describes microrelief on the soil surface created by seasonal swelling and shrinking of expansible clays in soils. The resulting soils are termed vertisols (new USDA soil taxonomy) or grumusols (superseded USDA soil classification). These soils are common in areas of the seasonally wet and dry tropical climates and have been described in such tropical areas as New South Wales (Jensen 1911) and Kenya (Stephen, Bellis, and Muir 1956).

In the dry season these soils shrink, resulting in open cracks which in turn fill with surface soil through animal activity, root movement, wind, and wash-in when rainfall first begins. With the occurrence of rain, the soil material in the cracks wets and closes. This closure creates appreciable lateral and upward pressures which may force the soil up in the area between the cracks, resulting in mounds (Buol, Hole, and McCracken 1973). This entire process is referred to as argilliturbation, that is, mixing by expansible clays. Such a process can sometimes be responsible for the redistribution of artifacts within the soil (Duffield 1970; Wood and Johnson 1978).

Gilgai formation is clearly not, however, responsible for the field forms observed at Pulltrouser. Even though a dry season exists in the area, the mean annual rainfall of 1,531 millimeters exceeds 1,150 millimeters, that annual rainfall amount above which vertisol development rapidly decreases (Duffield 1970). If gilgai were to be found in the swamp complex, it would be in the savanna area of PW, which experiences an annual cycle of severe saturation-desiccation. No patterns are discernible in the savanna from the air or on the ground. There is, however, limited vertic activity in the savanna of PW, where limited shrink-swell has resulted in the development of wedge-shaped features in the soil profile (fig. 5-5). Slickenside (pressure face) development does occur within the upper 30 to 50 centimeters. Moreover, the observed soil is apparently in equilibrium with the present hydrological conditions, that is, the magnitude of water table fluctuation. Although desiccation occurs, these soils will not form gilgai because of the limited capacity of the constituent clays to expand and contract. Since the soil contains both 2 : 1 and 1 : 1 silicate lattice clays, the shrink-swell potential is limited. The modest level of expansive clays is, in part, due to the advanced state of weathering of the limestone. The expansion-contraction potential of the clays is further reduced by the high concentration of carbonates and gypsum in the soil. Carbonates affect the cation exchange and flocculation-agglomeration of these soils, which effectively reduces the shrink-swell potential (Transportation Research Board 1976). Analysis indicated that the exchange complex is dominated by calcium.

Near the end of the dry season, soils were examined in excavations within the raised fields. The same observations were made one year after the pits were left exposed. No gilgai formation or any tendency toward that end was evident. Soil cracking which did develop occurred to a depth of only approximately 25 centimeters; it was contained primarily within the A horizon and was apparently limited to the excavations. Also, crack width and depth, distribution, and orientation were not conducive to vertic activity. Texture, color, structure, organic matter, and other characteristics of the profile indicate that the soil cracking observed during the 1979 field season was representative of that normally experienced by the raised-field soils. Further, if the features were gilgai, there would be no stratigraphy evident in the soil profile such as the mottled zone; this would not exist under vertic conditions. Finally, a foot survey of various sectors within the study area produced no evidence of gilgai formation.

The above discussion is not to be construed as a denial of the existence of gilgai in the Maya lowlands, only of its existence at Pulltrouser Swamp. However, if the soils of Pulltrouser Swamp are similar to those in other depressions, the existence of extensive well-developed gilgai elsewhere in the lowlands is doubtful. No major gilgai have been reported in the area, although small-scale heaving of the soil was reported at Tikal (Olson 1969). Further, Antoine and associates (1982) could find no evidence of gilgai formation, past or present, at Albion Island.

6. Macrofloral Remains of the Pulltrouser Area: Settlements and Fields

CHARLES H. MIKSICEK

In his review article on New World crop origins, C. Earle Smith stated that "Central America as a whole has not furnished plant remains" (1965: 323). The situation has not changed much since this statement was made, despite the emphasis on "environmental archaeology" in other parts of the world.

Reports of plant remains from lowland Mesoamerican sites are scattered in the archaeological literature. A small cob of Tepecintle maize dating to the Late Preclassic or Early Classic was recovered from Temple E-11 at Uaxactún (Wellhausen et al. 1957). Nal Tel–Chapalote maize kernels from a Late Classic context and possible bean, squash, and cacao seeds from Middle Preclassic horizons were recovered by Willey and colleagues (1965) from sites in the Belize River Valley. Coe and Flannery (1967) found mineralized Nal Tel–Chapalote maize cobs as well as avocado (*Persea americana*), matasano or white sapote (*Casimiroa edulis*), and jocote (*Spondias* species) seeds on Middle Preclassic floors at Salinas La Blanca in the Ocós area of Guatemala. Mary Pohl (personal communication) reports that remains of ramón (*Brosimum alicastrum*), maize (*Zea mays*), beans (*Phaseolus* species), and wild cocoyam (*Xanthosoma* species) were recovered from Late Terminal Classic rooms of the palace structure in Group G at Tikal. Recent work at the Cuello site in northern Belize (Miksicek et al. 1981) has revealed the unexpected potential of Maya sites for producing archaeobotanical remains when systematic sampling and water flotation are utilized. For example, maize (*Zea mays*), squash (*Cucurbita moschata*), wild chile (*Capsicum annuum*), cacao (*Theobroma cacao*), cotton (*Gossypium* species), mamey (*Calocarpum mamosum*), nance (*Byrsonima crassifolia*), hackberry (*Celtis* species), and avocado (*Persea americana*) macrofossils have been recovered from Preclassic horizons at Cuello. Perhaps, with the wider application of these techniques in the Maya area, this paucity of paleoethnobotanical data will be remedied.

THE NATURE OF THE ARCHAEOBOTANICAL RECORD
Wet tropical habitats have traditionally been considered poor environments for the preservation of plant remains. Tropical soils tend to be nutrient-deficient; most of the available nutrients are locked up in the standing biomass. Organic matter decomposes rapidly. Under such conditions plant remains have little chance of enduring for long periods of time unless they are carbonized, reduced to inert charcoal which is resistant to further decay. Only in a permanently wet, anaerobic environment, such as the lower stratum of a raised field, will uncharred plant material be preserved.

Unfortunately, plant material can be incorporated into archaeological horizons, including those of raised fields, by several natural processes such as bioturbation and pedoturbation. For example, leafcutter ants gather leaf fragments and small seeds which are carried into their nests to be used as food or as a culture medium for their "fungal gardens." Rotting palm trunks produce large cavities which could act as traps for forest detritus. Depressions created by the latter two processes can subsequently be filled by floods or surface erosion, sealing plant debris in lower horizons. Burrowing animals can transport plant material into their dens or create traps for forest floor litter. Even in wetland circumstances, occasional desiccation can cause soil cracks that may collect botanical materials. For these reasons, the uncarbonized plant remains from raised-field contexts (table 6-1) should be treated with caution. Carbonized seeds and stems of species exogenous to the contemporary biota are less likely to be intrusive, as the Pulltrouser depression, for the most part, has not been cleared for cultivation during historic times. However, carbonized plant remains could be imported with non-local soils used in the construction of the raised beds.

METHODS OF RECOVERY AND IDENTIFICATION
The project collected soil samples during the test excavations. These samples were processed in the field using the flotation system described by Minnis and LeBlanc (1976). Chemicals to increase specific gravity or deflocculants were not needed or utilized. The resulting flotation samples were dried and sent to the University of Arizona Archaeobotanical Laboratory for analysis. Leaf, wood, and charcoal specimens were also collected during the excavations.

In the laboratory, the dry flotation samples were first passed through a graded series of geological screens, which removes most

of the modern rootlets and sorts the material into similar-size particles that are easier to recognize and identify. The resulting fractions were then sorted under a low-power binocular dissecting
microscope, and identifiable seeds and plant fragments were removed. Seeds were identified at low power (7 to 20×) using modern
reference material collected by the author in Belize, Guatemala, El
Salvador, and southern Mexico.

Charcoal fragments were fractured to produce a fresh trans-
verse section and were examined under higher power (30 to 50×).
Species determinations were made by comparing reference slides
prepared by the author from material collected in the Pulltrouser
area and by using published anatomical keys (e.g., Record and Hess
1942–1948). Uncarbonized woody material was first softened by
being boiled in water for twenty minutes, dehydrated with an alco-
hol-acetone series, and embedded in Epon resin for sectioning on a
sliding microtome (Smith and Gannon 1973). Permanent slides
were prepared from these sections which were then identified at
100×. Several critical charcoal fragments were also resin-embedded
and thin-sectioned.

The macrofloral remains recovered during the Pulltrouser excavations reflect both background vegetation and economically important species. This discussion limits "economic species" to those
used for purposes other than timber or firewood. These remains
and their habitat preferences are summarized (tables 6-1 and 6-2).
There are sharp distinctions between the types of plants recovered
from raised-field versus habitation contexts.

ECOLOGICAL INDICATORS
The forb category (grasses and herbaceous plants) reflects the nature of the ground cover and to some degree the openness of the
forest canopy. Unfortunately, all the seeds in this category are uncarbonized and most likely reflect recent conditions. Habitation
contexts are characterized by a mixture of *Paspalum* and *Echino-
cloa* seeds (two very common grasses in open areas), tropical poke-
weed (*Rivinia* species), *Sida* (malva), and *Melochia* (escobilla, a
weedy Sterculiaceae). In contrast, float samples from the raised-
field excavations contain *Melochia* seeds and *Melampodium* seeds
but lack the grasses. *Melampodium* is a small yellow composite
that grows in disturbed areas and along forest borders. It is characteristic of early successional stages in moist areas.

The category of pioneer shrubs, the first woody species to in-
vade a cleared area, is fairly similar for both raised-field and habita-

Table 6-1. *Macrofloral Remains*

Suboperation-Unit-Lot	Sample	Depth (Cm.)	Remains
Operation II: Kokeal			
1-1-56	24	70–85	*Manilkara zapota* (sapodilla) ch
2-1-65	16f	65–80	dr, 1 frag. *Zea mays* (maize) cob*, 5 frags. *Sabal* (botan palm) ch
2-1-68	23	90–116	*Lysoloma* (guanacaste) ch
2-1-68	25	112	*Crysophila argentea* (escoba palm) ch
2-1-69	34	110–130	*Cordia* (siricote) ch, a.d. 60 ± 45
2-1-69	35	110–130	*Lysoloma* (guanacaste) ch, 20 b.c. ± 50
2-1-70	28	135	*Haematoxylon* (logwood) ch
2-1-70	29	143–151	*Acacia* (cockspur) ch
2-1-70	30	134	*Haematoxylon* (logwood) ch, 35 b.c. ± 55
3-1-72	37	15–40	*Lysoloma* (guanacaste) ch
3-2-?	54	Level 3	Euphorbiaceae (manioc family) root*
3-2-217	54f	82–95	dr, *Paspalum* (Dallis grass) s, *Melochia* (escobilla) 12 s
3-2-222	41	104	Meliaceae (mahogany family) ch
3-2-223	40	103	*Protium copal* (copal) ch, 120 b.c. ± 210
6-1-209	57f	35–50	dr, *Zea mays* (maize) stem*
6-1-296	82f	Burial	*Paspalum* (Dallis grass) 4 s, *Pimenta officinalis* (allspice) fruit unc, Leguminosae (legume family) s*
6-2-297	81f	30–60	dr, *Spondias* (hog plum) fruit*, *Paspalum* (Dallis grass) s, *Solanum* (nightshade) 2 s
7-1-268	58	266	*Theobroma cacao* (cacao) ch
7-1-270	56	295	*Crescentia* (calabash) ch
7-1-270	62	315	*Lysoloma* (guanacaste) ch
7-1-270	63	324	*Solanum* (nightshade) ch
77-2-411	89f	0-30/40	dr, *Carica papaya* (wild papaya) s
77-2-415	67	114	Meliaceae (mahogany family) ch
87-1-278	75f	Level 3	dr, 3 frags. *Terminalia (nargusta)* ch
Operation III: RF sites 1 and 2			
1-4-82	2	16	*Lysoloma* (guanacaste) ch
1-4-84	1	40–50	*Ficus* (wild fig) ch
1-5-86	3	20	*Crysophila argentea* (escoba palm) ch
1-5-87	11	20	*Crysophila argentea* (escoba palm) ch
1-5-87	12	50	*Crysophila argentea* (escoba palm) ch
1-7-103	6	24	*Cordia* (siricote) ch
1-8-106	7	16	Euphorbiaceae (manioc family) root*
1-9-108	4	26	*Cordia* (siricote) ch
1-9-108	5	31	Meliaceae (mahogany family) stump unc
3-1-252	52	35	*Bucida buceras* (bullet tree) ch
3-1-252	53	40–60	*Bucida buceras* (bullet tree) ch
3-1-252	53f	38	dr, *Bucida buceras* (bullet tree) 2 s
3-1-252	55	60–70	*Acacia* (cockspur) ch

Table 6-1, cont'd.

Suboperation-Unit-Lot	Sample	Depth (Cm.)	Remains
3-1-252	58f	38	palm leaf*, Solanum (nightshade) s, Melochia (escobilla) 2 s, Bucida buceras (bullet tree) 7 s
3-2-256	61	70	Hamelia patens (redhead) ch
3-3-309	62f	50	Bucida buceras (bullet tree) 9 s, Melampodium (flor amarilla) 7 s, pr
3-3-309	63f	50	Bucida buceras (bullet tree) 13 s, Solanum (nightshade) 3 s, pr
3-4-?	60	26	Euphorbiaceae (manioc family) root*
3-4-403	66f	82–95	dr, Paspalum (Dallis grass) s, Bucida buceras (bullet tree) 27 s
4-1-318	36	50	Meliaceae (mahogany family) stump unc, a.d. 1826
4-2-34	65	18	Euphorbiaceae (manioc family) root*
4-3-326	95f	20	pr
2-1-122	21	10	Lysoloma (guanacaste) ch
2-1-123	20	15	Lysoloma (guanacaste) ch
2-1-124	18	20	Solanum (nightshade) ch
2-2-131	22	35	Zea mays (maize) stem*
2-3-136	16	30–40	Persea americana (avocado) ch
2-3-137	17	35	Achras zapota (sapodilla) ch
2-4-142	38	30	Hamelia patens (redhead) ch
Operation IV: RF site 3			
1-3-158	49	30	Orbignya cohune (cohune palm) nut*
1-4-163	46	25	Cedrela mexicana (tropical cedar) ch
1-4/5-172	47	28	Euphorbiaceae (manioc family) root*
1-8-181	23f	50	dr, Melampodium (flor amarilla) s, Bucida buceras (bullet tree) 20 s
1-9-?	48f	55	dr, Bucida buceras (bullet tree) s, Solanum (nightshade) s
1-11-189	68f	56–74	pr
1-11-190	77f	50	dr, pr, legume seed unc (possibly Phaseolus), Trophis racemosa (white ramón) ch
1-11-191	34f	38	pr
1-11-191	43	38	Spondias (hog plum) ch
1-11-192	44	31	Spondias (hog plum) ch
Operation V: Kokeal			
77-2-411	64f	0–30/40	dr, Echinocloa (barnyard grass) 3 s
79-1-352[a]	91f	20–40	dr, Bucida buceras (bullet tree) 14 s, Guazuma ulmifolia (wild bay cedar) fruit unc, Melochia (escobilla) 12 s, Rivinia (tropical pokeweed) s, Spondias (hog plum) s, Solanum (nightshade) ch, Bucida buceras (bullet tree) ch, Sabal (botan palm) ch, Terminalia (nargusta) ch, Typha (cattail) leaf*
81-1-359	100f	125–140	dr, Bucida buceras (bullet tree) 2 leaves unc

Table 6-1, *cont'd.*

Suboperation-Unit-Lot	Sample	Depth (Cm.)	Remains
83-1-356	76f	30–50	dr, 2 frags. *Cornutia pyramidata* (fiddlewood) ch
83-1-357	71f	50–70	dr, 2 frags. *Zea mays* (maize) stem*, *Cordia* (siricote) ch, *Pinus caribea* (pine) ch, *Sida* (malva) s
92-1-374	64	93–118	*Cordia* (siricote) ch
111-1-485	70	130–145	*Curatella americana* (sandpaper tree) ch

Key: ch, charcoal; dr, modern dicot roots; f, flotation sample; pr, modern palm roots; s, uncarbonized seed (possibly intrusive); s*, carbonized seed; unc, uncarbonized; *, carbonized nonwood material.

[a]Suboperation 79 (operation V) was originally a mound on a raised field that was suspected to be an occupational site. Excavation revealed the mound to be an anthill. The number 79 was reassigned to a true structure at Kokeal. Because of the richness of the botanical remains, however, we processed the old, abandoned suboperation 79 soil samples. The results here, then, are from an anthill at RF site 1.

tion samples. The *Solanum* (nightshade) seeds were all uncarbonized and should be considered intrusive.

Wood from savanna and early successional trees was recovered only from excavations at Kokeal. Wood charcoal from these categories probably represents material collected for firewood. The calabash or jicara tree (*Crescentia* species) also produces large "gourds" which are used as all-purpose containers, dippers, and bowls. One or two calabash trees are usually planted around modern Maya houses for this reason. The nearest modern pine trees (*Pinus caribea*) are found in savannas about 15 kilometers south of Pulltrouser Swamp. Since pine pollen can be transported over long distances, its abundance in pollen profiles from Pulltrouser sediments (chap. 7) does not infer a closer distribution in the past. The soils of the Pulltrouser depression could not have supported stands of pines in the past, since the trees prefer acid, sandy soils. The pine charcoal fragment from structure 83 probably represents resinous branches imported to Kokeal to be used as torches or timber for construction.

Twenty percent of the wood charcoal from the raised-field excavations came from swamp trees, whereas 49 percent of the charcoal from Late Preclassic structures and 24 percent of the wood from Late Classic habitation units belonged to this category. These results may reflect extensive clearing of the marsh forest community for field construction during the Classic period, causing a reduced availability of timber from swamp trees. Admittedly, the

Table 6-2. *Comparison of the Ecological Associations of Plant Remains from Fields and Habitation Sites*

Fields	Habitation Sites
Forb	
Melochia (escobilla), *Melampodium* (*flor amarilla*)	*Melochia, Rivinia* (tropical pokeweed), *Sida* (malva), *Paspalum* (Dallis grass), *Echinocloa* (barnyard grass)
Pioneer shrubs	
Hamelia (redhead), *Solanum* (nightshade) wood & seeds, *Acacia* (cockspur)	*Acacia, Solanum* wood & seeds
Early successional trees	
None	*Cornutia* (fiddlewood), *Guazuma* (wild bay cedar) fruit
Savanna trees	
None	*Pinus* (pine), *Crescentia* (calabash), *Curatella* (sandpaper tree)
Swamp trees & marsh plants	
Crysophila (escoba palm), *Bucida* (bullet tree) wood & seeds, *Trophis* (white ramón)	*Crysophila, Bucida* seeds, *Terminalia* (*nargusta*), *Haematoxylon* (logwood), *Typha* (cattail)
Forest trees	
Lysoloma (guanacaste), *Cedrela* (tropical cedar), *Orbignya* (cohune palm) nut, Meliaceae (mahogany family)	*Lysoloma, Sabal* (botan palm)
Economic trees	
Cordia (siricote), *Achras* (sapodilla), *Spondias* (hog plum), *Persea* (avocado)	*Cordia, Achras, Spondias, Persea, Protium* (copal), *Theobroma* (cacao), *Pimenta* (allspice), *Carica* (wild papaya)
Field crops	
Zea (maize) stem, Euphorbiaceae (manioc family) root	*Zea* cob fragment & stems, Euphorbiaceae root

Note: All plant remains are wood charcoal unless otherwise specified.

total sample of charcoal remains is rather small, limited to sixty individual fragments, but this apparent trend is mirrored in the pollen data (chap. 7) by a decrease in *Terminalia*-type pollen (swamp tree) and an increase in disturbance pollen (Cheno-*Am* and low-spine Compositae). Bullet tree seeds (*Bucida buceras*) were recovered from almost all of the flotation samples from raised-field contexts, whereas they were recovered from only two samples from habitation contexts.

The bullet tree seeds were all uncarbonized, and most are probably intrusive. However, it is difficult to explain the *Bucida* seeds found at or below 50 centimeters in excavations of several raised fields (III-3-3, III-3-4, IV-1-9). These seeds were highly eroded and could be ancient, preserved by the continuous wetness and the low oxygen levels at this depth. *Terminalia* (*nargusta*) and *Bucida* trees produce dense wood which is usable for construction and firewood. White ramón (*Trophis racemosa*) has an edible fruit which can be used similarly to that of its close relative, the Maya breadnut or ramón (*Brosimum alicastrum*), an upland tree. *Haematoxylon* produces the red or blue logwood dye which was an important item of commerce before aniline dyes were developed. Most of the escoba palm (*Crysophila argentea*) charcoal comes from RF site 1 (III-1-5), along the edge of an ancient canal, and may represent clearing of the depression by fire during construction of the field platforms. During excavation, two stumps (mahogany family) were found in an upright position on the edges of raised-field platforms at about the same depth (31 to 50 centimeters). Initially these were thought to represent border trees similar to those found growing around modern chinampas in the Valley of Mexico. However, the radiocarbon date of a.d. 1826 (table 4-2) of one sample suggests a historic association. Perhaps these trees were cut or broken during logging operations. The carbonized *Typha* leaf from structure 79 at Kokeal probably reflects the use of cattail leaves for house thatching.

Wood charcoal in the forest tree category shows a trend similar to that evidenced by swamp trees. Thirty-two percent of the wood from raised fields came from forest trees, while 37 percent of the charcoal from Late Preclassic structures and 20 percent of the wood from Late Classic habitation contexts came from this category. Again this trend is reflected in the pollen data; samples that produced maize or abundant disturbance pollen had decreased frequencies of forest pollen (Moraceae) (chap. 7). Apparently there was an opening up of the local landscape resulting from the clearing of both swamp and upland forests between Late Preclassic and Late Classic times. Sixteen percent of the charcoal from raised-field contexts, 6 percent from Late Preclassic habitations, and 24 percent from Late Classic structures came from early successional trees or shrubs. Most of the wood charcoal in the forest tree category from the habitation contexts probably reflects usage for construction material. Guanacaste (*Lysoloma*) and tropical cedar (*Cedrela mexicana*) are both timber species. Botan palms (*Sabal*) produce trunks for house posts and guano leaves for thatching.

ECONOMIC SPECIES

Both the habitation and the raised-field samples share a number of species. *Cordia* (siricote wood for carving and an edible fruit), *Manilkara zapota* (a very hard wood for construction, an edible sapodilla, and latex for chicle), and *Spondias* (hog plum) were recovered from both types of contexts. Fragments of carbonized maize stem (*Zea mays*) were recovered from both habitation and raised-field samples, but only the site of Kokeal produced a fragment of maize cob.

The raised-field excavations produced only one distinct economic plant taxon, whereas Kokeal produced several possibilities. *Pimenta officinalis* (allspice, from a burial but uncarbonized), *Carica papaya* (feral papaya, also uncarbonized), *Protium copal* (copal incense, wood charcoal), and *Theobroma cacao* (cacao, wood charcoal) were recovered only from habitation contexts.

The five fragments of charred Euphorbiaceae root are a challenge for interpretation. Several pieces of this material were embedded in Epon resin for sectioning and anatomical study. They are about 1 centimeter in diameter with a fibrous exterior, a thin cortex, and no central pith. The internal structure is poorly lignified, with numerous large, latex-plugged vessels and abundant starch crystals. Anatomically the fragments are closer to *Cnidoscolus* than they are to *Manihot esculenta* (manioc) or *Jatropha* species (physic nut). *Cnidoscolus multilobatus* (*mala mujer*) is a noxious stinging nettle that invades cleared areas. *Cnidoscolus chayamansa* and *C. aconitifolius* (chaya or tree spinach), however, are cultivated forms, lacking or having very reduced amounts of stinging hairs, that were domesticated in Central America as an edible leafy vegetable (National Academy of Sciences 1975). A more precise identification is difficult at this time. Four of these specimens were recovered from approximately the same depth (16 to 28 centimeters), all from separate field areas. A fifth and smaller fragment came from structure 3 at Kokeal. The raised-field specimens are in an ideal stratigraphic position to represent cultivated chaya grown in the fields during ancient Maya times, or they could be nettles that invaded fallow plots that were later burned. Further confusion is introduced by the fact that a specimen from the solum-fill contact zone at RF site 3 which yielded a date of a.d. 1585 (table 4-2) was not identified before it was submitted for radiocarbon analysis. If this sample belonged to the same taxon, it would suggest Postclassic disturbance or utilization of the Pulltrouser depression. Ceramics from structure 83 at Kokeal (chap. 11) document a minor Postclassic presence in the area. However, it must be noted that the radiocarbon sample comes from a location that is adjacent to the main channel in which logs were floated out of PE and PW and that is the major route crossing the depression (chap. 4).

The uncarbonized legume seed from RF site 3, flotation sample 77f, presents another interpretative puzzle. Reniform in profile, similar to a very small kidney bean, this seed appears to be a representative of the genus *Phaseolus*, which includes many cultivated beans and their wild relatives. It was recovered from a depth of 50 centimeters, approximately the level of continuous saturation, from a channelized-raised field. Beans tend to be very poorly preserved in archaeological sites, so this seed could be intrusive, a product of recent agricultural activities in the area, or it could conceivably be an ancient Maya bean preserved by the high moisture and low oxygen of the field. Without dating the specimen directly by the accelerator methods now available for small radiocarbon samples, it would be difficult to resolve this dilemma.

PREHISTORIC CULTIVATED PLANTS
IN THE PULLTROUSER AREA

Neither the plant macrofossil data nor the pollen data (chap. 7) are sufficient to establish firmly which crops may have been cultivated on the raised fields. The presence of maize pollen and the fragment of maize stem from RF site 2 are tantalizing bits of evidence for maize cultivation, but further corroborative data are needed. *Gossypium* (cotton) pollen from the bottom of RF site 1 is also tempting, but as discussed in chapter 7 its presence could be misleading. The cultivation of chaya is also a possibility, but incomplete identification and uncertain association allow only speculation.

The cacao thesis postulated by Hammond (1978) and Dahlin (1979), which suggests that raised fields were constructed for cacao cash cropping, does not seem to be supported by the data because only a small fragment of carbonized *Theobroma* wood was recovered from an earth mound at Kokeal. This is a habitation site, not a raised field.

Based on the macrofossil evidence, it appears that Kokeal may have been similar to modern Maya villages with large numbers of economically useful tree species planted among the structures in small dooryard orchards. Plants such as avocado, siricote, hog plum, copal, sapodilla, and possibly also allspice and papaya would have provided food, shade, incense, latex, hardwood for woodworking, medicine, and deadwood which could be pruned for firewood. After abandonment of the site, feral descendants of these trees would account for the abnormal proportion of economic species associated with ruins noted by many workers in the Maya area (Lundell 1938).

It should be noted, however, that some of these species occur in upland regions without apparent habitation associations and therefore may not necessarily represent cultigens.

CONSTRUCTION OF THE RAISED-FIELD PLATFORMS

The integration of soil, ceramic, pollen, and plant macrofossil evidence provides a coherent scenario for the construction of the fields at Pulltrouser, as discussed in chapters 4 and 5. The channelized fields were formed by an extension of canals into the mainland at the edge of the Pulltrouser depression. Presumably solum from the canal excavations was piled on the planting beds. The plant macrofossils and pollen (chap. 7) suggest some mixing of swamp muck with upland (nonswamp) soils. Charcoal from sapodilla, guanacaste, and avocado, all upland tree species, was recovered from the B horizon of a channelized field at RF site 2. Charred stems of two early successional shrubs, *Hamelia* and *Solanum*, from the same stratum also may infer that some soil was imported from short-term-fallowed fields or other disturbed areas nearby. The pollen and plant macrofossil evidence may indicate that some upland soil, ash from field clearing, or mulch could have been added to the planting surface which was then mixed into the local solum during cultivation. Unfortunately, the maize stem found at 35 centimeters at RF site 2 could represent either a field cultigen or part of this exotic mulch.

The raised fields display a more complicated construction and provide a more clear-cut case of anthropogenic origins than do the channelized fields (chaps. 4 and 5). The plant remains from the fill zone attest to its nonlocal origin, as indicated by the recovery of charcoal from the pioneer shrubs *Acacia* and *Hamelia* and by disturbance pollen from such plants as *Trema*, *Celtis*, composites, and grass (chap. 7). The solum of the fields produced *Bucida* charcoal and a carbonized palm leaf, most likely from trees cut down and burned during the early phases of platform construction. Unit 5 of RF site 1 produced charred escoba palm stems. These data demonstrate that (1) the fill zone contains nondepression plant remains, (2) the solum contains plant remains indicative of swamps or inundated depressions and of uplands throughout the area, and (3) cultivation probably took place on the fields. The plant remains, coupled with the other data, provide support for the anthropogenic origins of the fields.

7. Analysis of Pollen from the Fields at Pulltrouser Swamp

FREDERICK M. WISEMAN

ARCHAEOLOGICAL POLLEN ANALYSIS
IN THE MAYA LOWLANDS

Pollen analysis, a technique used by Quaternary scientists to estimate change in past vegetation and climate (GARP 1975), has been
applied with varying degrees of success to archaeological problems.
Since pollen is present (at least initially) in virtually all terrestrial
and near-shore marine sediments, it follows that archaeological deposits such as middens, structure fill, canals, and other relics should
have the potential for the recovery of pollen in association with
cultural features. However, postdepositional processes such as oxidation, chemical degradation, and microbial activity often degrade
pollen or destroy it altogether. Even when pollen is found in the
sediments, the cultural paleoecologist is presented with a host of
problems. Is the recovered pollen *in situ* or redeposited? Was it
borne by wind or by water, or was it deposited by human agency?
Can we be sure that the pollen reflects a local and not a regional
event? What if climatic factors, not cultural activity, caused the
distinctive pollen assemblage? The cultural paleoecologist has to
worry about each of these issues and more, especially when working in a relatively unknown area. The case is not hopeless, however, because there are independent methods of verifying initial
palynological results, including cultural chronology, dating techniques, and other forms of paleoecological data such as phytolith
analysis, plant macrofossil analysis, zooarchaeology, and paleoped-
ology. Some confidence in results occurs when a pattern is found
and when agreement exists between types of evidence.

Pollen analysis in the Maya area has been practiced by paleo-
ecologists using techniques perfected for paleobiogeographic and
paleoclimatic research. This method includes finding a suitable
lake, sinking a piston corer into that portion of the lake deemed

most promising for recovery of a pollen section, extracting and counting the pollen, and reconstructing the vegetation history of the region from the results. Commonly, archaeological inferences are made from the reconstruction. Examples of such a method are found in the works of Tsukada (in Cowgill et al. 1966: 63–65; Tsukada and Deevey 1967), Deevey (Deevey et al. 1979), Bradbury (Bradbury and Puleston n.d.), and Wiseman (1978: 107–115). These works have provided the archaeologist with a fairly precise vegetation history of the lowlands, but they do not have the anthropologically desirable feature of cultural association.

The collection of pollen samples from archaeological contexts is another method which has become a powerful tool in the reconstruction of pre-Hispanic agriculture, room use, and food processing in the southwestern United States (e.g., Martin and Plog 1973). The aridity of this region often permits excellent preservation of cultivar, weed, and arboreal pollen in archaeological contexts. Such archaeological pollen methods have not been used much in the Maya area, to my knowledge. Perhaps the first attempt in the area was that by David P. Adam, now of the U.S. Geological Survey, while a student at the Laboratory of Paleoenvironmental Studies, University of Arizona. Adam extracted pollen from a Classic period chultun deposit at the site of Tikal. The sample was almost barren, but a few pine grains and fungal spores were observed (Adam n.d.). A later attempt on the same sample, using techniques perfected on southwestern archaeological pollen, proved more fruitful, although a desired statistical count of two hundred grains was not realized. However, with care in extracting and counting, approximately seventy grains were counted; this was interpreted as indicating that high forest was nonexistent at Tikal when the chultun was filled (Wiseman 1972).

In another study, Bradbury (Bradbury and Puleston n.d.) found maize and cotton in canal fill at a field system on Albion Island, suggesting that both cultivars were used on the field system (Puleston 1977a). There is need for caution with regard to this interpretation because the canal deposits date from the last dredging, which probably did not take place too long before field abandonment. In such studies from the Southwest, it is the convention to date finds from such contexts as postdating the fields. It is conceivable that pollen near the base of the fill could date to field use, but the profiles for the Albion Island work are not available. Despite these problems, the Albion Island work demonstrated the potential for palynology with regard to Maya agricultural artifacts.

Other such circumstances sampled in the mid 1970s provided

mixed results. Old soils in the Petén and terraces in the Copán Valley, Honduras, yielded little pollen (Wiseman n.d.a, n.d.c). However, archaeological samples from Yucatán, an area more arid than the central Maya lowlands, proved more promising for upland archaeological palynology. Fish (n.d.) found countable pollen at the sites of Edzna and Aguacatal, and Formative Dzibilchaltún samples contained some countable pollen (Wiseman n.d.b). Demonstration of pollen preservation in archaeological contexts was continued at Pulltrouser in context with the relic raised fields found there.

PALYNOLOGICAL RESEARCH DESIGN
The research design for Pulltrouser Swamp was formulated to provide a paleocultivation surface context for pollen analysis. There are several microgeomorphological environments within each raised-field system, each with its own potentials and limitations for pollen analysis (table 7-1). For several reasons, the interiors of the raised-field structures probably provide the best environment in the field-canal system for the close study of agriculture.

1. Anemophilous (wind-dispersed) cultivar pollen, such as that of *Zea* (maize), does not travel far from its origin by wind transport, although it may be moved and concentrated by water (Wiseman 1978: 93). Entomophilous (insect-dispersed) cultivar pollen types,

Table 7-1. *Sedimentary Environments and Pollen Potential at Pulltrouser Swamp*

Microenvironment	Geomorphic Processes	Remarks
Canal bottom	Silt & organic matter deposition, aquatic saprobes, slow water movement, possible drying out. Removal of bottom sludge by agriculturalists.	Good potential for pollen preservation—pollen has been found in such zones, incomplete association with agriculture
Canal sides	Water-level fluctuation, slumping	Poor pollen preservation environment—chance for oxidation
Raised-field structure	Possible erosion, probable anthropogenic deposition by agriculturalists, decayed organic deposition in postagricultural times	Possibly good pollen preservation—clays retain interstitial water preventing general drying out & oxidation
Raised-field surface	Modern deposition	Good pollen from current vegetation

such as that of *Manihot* (manioc), *Gossypium* (cotton), and *Theo-broma* (cacao), are unlikely to be found in sediments due to their specialized pollen vectors. Therefore, the discovery of these pollen types within the field itself would tend to indicate the proximity of the cultivar to the raised field.

2. The clay and sascab matrix of the raised field would tend to hold water by capillary and ionic means (chap. 5), preventing an alternating wet-dry environment that would oxidize pollen.

3. Pollen profiles could be tentatively dated by association with artifacts and carbon samples found within the field.

In addition to the raised-field sample suite, a series of short cores in canals or interfield basins was to be taken to reconstruct postagricultural pollen sequences. Such a reconstruction was deemed necessary to provide a control with which to compare the samples taken from supposedly agricultural contexts. Such comparisons were thought to provide a clearer understanding of the putative ag-ricultural profiles by potentially separating natural from artificial pollen inputs.

A third portion of the research design involved the collection of modern pollen from the described vegetation zones in order to correlate the abundance of a species with the amount of pollen de-posited within a vegetation stand. Species lists and plotless sam-pling were to be used to characterize the potential pollen-producing vegetation types.

FIELD AND LABORATORY TECHNIQUES
Sediment coring Pulltrouser Swamp was fraught with problems for, unlike deep lake sediments in the Petén, fallen branches, tree roots, and heavy clays hindered penetration of the core barrel. The instru-ment used was a 2-inch-by-1-meter Livingstone piston corer, whereas a Hiller instrument would have been more appropriate for use in the peaty deposits (Faegri and Iversen 1975: 89). A small (half inch) slit-sided core tool was more effective in penetrating the sediment, but it did not have the depth potential of the Livingstone. The core barrel was pushed and pounded into the sediment until it came to a stop, after which it was retrieved and taken to dry land where the core was extruded onto a flat surface, measured, and sampled. Sam-pling the core consisted of scraping away the outer centimeter of sediment with a sharp knife. This process removed the part of the sample most likely to have been contaminated or distorted by the passage of the core barrel through the sediment. The column was then measured and the stratigraphy noted. Subsamples were taken from the core with a pocketknife at 5-centimeter intervals. The

knife was cleaned between each use to prevent cross-contamination of samples. The samples were placed in labeled plastic bags (Whirl-paks) for shipment to the laboratory.

Sampling from the raised fields was done in conjunction with their excavation in order to provide stratigraphic and chronological controls for the pollen data. One wall of a completed excavation at RF site 1 was chosen as a pollen profile. The wall was scraped clean (using the sideways motion of a trowel) to a depth beyond which shrinkage cracks penetrated. This procedure exposed moist sediments. The scraped section was measured and the stratigraphy recorded in the field log. Samples were taken at 10-centimeter intervals, except when an unconformity was evident. Samples were taken on each side of the juncture.

Pollen extraction was performed at the Quaternary Paleoecology Laboratory, Louisiana State University. On arrival, the sediment samples were split (to preserve half of the sample for later analysis), and the palynological fraction was placed in distilled water. The extraction technique, described in appendix 7-1, consisted of treating the sediment with hydrochloric acid, hydrofluoric acid, nitric acid, and potassium hydroxide. This process removed successive fractions of carbonates, silicates, and organic residues from the sample, hopefully leaving a pollen-rich residue. The residues were decanted into storage vials for later analysis.

Classification of the pollen was performed under a binocular microscope having magnifications ranging from 100× for scanning, through 400× for pollen counting, to 1,000× oil immersion for identification of unknown types based on minute characters. Each sample was tallied, with a total number of classified pollen grains equaling two hundred grains or more if possible. Unfortunately, many samples were barren of pollen or contained too few grains for a count of two hundred. The resulting counts were then recorded on computer cards and added to a palynological data bank being assembled by the laboratory.

RESULTS

The modern pollen rain found under the swamp vegetation reflects both the local and the regional (pine and oak) pollen rain. The two dominant local tree taxa, Moraceae and *Terminalia*-type, were represented by *Chlorophora* (Moraceae) and *Bucida* and *Terminalia* (Combretaceae), all found within 5 meters of the sampling sites.[1] Pollen from the adjacent marsh is represented by sedge (Cyperaceae) and occasional cattail (*Typha*) pollen. The heavily disturbed uplands, covered by sugarcane fields and secondary scrub, are rep-

resented by large percentages of Chenopodiaceae (+ *Amaranthus*),
Compositae, Gramineae, and *Trema*. The proportions of these pollen types are good estimators of the local diversity of vegetation
found in the Pulltrouser Swamp area (see top samples, tables 7-2
and 7-3).

The fossil pollen data are more confused and fragmentary. Both
the archaeological pollen series (table 7-2) and the short-core series
(table 7-3) had only sporadic strata containing countable pollen (six
of thirteen and three of ten, respectively). The core samples (table
7-3) are almost certainly postagricultural. The high percentages of
Moraceae and *Terminalia*-type at the lowest sample (30 centimeters) argue against significant clearing of the escoba-botan forests.
These taxa are not known to have been used in ethnohistoric times
(e.g., Hellmuth 1977) and were probably early casualties in the construction of the raised fields. Unless stands of these trees were
spared, it is difficult to justify such amounts of these types of pollen during field usage. However, weedy, herbaceous vegetation is
well represented, indicating open vegetation in the vicinity, possibly as milpas on upland surfaces adjacent to the basin (Compositae)
and the central marsh itself (Gramineae, Cyperaceae). The data in
the core samples may provide a good view of Late Postclassic–
colonial land use, but without any reliable dating this statement
remains largely speculation.

The palynological data from the interior of a raised field at RF
site 1 are associated with construction and use of the fields and are
independently dated by artifacts. While the degree of contamina-
tion of the top few centimeters of the fields is uncertain, the samples at 70 to 110 centimeters are undisturbed and probably represent the landscape during construction and maintenance of the
raised fields (table 7-2). Here, the swamp forest taxa are reduced,
and weedy, agricultural indicators are abundant. Pollen of *Zea, Solanum*, and *Gossypium* found in these lower levels may represent
cultivars.

INTERPRETATIONS
Inferences from the Data.   At the time of construction of the system, Pulltrouser Swamp was probably an open body (nonforest) of
water containing water lilies (*Nymphaea*) whose remains (both
phytoliths and pollen) were incorporated in later field construction.
Nymphaea cannot compete with marsh graminoids and does not
do well under a closed swamp canopy due to its high light requirements (Graf 1973: 1663), although it can be found growing in the
deeper, water-filled canals along the forest-covered fields at Pull-

Table 7-2. Pollen Percentages from Raised-Field Site 1, Field 3

Depth (Cm.)	Pinus	Acacia	Bombacaceae	Bursera	Celtis	Coccoloba	Moraceae	Myrica	Quercus	Sapotaceae	Spondias	Terminalia-Type	Trema	Cheno-Am[a]	Cyperaceae	Compositae, High Spine	Compositae, Low Spine	Senecio	Gramineae	Zea	Solanum	Gossypium	Nymphaea	Other	Unidentified	Total Pollen in Second Sum	Nymphaea Biosilicate
0	71	0.5	1.6	0.5	2.1	1.1	6.3	0.5	7.9	0.5	1.6	16.4	1.6	4.2	11.1	5.3	21.2	2.1	14.8	0.5	0.0	0.0	0.0	21	18	189	*
5	48	1.2	0.6	0.0	3.6	0.0	33.7	0.0	11.2	1.8	0.6	17.2	1.2	1.2	10.1	3.6	7.1	0.6	5.9	0.0	0.6	0.0	0.6	7	6	169	*
10																											***
20	82	0.7	2.1	0.7	3.5	0.7	25.5	1.4	7.1	2.8	1.4	11.3	5.0	7.1	4.3	2.1	10.6	2.1	11.3	0.0	0.0	0.0	1.4	36	19	141	****
30	69	2.0	0.5	0.5	4.5	0.0	14.4	0.5	5.9	2.5	0.5	5.9	0.5	10.4	14.9	2.5	10.4	2.5	20.8	0.5	0.5	0.5	0.5	12	17	202	**
40																											***
50																											*****
60																											*****
70	58	0.5	0.0	1.4	5.6		3.3	0.5	9.8	3.3	0.5	7.0	4.7	1.4	5.6	4.7	17.3	3.3	28.0	0.9	0.5	0.8	1.9	41	22	214	****
80																											**
90																											*
100																											***
110	63	1.2	0.4	0.4	4.0	1.2	5.6	1.2	12.4	0.4	3.2	4.8	0.4	2.4	14.4	4.8	20.4	4.8	15.6	0.4	1.2	0.0	0.5	16	30	250	***

Note: Pine, other, and unidentified types are a percentage of the total pollen. The rest are counted as a second sum excluding these types. The asterisks indicate a subjective assessment of relative abundance.

[a] Cheno-Am is an artificial pollen taxon combining the pollen of the goosefoot family (Chenopodiaceae) with the almost palynologically identical pollen of the pigweed (*Amaranthus*).

Table 7-3. Pollen Percentages from Raised-Field Site 2, Core 1: Post-Maya Sedimentation

Depth (Cm.)	*Pinus*	*Acacia*	Bombacaceae	*Bursera*	*Celtis*	*Coccoloba*	Moraceae	*Myrica*	*Quercus*	Sapotaceae	*Spondias*	*Terminalia*-Type	*Trema floridana*	Cheno-Am	Cyperaceae	Compositae, High Spine	Compositae, Low Spine	*Senecio*	Gramineae	*Zea*	*Solanum*	*Gossypium*	*Nymphaea*	Other	Unidentified	Total Pollen in Second Sum
2.0	91	0.6	0.6	0.6	1.1	1.7	9.4	0.6	5.6	1.1	2.8	25.6	1.1	3.3	6.7	8.3	17.2	5.6	7.2	1.1	0.6	0.0	0.0	8.0	16	180
5.0	+						+		+			+		+	+	+	+	+	+		+			1.6	10	21
8.0	58	0.0	0.8	1.3	3.0	0.8	15.2	0.0	6.8	0.8	0.4	12.7	3.0	5.1	6.8	8.4	14.3	17.7	2.5	0.0	0.4	0.0	0.8			237
10.0																										16
12.5																										4
17.5	+																									6
20.0	+		+	+	+		+		+			+		+	+	+	+	+	+		+		+			32
23.5																										
25.0																										
30.0	79	0.5	0.5	1.4	0.5	2.7	22.3	1.4	8.6	3.6	3.2	21.0	2.7	1.4	9.5	6.4	7.3	2.3	5.5	0.0	0.0	0.0	0.5			220

Note: Pine pollen figures are a percentage of the total pollen, as are the other and unidentified classes. A second sum was used for the rest of the taxa. The plus signs indicate pollen present but in amounts too small for a statistical sample.

trouser where the canals apparently allow sufficient sunlight to penetrate the canopy level. The materials apparently used for field construction and maintenance contained *Nymphaea* remains, suggesting that at least partly open water situations with some sun were available. Analogous habitats can be found throughout the Maya lowlands: shallow lakes with water lilies along the edge in about 1 to 3 meters of water, grading into a marsh composed of large sedges such as *Cladium*, *Cyperus*, and *Eleocharis*, carrizo (*Phragmites communis*), and cattail (*Typha dominguensis*). Such a habitat description is supported by abundant remains of monocot leaves and panicoid grass phytoliths, probably from the marsh plants in shallower water. These materials may have been used as mulch or carried to the fields in muck.

The abundant weed pollen embedded in the raised fields may be interpreted as reflecting artificial, open vegetation close to the fields because agriculturalists presumably did not allow a large weed component to flourish on the platforms. The presence of Compositae pollen reflects an alteration of adjacent upland vegetation, from either habitation disturbance from occupation sites, such as Kokeal, or upland agriculture. I submit, as an educated guess, that the weed pollen comes from agricultural fields that were undergoing some type of fallow period. This guess is founded on a comparison of the pollen of weed flora of modern towns and fields with that of the construction fill. The latter pollen seems to resemble an agricultural weed pollen spectrum (more Compositae and Gramineae) more than a village weed pollen spectrum (more Cheno-*Am* and Euphorbiaceae). However, since these data are tentative, any argument must be presented cautiously.

Maize (*Zea*) pollen was found in all raised-field samples, both on the surface and at depth, and a piece of corn stalk was found at depth (chap. 6). These data are strong evidence of the association of the fields and that cultivar. *Gossypium* (cotton) pollen was also found within the fields. However, there may be wild *Gossypium* species in Belize, or the pollen may come from another Malvaceae. The pollen of *Amaranthus* and *Solanum* may also represent native noncultivars. Until more research is done, I would hesitate to say that these are undoubtedly cultivar pollen types.

Broader Implications.   Although the pollen data are fragmentary, due largely to postdepositional degradation in many samples, several implications regarding Maya subsistence research may be presented. First, the raised fields were constructed within a littoral environment decidedly different from that encountered today. The fields were built and maintained within a marshlike environment, not within escoba-botan swamp forests. Lines of evidence to support this statement include a lack of swamp tree pollen (either as *in situ* or as redeposited pollen) as well as the presence of water-lily pollen and phytoliths in the samples from lower strata which likely date to the initial construction of the fields. Since marshy habitats are easier to channelize and mound than root-bound arboreal swamps, they were probably selected by agriculturalists for raised-field construction, unless an overriding limiting factor such as poor soil fertility, inadequate water, or pests forced selection of swamp forest zones. These data are, at present, perhaps the best evidence for the initial setting of the fields but are not necessarily supported by the soils and the plant remains (chaps. 5 and 6). The reconstruction offered here is a preliminary hypothesis to be tested in later research.

Second, the surprising dearth of upland and escoba arboreal pollen within the raised-field fill, compared to that within the canal sediments, may be attributed to two factors. The first factor is surface-to-fill bioturbation by rodents or invertebrates (chap. 6) and/or by root disturbance—tree fall, as was evident at RF site 3. Post-Maya arboreal pollen was found in the upper 30 centimeters of the raised-field profile, where bioturbation is most likely to occur. It seems unlikely that bioturbation would occur at depth, and arboreal indicators were virtually absent in the lower section of the profile.

Another, less localized factor is that the major source area for arboreal pollen, the uplands or mainlands surrounding Pulltrouser Swamp, was denuded of trees and apparently covered with herbaceous flora. If this condition existed at the time of raised-field construction, it suggests that the mainlands were extensively cultivated. These data may be viewed as preliminary support for the assumption that at Pulltrouser littoral habitats were not exploited by settlers using a raised-field subsistence system before the use of uplands. However, this interpretation is based on a small sample from fields that are later in date than other such systems in Belize are projected to be (Puleston and Puleston 1971).

A third major implication of the palynological research—that pollen is an indicator of economic activity within the field system—is less secure. Although there is maize pollen throughout the sample suite, its source is equivocal. It is tempting to state that maize was the major crop raised on the platforms, but its very ubiquitousness makes that hypothesis suspect. Consider the sample from 110 centimeters at RF site 1 (table 7-2). It is almost certainly a prefield sample or a sample associated with the initial construction, not a later deposit of fill made during maintenance of the field (such as the upper samples). The presence of maize pollen, if an *in situ* deposition, indicates that it was incorporated into the fill as a construction characteristic. The pollen at 30 and 70 centimeters is almost identical to the 110-centimeter sample. We would expect a significant increase in maize pollen in the higher zone if the fields were maintained under a maize agricultural regime. An alternative hypothesis that would explain the sample similarity is that refuse from nearby upland maize fields, including maize stalks and husks, was used as a mulch to improve the physical and chemical properties of the structure fill.

Another economic implication concerns the water-lily evidence in the upper samples, which probably are from maintenance additions, as opposed to initial construction. This plant, while not a primary economic taxon, may have been an important second-level component of the raised-field system. First, it provides a suitable microenvironment for numerous invertebrates, recycles organic detritus, and produces dissolved oxygen. These factors provide an ideal habitat for fish, an important protein source for the Maya. This association between fish and *Nymphaea* is often represented in Maya art (Puleston 1977a: 458). Second, the rapidly growing water lily provides an on-site, abundant source of mulch. Puleston, in a discussion of his experimental raised fields, noted:

> . . . the water lily is common in slow-moving and still water throughout the Maya lowlands. Colonies were quick to establish themselves in the re-excavated canals around our experimental fields and by the fall of 1975 were so thick that we had to uproot them to enable easy passage of our canoe loads of sawgrass mulch and palmetto to the plots under cultivation. (1977a: 458)

If conditions were similar in the past, the Maya could have short-circuited Puleston's technique and mulched with the water lily. Pollen and the much more abundant biosilicate remains of *Nymphaea* in the upper samples (assumed to date after initial construction) indicate an incorporation of lily plants into maintenance fill. The water lily may have been as important in Maya agriculture as it was in Maya art.

Two other taxa found in raised-field structure fill have been cited as important economic pollen types: *Gossypium* (Puleston 1977a: 454) and *Amaranthus* (Puleston, personal communication). *Gossypium* is an entomophilous plant and does not shed much pollen into the environment, so its discovery in raised-field situations has led to the supposition that cotton was a crop of the raised field. This assumption is probably valid to a certain extent, but a caveat is warranted. There are many noneconomic Middle American members of that genus which have pollen indistinguishable from the cultivar pollen. Most of these are secondary successional plants which are highly correlated with other agricultural indicators. These facts may give cotton a palynological image that is somewhat inflated. Until much more work is done on the biogeography and pollen taxonomy of tropical New World cottons, I cannot state with certainty that cotton was a raised-field crop at Pulltrouser.

The same caveat must be issued for the genus *Amaranthus*, only more emphatically. Grain amaranth comes from a genus composed of a host of species, all of which are aggressive old-field colonizers and prolific producers of pollens that are indistinguishable at the specific level. Also, the pollen is almost identical to that of the family Chenopodiaceae, another aggressive weedy family. With so much chance for error, I would consider the pollen as indicative only of disturbance, not of a cultivar.

The crops grown on the raised fields remain uncertain. The archaeobotanical record contains several arboreal crops, including siricote, sapodilla, hog plum, and avocado (chap. 6). Except for avocado, all these taxa are also present in the secondary forests in the environs of Pulltrouser Swamp and may be of natural origin. Therefore, at best the paleobotanical evidence for crops is equivocal.

Ethnohistoric data concerning the highland version of raised fields, the chinampa, may provide insight into the problem. Plants used on modern chinampas serve two purposes: structural reinforcement of the platform and economic productivity. Arboreal species such as willows (*Salix*) are planted on the platform's margins. The matted, entwined roots prevent slumping or erosion of the clay platform, thereby stabilizing the structure. Additionally, the plants provide shade for canals and fields, act as windbreaks, and support scandent crops (such as vanilla) and human structures. If the raised fields were analogous, then we may postulate the use of stabilizers. The remains of these fields are today bordered by stands of bullet trees (*Bucida*), perhaps descendants of original stabilizers. However, it is more likely that they merely colonized this microhabitat long after field abandonment.

The economic taxa possibly used on the fields are just as hard to visualize. One approach is to attempt to isolate those species of cultivars that tolerate the soils of the lowland swamps. However, with proper mulching and management, the raised-field soils (haplaquolls) would support almost any crop (chap. 5). At least fifteen species may be likely candidates for raised-field cultivation, based on ethnohistoric data on Maya crops from the neighboring Petén (Hellmuth 1977: 433–436). These are *Ananas cosmosus, Bixa orellana, Capsicum* species, *Dioscorea* species, *Gossypium* species, *Ipomoea batatas, Manihot esculenta, Nicotiana* species, *Pachyrhizus erosus, Phaseolus* species, *Sechium edule, Theobroma cacao, Vanilla planifolia, Xanthosoma yucatanense,* and *Zea mays.* Excluded here are trees which are too large to have been accommodated by the fields (*Brosimum, Manilkara, Protium*) and xerophytes (*Agave*).

Raised fields require a relatively large initial and continuing labor investment to refurbish, mulch, and plant (chap. 13). Therefore, it was probably not in the farmer's best interest to plant crops on the platforms that did not give a high return on this investment. Due to their market prestige in the contact period, I suspect that *Ananas* (pineapple), *Gossypium, Nicotiana* (tobacco), *Theobroma, Vanilla* (vanilla), and *Zea* would have been selected for planting on the fields, unless overriding limiting factors forbade their use. Of these cultivars, the evidence from Pulltrouser and elsewhere supports best the case for maize (*Zea*) and, perhaps, cotton (*Gossypium*).

If the Maya elite dictated the cultivar suite for raised fields, any crop could have been used, regardless of habitat requirements or market value. I suspect that this may have been the case, but a bias toward the six crops listed above may have existed because of their transportability and market value. After all, Pulltrouser Swamp's productivity was but a small cog in the bewilderingly complex subsistence system that supported the Maya civilization.

ACKNOWLEDGMENTS
Partial support for the fieldwork and laboratory analysis was provided by the project and by a Louisiana State University summer faculty research grant. I thank project members for their comments and field support, particularly William C. Johnson. This chapter is a revision of Quaternary Paleoecology Laboratory's report 6, Louisiana State University.

NOTE
1. There is some question regarding the identification of *Terminalia* pollen. Until this problem is resolved by modern pollen sampling in Belize, I will refer to the pollen as *Terminalia*-type. Ecologically, the pollen taxon "behaves" as a swamp plant, so inferences may still be used regardless of the identity of the producing plant.

APPENDIX 7-1. POLLEN EXTRACTION TECHNIQUE

A. *Sediment deflocculation and pollen concentration*

1. Break up the sample and screen it through at least a twenty-mesh standard sieve to remove larger sand and gravel particles.
2. To about 50 grams (weighed; weight recorded) of the screened sample, add 50 milliliters of distilled water in a 500-milliliter beaker.
3. Add 25-milliliter portions of concentrated HCl, stirring the mixture slowly. If the mixture fizzes, add another 25 milliliters of concentrated HCl; continue adding portions until fizzless. As the fizzless state approaches, stir more vigorously to be sure all particles are subjected to HCl.
4. When the mixture is fizzless, stir it vigorously with a stirring rod until a vortex forms.
5. Let stand thirty to sixty seconds while boulders, etc., settle out. While the mixture is still slowly turning, pour the supernatant through a hundred-mesh screen into another beaker. Wash the screen with distilled water (from a squirt bottle) into the beaker. Repeat the process one more time (swirl); then discard the sediment.
6. Swirl the supernatant in the second beaker until a vortex forms; let stand one to two minutes (do not let the motion completely stop); pour into a 50-milliliter centrifuge tube. Balance the tubes in a centrifuge-tube balance; stir the sediment; centrifuge for three minutes; decant (the abbreviation BSCD is hereafter used to refer to this process). If more centrifuge tubes are necessary, use several tubes; BSCD; wash all materials into one tube; BSCD.

B. *Matrix destruction*

1. Wash with 10 percent HCl; BSCD.
2. Wash with 30 percent HCl; BSCD.
3. Wash with distilled water; BSCD.
4. Add 10 milliliters of 50 percent HF; stir gently once or twice. Wait several minutes (the reaction may be delayed). Then stir gently until all the material is well mixed. If a reaction occurs, break the bubbles gently with a stirring rod as they reach the top of the tube. After the reaction dies down, stir again gently and, if no further reaction occurs, add 10 milliliters of 50 percent HF and stir gently. Repeat this step until there is no further reaction. If there is no reaction at all, add another 30 milliliters of 50 percent HF.

Cover with paper towels and let stand six to twenty-four hours.

5. BSCD; add 30 milliliters of 70 percent HF (there will be no reaction at this stage); let stand six to twenty-four hours.
6. Stir; gently boil in water bath twenty to thirty minutes.
7. BSCD; add boiling water; BSCD.
8. Add boiling water; BSCD.
9. Add 25 milliliters of 20 percent HNO_3; let stand ten minutes.
10. BSCD; add boiling water; BSCD.
11. Add boiling water; BSCD.
12. Add 30 milliliters of concentrated HCl; boil in water bath two minutes (or until the solution begins to bubble); BSCD.
13. Add boiling water; BSCD.
14. Add boiling water; BSCD.
15. Acetolyze here, if necessary.
16. Add 5 percent KOH; place in boiling water bath for three minutes; BSCD.
17. Add water; BSCD at least twice. Repeat until the decanted solution is water-white and clear (as many as ten or fifteen times).

C. *Preparation for storage*
1. Add distilled water; BSCD.
2. Wash the residue into a vial with distilled water.
3. Centrifuge the vial (half speed).
4. With a disposable pipette, remove the supernatant.
5. Add glycerol of equal volume to the residue.
6. Label the vial with the following data: provenience; extractor, date extracted; acetolysis number.

8. Mollusca: A Contrast in Species Diversity from Aquatic and Terrestrial Habitats

ALAN P. COVICH

One of the most challenging questions in biology currently is, How do biotic communities originate and develop their structure? Just as the form and function of human cultural communities provide an active area of research in the social sciences, the mechanisms that regulate natural species interactions and their persistent, recurring assemblages are under intensive study. A possible topic of interdisciplinary exchange, then, is evident when archaeologists, geomorphologists, and geographers begin to work with biologists on the exploitation and distribution of such widespread species as the mollusks.

From the biological viewpoint, there is an apparent paradoxical contrast in the high number of different species among the tropical marine mollusks (e.g., Vermeij 1978) relative to the low number of species among the tropical freshwater mollusks (e.g., Covich 1976). Although many potential mechanisms exist for regulating the number of individuals of each species and the total number of different species in each assemblage, one of the most important regulators appears to be the higher rates of removal of certain individuals from multiple-species communities while other individuals avoid removal. In the biological literature, the rate of removal is usually thought to be related to certain genetic differences in longevity or to major differences in vulnerability to predators (Vermeij and Covich 1978). The likely impact of harvesting mollusks by both ancient and modern human populations obviously needs to be considered before the significance of nonhuman predation can be evaluated in present-day ecosystems. Simultaneously, it is impossible to evaluate the cultural exploitation of mollusks as food, ritual items, or ornamental resources until predation on these species by many diverse natural, nonhuman consumers is well understood. This chapter focuses primarily on the major differences in species diversity as they relate to habitat modification in the lowland Maya area.

Because molluscan shell remains are frequently abundant in archaeological deposits, the spatial and temporal distributions of species are reported and currently provide a rapidly increasing data base for broad-scale ecological interpretations. Usually, the shell deposits are dominated by terrestrial, lung-bearing (pulmonate) snails at inland sites or by aquatic, gill-bearing (prosobranch) and lung-bearing snails at coastal sites. Pelecypods (bivalves) also typically dominate aquatic assemblages and often occur in localized high densities that are interpreted as culturally deposited middens.

In the first case, the species assemblages are typically considered to represent paleoenvironmental indicators of past rainfall, temperature, and vegetation. Because the habitats of most terrestrial gastropods are widely and readily studied, considerable data exist on how these species select their optimal food and location. Their seasonal distributions are well known, especially in temperate zone ecosystems (e.g., Baerreis 1973; Evans 1972; Miller 1978; Sparks 1964). In the second case, the distributions of aquatic mollusks in archaeological samples are more frequently used to analyze food resource utilization or to trace ancient trade routes (e.g., Andrews 1969; Moholy-Nagy 1978; Nations 1979; Parmalee and Klippel 1974; Voorhies 1976; Zeitlin 1978).

BIOGEOGRAPHICAL RELATIONSHIPS

The known biogeographical distributions of the land snails in northern Belize thus far appear to be generally similar to those in Yucatán and Guatemala. Not unexpectedly, the lack of any effective physical barrier has permitted widespread dispersal over long periods of time (Basch 1959). In some cases this dispersal may have been enhanced by Maya traders, either intentionally or accidentally. It has been apparent since the earliest studies on the malacological fauna of Central America that there are minor morphological shifts in traits, such as shell sculpture, size, and pigmentation. This plasticity characterizes many of these relatively large species complexes. Generally, there is a low degree of restricted, endemic species distributions within Central America (cf. Bequaert and Clench 1933, 1936, 1938; Goodrich and van der Schalie 1937; Haas and Solem 1960; Pilsbry 1891; Martens 1890–1901). Many of the genera extend from central and northern Mexico into the West Indies and to northern South America.

It is possible that many of the dominant land snails are "weedy" species associated with agricultural disturbance and tolerant of a wide variety of habitats. Andrews points out that "they form an almost ever-present normal component of the materials used for construction fill in Maya architecture. Once favored living conditions such as open rubble have been established, they migrate into these artificial environments in enormous numbers" (1969: 34). A review of the specific habitats of the dominant land snails found in the present study follows in the discussion below.

The marine gastropods also comprise a widely distributed group that has representative species throughout the Caribbean and Gulf habitats. Parodiz reports that the beaches of Yucatán "are literally covered with shells of large species of *Busycon, Strombus*," and others that are washed ashore (1979: 5). Similar high densities of large marine conchs occur in northern Belize along with abundant bivalves. Biogeographic and taxonomic study of marine mollusks around the area of Carrie Bow Cay on the barrier reef of Belize is currently under way as part of a ten-year project by R. S. Houbrick, D. Young, and T. Waller, organized through the Smithsonian Institution by Klaus Ruetzler, project coordinator. When complete, Houbrick's analysis of the marine prosobranchs, especially *Cerithium*, will elucidate relationships among species in Belize relative to other distributions throughout the western Atlantic (Houbrick 1974). Much of the information on the distributions and ecology of species found by Andrews (1969) along the Caribbean coast of Yucatán applies directly to Belize. He also places these species in an archaeological context and summarizes the distribution of approximately 15,000 specimens of 192 species from eighteen archaeological sites. Parodiz (1979) discusses Andrews' findings and notes that the number of species reported from both archaeological and present-day beach deposits totals 291.

Apparently, in northern Belize, the freshwater mollusks are locally more restricted in their preferences for microhabitats than are many of the terrestrial snails. Most of these freshwater species, however, share the wide geographical distributions typical of the terrestrial and marine mollusks. The freshwater mollusks are also equally plastic in their morphological variability. For example, one of the most abundant ampullariid species, *Pomacea flagellata* (Say), has tremendous variability in coloration and size among widely scattered populations. Many of these freshwater species are now under study by Arthur H. Clarke, who recently collected new material in Belize.

Patterns in spatial and temporal distributions of these very different types of shell remains can provide information on certain large- and small-scale environmental changes or cultural uses of mollusks. There are, however, several limitations that restrict broad interpretations. First, the sample size must be large enough and sufficiently complete to represent the original community composition of all the molluscan species that simultaneously co-occurred. If only thicker-shelled or more solution-resistant shells are preserved, then the assemblage is incomplete and comparisons with present-day distributions are less reliable (Covich 1978). A second but related restriction can be imposed by inadequate analysis of the associated faunal evidence (e.g., from fish, turtles, waterfowl, and aquatic mammals) needed to assess the potential for the predatory removal of thin-shelled or behaviorally vulnerable species of mollusks. Third, all sources of the freshwater and marine species must be adequately identified. Because geological deposits of shells of various ages can be redeposited and mixed with contemporaneous shells by a variety of natural and cultural processes, it is important to have information on the distributions of fossil molluscan assemblages near the sites of deposition under study. Finally, ethnographic information on the use of mollusks for tools, ornaments, or food is needed for projecting ancient cultural patterns of shellfish exploitation. In some cases past uses of mollusks may have been lost or replaced by new resources, and the paleoecological interpretations may tend to underestimate these cultural uses. Because of all these limitations, there is little likelihood of using shell distributions as chronological markers or of documenting highly localized patterns of trade in food resources or shell ornaments. Only major changes and trends of species shifts are likely to yield reliable estimates of environmental fluctuations or cultural patterns of exploitation.

AN ANALYSIS OF DIVERSITY

The present chapter focuses on the proportional mix of terrestrial, freshwater, and marine molluscan shells collected in northern Belize from excavations at northern and southern Kokeal (Op. II and Op. V) and from along the edge of PS (Op. III). Only a few shells were found along the southwest edge of PE. These locations are described in detail elsewhere in this volume (chaps. 4 and 11). A team of workers used direct visual sorting, sieving, and flotation (especially effective for separating small specimens) to collect both broken and intact shells. I briefly surveyed the present-day distributions of the freshwater snails that were found living in the canals adjacent to Pulltrouser Swamp and the New River. Another brief survey sought terrestrial snails from the disturbed secondary forest and sugarcane fields near the archaeological excavations.

The long-term goals of this study were to reconstruct the original environment of deposition and to interpret the impact of the early Maya agriculture, general land use, and molluscan exploitation on the snail and bivalve community. The choice of mollusks for this research is based on several criteria: (1) the taxonomy of the molluscan species is sufficiently well known for this section of the neotropics to allow for reasonably consistent identifications based on shell remains, usually to the generic and often to the specific level (only rarely to the subspecific level); (2) durable shells are present in sufficient quantities throughout long sequences of sedimentary deposits both on land and in sublacustrine mud, so that relatively continuous data on the composition of these communities can be obtained; and (3) habitat preferences are relatively well studied, permitting at least broad interpretations of past environmental conditions with respect to such major parameters as rainfall and vegetation composition. In using each of these criteria, certain assumptions must be carefully tested to maximize the reliability of any interpretation. Ongoing studies of the present-day molluscan communities continue to improve the data base needed for environmental reconstructions.

Of the 140 samples containing molluscan material from the three study areas, there were 3,988 complete shells identified and 3,379 fragments that could be tentatively identified. "Complete" shells were often whole and intact, but all specimens containing adequate shell structure (e.g., diagnostic traits such as hinge elements among pelecypods or characteristic spires among some gastropods) were counted as "complete" individuals for estimating shell density. The ratios of complete to fragmented shells (tables 8-1 and 8-2) allow for some overall comparisons of the type and degree of shell preservation at each location.

FRESHWATER GASTROPODS

Pomacea flagellata (Say).   This species of amphibious gastropod (fig. 8-1a) was most commonly collected in near-shore deposits, and it is also the most abundant gastropod in the area today. Numerous large shells (up to 78 millimeters in length) are found on the modern soil surfaces. These prosobranch snails of the family Ampullariidae are well known for their potential to reach very high population densities in areas with fluctuating water levels (Burky 1974; Guedes, Fiori, and Diefenbach 1981). One part of their mantle cavity contains a ctenidium or gill, while another portion is modified into a gas-filled lung; this family is unique among the gill-bearing prosobranchs in having both gills and lungs. They are

Table 8-1. *Molluscan Remains from the Pulltrouser Area*

Species	Near-Shore Freshwater Habitat: Pulltrouser South	Terrestrial Habitat: Southern Kokeal	Northern Kokeal
Freshwater gastropods			
Pomacea flagellata (Say)	613(2,236)	30(142)	14(35)
Pachychilus glaphyrus (Mor.)	0(0)	32(0)	0(0)
Pyrgophorus coronatus (Pfr.)	76(3)	0(0)	0(0)
Biomphalaria havanensis (Pfr.)	75(0)	0(0)	0(0)
Stenophysa spiculata (Mor.)	3(0)	0(0)	0(0)
Gundlachia spp.	2(0)	2(0)	0(0)
Freshwater bivalves			
Cyrenoides americana (Mor.)	204(300)	71(36)	0(0)
Nephronaias sp.	0(0)	0(1)	0(0)
Marine gastropods			
Strombus gigas (L.)	0(6)	10(4)	0(1)
Melongena melongena (L.)	0(0)	5(1)	0(0)
Cerithium sp.	0(0)	2(2)	0(0)
Marine bivalves			
Lucina pectinata (Gmelin)	0(0)	8(91)	0(7)
Dinocardium sp.	14(1)	0(7)	0(0)
Terrestrial gastropods			
Neocyclotus dysoni (Pfr.)	184(163)	2,162(164)	314(11)
Orthalicus princeps (Sow.)	6(118)	31(42)	0(0)
Euglandina cylindracea (Phil.)	0(0)	27(6)	6(2)
Helicina amoena (Pfr.)	0(0)	8(0)	0(0)
Polygyra yucatanea (Mor.)	3(0)	11(0)	0(0)
Bulimulus sp.	0(0)	75(0)	0(0)
Total complete specimens	1,180	2,474	334
Total fragmented specimens	(2,827)	(496)	(56)
Total samples per site	60	50	30

well adapted for surviving in shallow water that becomes very warm and is seasonally deoxygenated by decomposing vegetation. These snails can also survive complete desiccation of the water by burrowing into the mud to considerable depths. They reach high densities in part through avoidance of predators—they burrow into the mud in response to chemical alarm pheromones given off by several species of predators, such as snapping turtles, sunfish, and decapod crustaceans (Snyder and Snyder 1971). They also lay their eggs above the water level on vertical structures such as emergent

Table 8-2. Frequency of Distribution of Pachychilus and Cooccurring Gastropods from Southern Kokeal

Operation-Suboperation Unit	Lot	Depth (Cm.)	Number of Complete & Fragmented ( ) Specimens per Sample				
			Pachychilus	Pomacea	Neocyclotus	Orthalicus	Euglandina
II-2-1	62	0–35	3(0)	0(8)	149(46)	0(4)	0(0)
II-2-1	63	35–55	5(0)	0(27)	64(20)	0(2)	1(0)
II-3-2	74	0–50	1(0)	1(13)	480(110)	3(0)	12(12)
II-7-1	251	0–30 (topsoil)	5(0)	1(1)	60(0)	0(0)	0(6)
II-7-1	252	0–30 (topsoil)	1(0)	0(3)	113(15)	2(0)	2(0)
II-7-1	260	15–240	13(0)	2(3)	189(9)	2(0)	22(0)
II-7-2	280	0–30 (topsoil)	1(0)	0(0)	102(7)	0(0)	0(1)
II-7-2	281	0–30 (accumulated soil)	1(0)	4(11)	73(11)	0(0)	0(5)
II-77-2	417	90–130	1(0)	0(5)	45(2)	0(0)	0(0)
II-IH-1[a]	461	0–20	1(0)	0(1)	8(0)	3(1)	2(1)
Total			32(0)	8(72)	1,283(220)	10(7)	39(25)

[a] This operation was a test pit in a structure to the south of southern Kokeal.

Fig. 8-1. Representative specimens of subfossil gastropods from southern Kokeal: a, *Pomacea flagellata* (Say); b, *Pachychilus glaphyrus* (Mor.); c, *Cerithium* species; d, *Neocyclotus dysoni* (Pfr.); e, *Euglandina cylindracea* (Phil.).

vegetation, apparently as a mode of avoiding deoxygenated water and predation on the juveniles. There is some evidence that the egg masses are distasteful to predators; some species' eggs have bright colors that may warn or remind potential predators that the eggs or egg yolks are toxic (Snyder and Snyder 1971).

The apple snail is widely distributed. There are probably twenty to twenty-five species throughout the neotropics (Boss and Parodiz 1977). The exact number of forms and subspecies is unknown because of the great variation in size and shape. Pain (1963) recognizes four subspecies in Central America for *P. flagellata*: *P. f. flagellata*, *P. f. livescens*, *P. f. erogata*, and *P. f. dysoni*. Rehder (1966) states that specimens from Yucatán show considerable variation in form and color, which casts doubt on the validity of most named subspecies. Branson and McCoy (1963) note that approximately thirty specific and subspecific epithets have been applied to the "races" that were supposedly separable just by size differences.

Goodrich and van der Schalie (1937) suggest that large-shelled forms occur mainly in larger lakes while smaller and thicker-shelled forms occur mainly in small streams and ponds. Moholy-Nagy (1978) recognized two forms: *P. f. arata* (thin-shelled and small) and *P. f. tristrami* (thick-shelled and large). Both forms were found in archaeological contexts at Tikal. Shell frequencies changed stratigraphically and were most common in Preclassic and Terminal Classic deposits.

Several archaeologists (Andrews 1969; Feldman 1978; Moholy-Nagy 1978) suggest that *Pomacea* was used as a food resource by the Maya. Nations (1979), however, reports that the Lacandon Maya ignore *Pomacea* as a food and claim that eating these snails can cause illness. Currently, it appears that the use of *Pomacea* as a food requires further study. The variability in feeding behavior observed by Snyder and Snyder (1971) among various natural predators suggests that there may be developmental changes in the palatability of *Pomacea*.

Four times as many shell fragments as complete shells were collected. This high proportion of breakage despite this species' relatively thick shell suggests that the shells were either redeposited as construction fill (as was the case at Tikal according to Moholy-Nagy 1978) or broken in midden debris. Predation by birds or other vertebrates (Snyder and Snyder 1971) also probably added to the proportion of shell breakage. The much greater concentration of *Pomacea* shells in the near-shore habitat relative to the excavations at Kokeal suggests that perhaps *Pomacea* was not used for food but was generally incorporated into the construction fill of the raised fields. The environment of deposition was likely a fluctuating shoreline characterized by dense aquatic vegetation, similar to that habitat which encircles the modern-day swamp.

Pachychilus glaphyrus (Mor.).   In contrast to *Pomacea*, this aquatic species (fig. 8-1b) was found only at southern Kokeal; no specimens were found at Pulltrouser. *Pachychilus* is typically a riverine prosobranch and would not be expected to occur naturally in the swamp. It is found in some large, wave-swept lakes but generally is most common in fast-flowing streams. All the shells found at Kokeal were intact but had the uppermost apex broken off. This breakage could be a result of natural predation, especially by fresh-water crabs, but, because of the cultural context and the considerable distance from any known natural source of living specimens in this area today, I presume the breakage was the result of Maya preparation of the snails for boiling in a soup. Initially, *Pachychilus* may have been harvested from the New River or some distant source and brought to the site for cooking. Nations reports that the Lacandon rely on *Pachychilus* as a "supplementary food source (chiefly for women and children) when no other animal protein is available" (1979: 569). He also notes the use of these shells for powdered lime, which is added to water for boiling maize. Baer and Merrifield (1971) also report on techniques used by the Lacandon for collecting and cooking riverine snails.

The shells were relatively scattered and in low density at Ko-keal, suggesting either the infrequent use of *Pachychilus* as a soup snail or its very frequent use as a source of powdered pure lime. Feldman (1978) suggests that *P. glaphyrus*, whose broken remnants are encountered among the structures at Seibal, was perhaps used by the seventeenth-century Cholti Lacandon of the Usumacinta drainage. Moholy-Nagy points out that at Uaxactún "*Pachychilus*, a nonlocal genus, outnumbered *Pomacea*, a local one," and that this disproportionate representation may be of considerable importance (1978: 72). A total of 805 shells of *Pachychilus glaphyrus* and *P. largillierti* was found in excavations in the Belize River Valley, along with 765 specimens of the clam *Nephronaias ortmanni* (Willey et al. 1965). These shells were scattered throughout the stratigraphy, although the heavy preponderance was in the Pre-classic phases, after which the supply diminished from either over-exploitation or habitat modification (silting of the stream and riverine substrata).

Pyrgophorus coronatus (Pfr.).   This genus in the family Hydro-biidae is distributed throughout the Caribbean and coastal areas of the Gulf of Mexico; it extends from Texas southward to Venezuela. In some previous studies this species was placed in the family Am-nicolidae and in the genus *Potamopyrgus* (e.g., Goodrich and van der Schalie 1937; Harry 1950). Reported from at least sixteen locations in Yucatán, it is typical of permanent, relatively deep lakes, cenotes, and *aguadas* (sinkhole depressions). It is the dominant gastropod in Laguna Chichancanab in Yucatán (Covich and Stuiver 1974), and large numbers of shells are found in Laguna Petén Itzá (Goodrich and van der Schalie 1937). I found live specimens in the littoral zone of Pulltrouser in May 1979. Most specimens are in the 3-millimeter range, with the largest specimens being only 5 milli-meters in shell length. Although preyed upon by small fish and crayfish, these gastropods are not used by humans. The shell sculp-ture varies from several rows of conical, elongate spines to smooth or slightly carinate (Covich 1976). There is no consensus among investigators regarding any possible ecological significance of this shell variation. A single specimen may display abrupt transitions from smooth to spinose morphology.

The presence of seventy-six complete specimens in the near-shore deposits and the absence of any from Kokeal suggest that this species is typical of aquatic sediments and possibly of reworked sediments that could have been used for raised-field construction. Periodic transfer of organic enriched mud from the canals to the surface of these raised fields would probably mix shells of *Pyrgophorus* and *Pomacea* in proportions typical of those encountered. The relative lack of breakage in this species is no doubt due to its smaller size and relatively thick shell as well as to the low probability of recovering many shell fragments from such small specimens.

Typically, in an undisturbed lake profile, the nearest-shore zone would be dominated by *Pomacea*; *Pyrgophorus* would dominate in the next deepest zone and extend in lower densities to the center of the lake. However, if the lake level fluctuated due to marked seasonal or interannual variations in rainfall and evaporation, then both *Pomacea* and *Pyrgophorus* could be found in more equal proportions. This is because of the additive nature of the shell deposits produced over several years that can be mixed together naturally through burrowing activities of aquatic and terrestrial animals.

Biomphalaria havanensis (Pfr.).   The taxonomy of this genus has been well studied because some species are intermediate hosts of such human parasites as *Schistosoma mansoni*. Over 250 species have been described from the neotropics, and the status of this genus is reviewed by Malek (1969). As members of the family Planorbidae, these pulmonates occur in relatively shallow waters and are found most frequently in lakes and ponds, although they are also collected in some streams and irrigation canals.

The shell morphology of ramshorn snails is flat-spired and unsculptured. All these forms have shells that are flat and compressed on both sides; maximal shell height is 2.5 millimeters and maximal diameter is approximately 11 millimeters. Correct species identification will require study of preserved live specimens and their internal anatomy. Thus, the use of *B. havanensis* is tentative. Malek (1969) reports *B. albicans* from Belize, although that species is smaller than specimens I collected from Pulltrouser. Malek refers to a "*B. obstructa* group" for a number of related taxa and states that *B. obstructa* and *B. havanensis* are closely related species.

The lack of fragmented *Biomphalaria* is probably a result of a thicker shell and an architecture that is resistant to crushing. Field observations of predators are limited, but Sturrock (1974) notes that freshwater shrimp and other natural consumers may reduce the densities of *Biomphalaria*. There is no reported cultural use of this species as food or ornament. Presence merely of the genus is not evidence for past occurrence of the parasitic disease schistoso-miasis because in this area only *B. glabrata* is a suitable intermedi-ate host, and without it the life cycle of the parasite is interrupted.
Stenophysa spiculata (Mor.).   These very thin-shelled pulmonates of the family Physidae are distributed throughout the Yucatán Pen-insula and into northern Guatemala and Belize. Shell characteris-tics are variable, and distinguishing species on the basis of external morphology alone is difficult (Rehder 1966). Again, this identifica-tion is tentative and will require additional material for study. The low number of specimens is no doubt influenced by the fragile na-ture of this species and the low probability of its preservation in or retrieval from the sediments.
Gundlachia Species.   These small, thin-shelled species are also found in low numbers at Pulltrouser. Live specimens are infre-quently collected because they are small and typically are well con-cealed in aquatic vegetation or under stones in lakes, ponds, and streams. The occurrence of two specimens at southern Kokeal may have been associated with the transport of plants from the swamp to the site by the early Maya. The species are often referred to as freshwater limpets because of their patelliform, streamlined shells. Goodrich and van der Schalie (1937) report three species from Gua-temala, while Bequaert and Clench (1936) report two species from northern Yucatán.

FRESHWATER BIVALVES
Cyrenoides americana (Mor.).   These pelecypods of the family Cyrenoididae are widely distributed in the southern United States and along the Gulf of Mexico coasts as subfossils, but live speci-mens are difficult to collect in many areas where dead shells are abundant. They live in sediments and carbonate concretions to wa-ter depths of 3 or more meters in Laguna Chichancanab, but their habitats in Belize are unknown. The high percentage of broken shells (although the species is relatively thick-shelled and small) suggests again the possibility that much of the sediments were re-worked. It is not known if these bivalves were ever eaten by the Maya, but it seems unlikely.
Nephronaias Species.   The fragmented shells found in a ceramic

bowl cache in structure I (chaps. 10 and 12) at Kokeal lacked the shell covering or periostracum. The white nacre and overall appearance are typical of *Nephronaias*, although the identification is tentative. The pelecypod fauna is very poorly known; only a few archaeological studies report freshwater bivalves. Andrews (1969) lists *Nephronaias* and *Psoronaias* from four sites; Feldman (1978) lists *Psoronaias semigranosus* from Seibal and Altar de Sacrificios. The potential usefulness of both freshwater and marine bivalves for the production of ornamental shells is significant in some archaeological sites. Zeitlin (1978) finds a marked positive correlation between flaked quartz and ornamental shells in deposits from Laguna Zope where *Nephronaias* and *Sphenonaias* occurred. Although these freshwater pelecypods are likely to have also provided food as well as ornamental shells, their importance as a source of protein must be evaluated in light of the relatively low values found from chemical analyses of several temperate zone bivalves (Parmalee and Klippel 1974).

MARINE GASTROPODS

Strombus gigas (L.).   This very large conch is found commonly along the Caribbean coast and has been reported from Tikal, Barton Ramie, and a midden at Isla Cancún (Andrews 1969). At this last site, it clearly dominated a midden and was found commonly co-occuring with *Melongena corona*. The broken body whorl of the largest of the ten complete *Strombus* shells found at Kokeal (fig. 8-2) is a possible indication of harvest by humans. This slow-moving species is readily observed along the shallow beaches off Belize and near reef areas. The larger shells are used for a wide variety of purposes from hoes for cultivation to ornamental designs. This species is currently a major food source.

Melongena melongena (L.).   This large conch is also abundant along the coast of Belize (Clench and Turner 1956) and, like *Strombus*, it is a major food item. Shell deposits were also common at Tikal, Barton Ramie, and Dzibilchaltún. Andrews (1969) notes that *Melongena* was very common in the Formative period but was almost totally absent from later deposits at Dzibilchaltún. He reports that *Melongena* was not worked into utensils or ornaments as was *Strombus*. Three of the five complete shells found at Kokeal illustrate the four rows of spines on the intact shell and the pattern of shell breakage (fig. 8-3). The relatively thin body whorl or outer shell is chipped away by the human consumer or a marine crab (Zipser and Vermeij 1978) or some other animal. Although it is quite likely that these shells were remnants of human use, it is

Fig. 8-2. *Strombus gigas* (L.) from southern Kokeal. All ten complete specimens from lots 58 and 59 were broken, indicating probable use of these large conchs as food. Shell length is 19.5 centimeters.

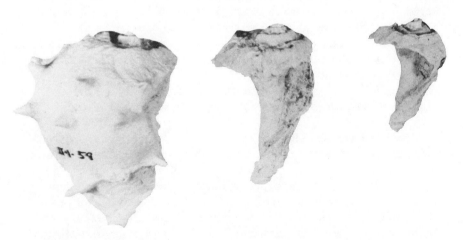

Fig. 8-3. *Melongena melongena* (L.) from southern Kokeal. Several of the shells from lot 58 were broken either by natural predators, such as crabs, or by the early Maya, who probably used these smaller conchs for food.

also possible that they were redeposited from marine limestone as fossils and are much older than the other Kokeal shells.

Cerithium Species.   The few specimens of this relatively small marine gastropod (fig. 8-1c) may have been accidentally transported into the Kokeal site, or they may have been redeposited from ancient marine limestone that had weathered and left the fossils intact. The few specimens reported from archaeological collections are typically unworked shells, but Andrews states that those from inland sites were "clearly destined for votive use" and notes that they were reported from various caches (1969: 8). Houbrick (1974) reports on modern-day ecological distributions in the waters off Florida and Belize.

MARINE BIVALVES

Lucina pectinata (Gmelin).   This small pelecypod appears to be mixed in with other shell debris and probably was an accidental introduction. It is not known to be edible. Andrews (1969) uses *Phacoides pectinatus* as a synonym and notes its wide and common occurrence on the entire littoral of the Yucatán Peninsula extending from Chapel Cay, Belize.

Dinocardium Species.   These ridged shells are very distinctive and, even though frequently broken, they can be readily identified. The presence of fourteen relatively whole shells and one small fragment at PS is puzzling as few other marine shells were encountered. They may have been used as cutting tools for small vines or twine. Perhaps they were associated with other activities as well, such as the production of striated patterns on pottery. Andrews (1969) notes that there were very large numbers of unworked shells in the Formative at Dzibilchaltún and speculates that *Dinocardium* may have been used for food. As with *Cerithium*, these shells could be redeposited from weathered marine limestone.

TERRESTRIAL GASTROPODS

Neocyclotus dysoni (Pfr.).   By far the most abundant shell at Kokeal and very common (as the third most abundant shell) at PS, *Neocyclotus* (fig. 8-1d) appears as a ubiquitous component of the deposits. This genus is distributed from Veracruz southward to Venezuela, Ecuador, and Colombia as well as on the West Indian islands. Basch (1959) reports that *N.d. cookei* (Bartsch and Morrison) was common at Uaxactún, Tikal, and several localities in Belize. He found live snails aestivating in rotting logs. Solem (1956) suggests that the subspecies *cookei* is closely related to larger forms (*N. d. ambiguum*) in southern Mexico.

Hammond and colleagues (1979) interpret the presence of *N. d. cookei* as an indicator of swidden agriculture, because they suggest that this snail is associated with burned land. My own interpretation differs from theirs. This species is not restricted to recently burned milpas but is only much more visible after the fire has temporarily removed the vegetation that normally precludes easy collection of the numerous empty shells. Fire also tends to destroy the thinner-shelled species of land snails that may be even more frequently associated with human disturbance than is *Neocyclotus*. A study of notes from museum collections of this species in Belize and Guatemala demonstrates that it is very widely distributed outside of swidden habitats (such as stream beds and around coves) as well as in a variety of partially cleared forest areas where moist leaf litter is available.

Orthalicus princeps (Sow.).   This common arboreal species is often reported from archaeological sites. Andrews notes that "the largest, most attractive and thickly shelled of these [land snails], *Orthalicus princeps princeps* (Broderip), was frequently encountered, but never with evidence of intentional alteration" (1969: 34). The dark brown bands on a white shell make this readily distinguishable from other species even if only shell fragments are found. The abundance of broken pieces in the near-shore deposits is interpreted as further evidence of sediment reworking. The snails probably entered the canals and raised fields from the overhanging trees that lined the canals. Basch (1959) often found *O. princeps* aestivating on *Cecropia* trees, in recent secondary forest regrowth. Bequaert and Clench (1933) suggest that this elusive species is "rarely seen alive, owing to its strictly arboreal habits."

Euglandina cylindracea (Phil.).   The occurrence of this voracious predator (fig. 8-1e) at Kokeal is a natural distribution of a carnivore associated with its prey species. These common land snails, widely reported from such archaeological sites as Tikal and Barton Ramie (Andrews 1969), typically cooccur with *Neocyclotus*. *Euglandina* occurs on the trunks of trees, on leaves, and on larger shrubs. Goodrich and van der Schalie (1937) record that this species is typical of disturbed or cleared habitats. Basch (1959) notes that one lively *E. cumingi* ate fourteen *Bulimulus* in about forty-five minutes. Ingram and Heming (1942) point out that *E. rosea* is cannibalistic as well as predaceous and is somewhat selective about which species of snails it consumes.

Helicina amoena (Pfr.).   Another relatively common tree snail, this species occurs in most parts of Central America and extends from southern Mexico to Panama (Basch 1959). Goodrich and van der Schalie (1937) report this species as one of the most common land snails in Guatemala. Its rarity at southern Kokeal makes its distribution difficult to interpret.

Polygyra yucatanea (Mor.).   The distinctive striations and complexly toothed aperture make this species easy to identify, and its modern distributional ecology is relatively well known. Goodrich and van der Schalie were the first to record its occurrence in the Petén, where it is widespread. They found it "invariably close to lakes or drainage systems . . . not once were these found at any great distance from either a lake shore or banks of a river." Along with *Helicina, Euglandina,* and *Neocyclotus,* they also found *Polygyra* in cleared areas. They note that milpa farming "is naturally very disadvantageous to any land shells inhabiting the area. Some time after the clearing process, however, a number of species adapt themselves to the altered surroundings, and live under logs and stones strewn about the premises" (1937: 15). Apparently, these common land snails migrate into the patches of recently cleared secondary forest from the surrounding vegetation. The relatively low densities of *Polygyra* and *Helicina* in comparison with the very high densities of *Neocyclotus* may well be a characteristic of the type of secondary vegetation or soils in the area, rather than any direct or indirect effect of fire generally. Proximity to water does not appear to influence the *Polygyra* distributions at Pulltrouser Swamp.

Bulimulus Species.   This small terrestrial species was found in flotation samples from southern Kokeal. Its ecological distributions appear very broad; culturally, it may be associated with thatch housing material. Charles Miksicek (personal communication) noted that these snails commonly appeared at the onset of the rainy season in thatch-roofed houses at Cuello. Naturally they appear commonly associated with palms. This group was relatively abundant archaeologically, especially in the Preclassic deposits in the Belize River Valley (Willey et al. 1965).

CONCLUSIONS AND NEW DIRECTIONS

The cooccurrence of *Biomphalaria* with *Pomacea, Pyrgophorus,* and *Gundlachia* at Pulltrouser is typical of shallow fresh waters throughout Central America and the West Indies (e.g., Covich 1976; Sturrock 1974). Only *Pyrgophorus* appears relatively slow in its dispersal ability and may be restricted to relatively permanent or deeper bodies of water. The other three gastropod species can rapidly disperse into both flowing and standing waters and appear to reach relatively large populations in waters that fluctuate seasonally.

The gill-bearing *Pyrgophorus* is less adapted to survive complete desiccation. It can enclose its aperture with an operculum and partially seal off the shell during periods of long-distance transport. It can disperse, as do the other freshwater gastropods, primarily by movement along watercourses or by aerial routes if attached to the feet and feathers of waterfowl (Rees 1965). The pelecypods too can be moved by other animals over considerable distances, but they are not well adapted to dry conditions. However, given enough time these molluscan migrations can passively disperse enough new individuals into a habitat that the species assemblage increases its diversity over long periods. The equilibrium number of individuals and the number of distinct species will reflect the distances from recolonizing source areas, the intensity of competition among resident and dispersing species, and the size of the habitat available for colonization. Studies in temperate zone lakes and ponds (Aho 1978; Browne 1981; Lassen 1975) suggest that this equilibrial composition is predictable, using the MacArthur-Wilson model of island biogeography, and that these islandlike aquatic habitats accumulate different numbers of species in relation to distances from source areas (other aquatic habitats) and their size. Size alone is probably not as important as the extent of the shoreline habitat that is densely occupied by most molluscan species or as the age of the lake and intensity of predator activity.

Data for tropical assemblages of mollusks have not been analyzed in terms of equilibrial composition as predicted by the MacArthur-Wilson model, but it appears that a large, densely vegetated, and relatively permanent body of water such as Pulltrouser Swamp has attained some level of stable association among its molluscan species. If the swamp has been filling in with sediments for several thousand years, it may have once been much deeper (4 to 6 meters) in its central open-water reaches. But exactly how deep and how fast it accumulated sediments and shell deposits can be determined only by digging additional trenches at various distances from the modern shoreline and by coring into the deepest sediments along transects. If the Pulltrouser Swamp began as a relatively deep, permanent lake we might expect the community to be dominated by gill-bearing prosobranch species such as *Pyrgophorus* and by pelecypods. The proportion of prosobranchs (perhaps including *Pachychilus* as well as *Pyrgophorus*) to pulmonates would be expected to shift over time as the habitats became shallower, warmer, and more densely covered with aquatic plants. The *Pomacea* densities would be expected to remain high around the perimeter in the shallow littoral zone; incorporation of this species into the samples would depend on the core or trench location relative to the shoreline over periods of shell deposition.

As the plants grow and decompose, they cause severe depletion of dissolved oxygen (especially at night when the submerged plants are not photosynthesizing but respiring and using up the dissolved oxygen). Floating and emergent plants can cause rapid depletion of oxygen in shallow waters as their leaves decompose. All this plant debris is slowly deposited and, along with clay and carbonate mineral deposits, fills in the lake basin.

Until more of these types of samples are available, it is not possible to infer how the diversity of freshwater molluscan communities is regulated. It is clear, however, that in comparison to marine (and perhaps even terrestrial) habitats the spatial and temporal instability of freshwater habitats places severe limitations on the entry of new species into these molluscan communities, despite the array of adaptations to avoid desiccation or predation that these species have evolved.

A possible technique that has not yet been attempted in analyzing large shell deposits in the Maya area is a comparison of oxygen isotopes from mollusks that lived in freshwater or marine areas with diagnostic ratios of oxygen-16 and oxygen-18 in their shell carbonates. Shackleton (1973) and Killingley (1981) have examined marine shell middens in attempts to determine the source and seasonality of the collected shells. Growth rates of individual clams or snails can also be determined by analysis of oxygen isotope ratios. Mean longevities of *Strombus gigas* are known to be about six years; thus a series of individual shells can yield information about seasonal changes in temperature and growth over a relatively long time (Wefer and Killingley 1980). In Belize it may be possible to compare lake, riverine, and estuarine waters for distinctive differences in isotope ratios and then match up shell ratios with these habitats. If relatively constant temperatures are assumed, then the only variables influencing the isotope ratios will be rainfall and evaporative enrichment of oxygen-18 relative to oxygen-16 (Covich and Stuiver 1974). Very large differences in these enrichments of oxygen-18 from location to location would allow for a more detailed analysis of the spatial relationships among the living areas, feeding sites, and sources of various molluscan foods.

Perhaps the most pressing need for additional study remains a systematic exploration of microhabitats and their use by land and freshwater mollusks. At present only general environmental reconstructions are possible. Once environmental heterogeneity is matched with community structure, and differences in shell preservation are understood, it may be possible to define much more precisely the relationships between numbers of species and their relative and absolute abundances. I anticipate that the generalized ecological requirements of many of these species (Hubendick 1958, 1962) will preclude their use for more exact environmental interpretations. However, some species will undoubtedly have very specialized adaptations for particular ecological niches that will yield useful information and insight regarding the cultural impact not only on molluscan communities but on the tropical biota generally.

ACKNOWLEDGMENTS
In addition to the help of the entire project group in collecting the fossil shell material, I was also aided greatly by malacologists at several museums who shared their collections and information on species distributions in Belize: John B. Burch, Museum of Zoology, University of Michigan; George M. Davis and Arthur E. Bogan, Academy of Natural Sciences, Philadelphia; Arthur H. Clarke, Smithsonian Institution, Juan J. Parodiz and Clarence J. McCoy, Carnegie Museum of Natural History, Pittsburgh; and Ruth D. Turner, Museum of Comparative Zoology, Harvard University. Zenith Marsh assisted with photography, and Melanie Davis typed the original manuscript.

9. The Pulltrouser Settlement Survey and Mapping of Kokeal

PETER D. HARRISON

The principal objective of the settlement study was to identify and map the nearest settlement to a major site of raised-field studies (RF site 1) along the western edge of PS and to test several structures at that site.[1] A secondary objective was to survey as much as possible of the environs surrounding Pulltrouser Swamp. The purpose of these efforts was to establish the rudiments of the pattern of settlement adjacent to the depression and to provide an indirect and/or a complementary basis for dating the fields at Pulltrouser, depending upon the success of directly dating them.

The move to Pulltrouser invoked circumstances which were unknown to the project and to the archaeological community at large.[2] Previous surveys of northern Belize (Hammond 1973, 1976a) were of a macronature; no microlevel studies which included the Pulltrouser area were available. Norman Hammond (personal communication) had identified a set of structures near the confluence of the three arms of the depression on the west side and a potentially large plaza group on the east side of PS (fig. 9-1). The former site had been labeled Mile 70, after its distance from Belize City along the northern highway. Despite project constraints, the amount of the survey completed and the artifactual materials excavated were substantial. We are confident that the survey of the western side of PS is largely completed with regard to surface structures.

AREA SETTLEMENT
At least three loci of settlement occur immediately around Pulltrouser Swamp (fig. 9-1). Another, Yo Tumben, is situated south of Kokeal. Of these only Kokeal has been completely surveyed. A site on the east side of PS has been seen from the air by Norman Hammond (personal communication) and by myself on aerial photo-

graphs. A third site observed is located on the west side of PE near its southern terminus. A possible fourth site (Mile 70) located on the northwest side of PS has been examined subsequent to the 1979 season, but its status as a settlement has not been determined. On a local regional basis, at least three "major" sites form a triangular pattern distant from the depression: Nohmul, Cuello, and San Estevan (fig. 9-1).

SURVEY METHOD AND MAPPING

The survey and discovery of mounds-structures and the mapping process in general were strongly regulated by the cycle of the sugarcane harvest, which coincided in the immediate area with the excavation season (February to June).[3] Individual cane fields could be explored and mapped only after the cane was burned and cut. This factor led to an uneven procedure of mapping, in which the squares of the checkerboard were not necessarily surveyed in order. As the season progressed, so did the rate of cane cutting. New portions of the site would become visible as the older, already surveyed parts disappeared under new growth. Despite this handicap to orderly progress, we are reasonably certain that, if any mounds were missed in the final count, it was due not to the cane cover but rather to those portions of the survey area under dense secondary growth. For example, the east end only of structure 15 (fig. 9-2) was noted on the final day of survey due to the expansion of a cane field into an area of dense growth. The remainder of the structure could not be determined without considerable *brecha* work, which time constraints did not permit. That this structure appears only as the end of a patio platform in a rather critical location in terms of immediate structure distribution is the result of this kind of limitation.

Approximately 25 percent of the 1.08 square kilometers which Kokeal covers was not cleared for cane cultivation but overgrown with forest cover. In these areas some structures may have been overlooked. Uncleared secondary forest regularly occurs over larger structures, such as the acropolises of Kokeal, since constructions of this scale inhibit farming. We are confident that such large structures have all been identified. Secondary and other forest growth occasionally occurs without apparent explanation, sometimes surrounded by cane fields, sometimes close to the swamp littoral. One zone of dense growth north of structure 56 (fig. 9-2) was found to contain two small structures which could not later be relocated. In areas of dense secondary vegetation, one barbed, indigenous vine in particular played an inhibiting and often painful role. Consultation

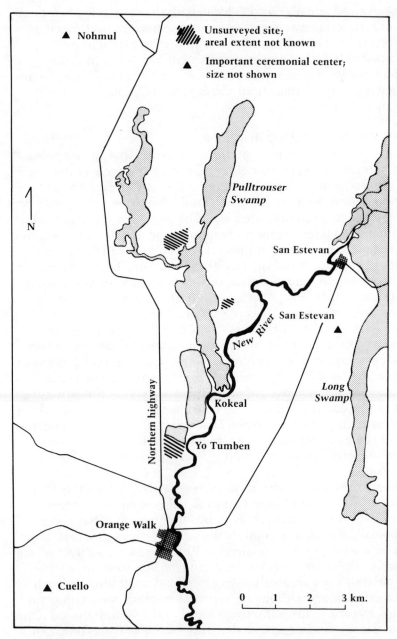

Fig. 9-1. Settlements adjacent to the Pulltrouser Swamp area. Adapted from *Science* 213 (1981): 403, copyright © 1981 by the American Association for the Advancement of Science.

with Yucatec-speaking Maya assistants confirmed that the name of this offending vine was *koke*, hence the name Kokeal for the site.

Mapping was accomplished by pace and compass for individual mounds, utilizing an established, standard pace length.[4] Interstructural distances were directly measured by tape and compass from a central stake placed at the top of each mound in a series of traverses, assuring that the structures have been mapped accurately relative to each other. The one fixed point on the site map which marks the edge of PS is located at the northern end of the site. Near this point, structure 80 appears to be a relic field, rather than a habitation structure, but it is numbered on the site map in order to establish the proximity of habitation to agricultural constructions.

The structures were numbered in the order of discovery, and the progression is generally from south to north. A number of discrepancies occur in the order because some components of certain patio groups were numbered before the whole patio was explored, for the reasons explained above. A verification program was undertaken to insure that doubtful features were not anthills or other nonstructural features. Anthills in this area do achieve a height of up to 1.5 meters, can be regular in shape, and even simulate plaza formations. Such formations of a noncultural nature were noted during the survey of Albion Island, 13 kilometers to the west (Puleston 1977a). During survey verification, mounds numbered 25 and 27 through 31 were found to be anthills and were therefore omitted from the map. Of the 124 numbered mounds, 117 are verified as ancient Maya-made structures, one of which appears to be a relic field (80). Orientations and heights are given in table 9-1.

SETTLEMENT AND TOPOGRAPHY

The use of local geography in the selection of advantageous construction sites is notable at Kokeal. This selection is a question not only of favoring high ground and avoiding the bottoms of the reentrant channels but also of favoring gentle slopes in such a way as to minimize the construction effort necessary to produce a sizable building platform. The most dramatic example of such contour exploitation is found in the structures of Yo Tumben, an associated site to the south of Kokeal discussed below (fig. 9-2). In this case, the utilization of hillsides and slopes maximizes the external appearance of height while minimizing the amount of construction required to achieve the effect. The other form of utilization of terrain is found in the clustering of structures on the low escarpment or terrace (chap. 2) which runs roughly parallel to the western side of the river and depression. This escarpment constitutes an eleva-

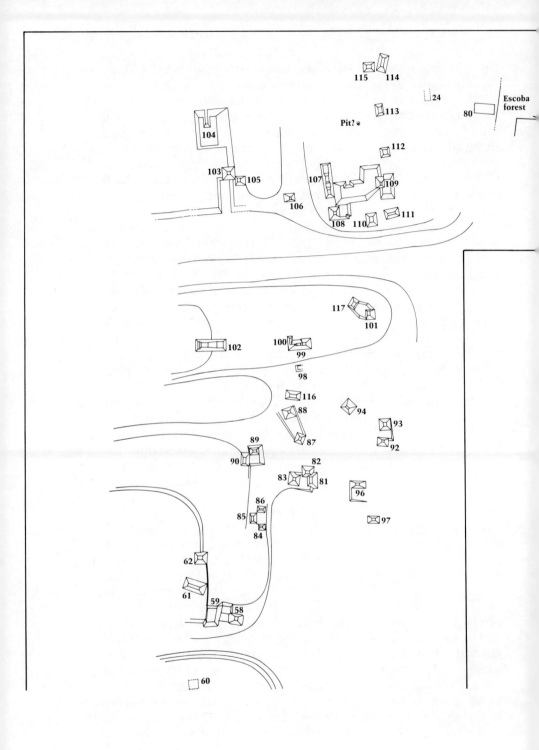

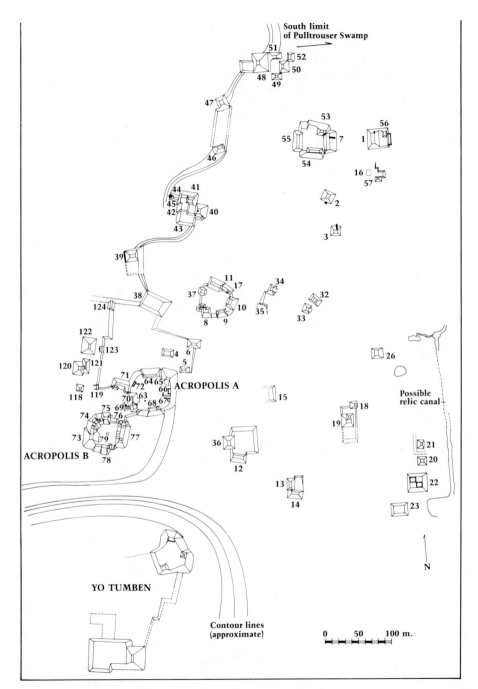

Fig. 9-2. Kokeal. *See also figure 4-4, pages 34–35.*

Table 9-1. *Mound Heights and Orientations at Kokeal*

Structure	Estimated Orientation (Magnetic Degrees East of North)	Elevation & Side Viewed
1	1.5	0.60 m./W
2	30.0	1.10 m./E
3	95.0	1.20 m./N
4	98.0	1.10 m./E
5	102.0	1.00 m./N
6	99.0	1.00 m./S
7	1.0	0.60 m./W
8	3.0	1.00 m./N
9	82.0	0.25 m./N
10	30.0	0.50 m./W
11	119.0	1.00 m./S
12	88.0	0.30 m./N
13	4.0	0.40 m./E
14	100.0	0.40 m./N
15	90.0	0.40 m./E
16	90.0	0.15 m./E
17	131.0	0.50 m./S
18	83.0	1.00 m./S
19	93.0	1.00 m./N
20	92.0	1.30 m./E
21	6.0	1.10 m./W
22	1.0	0.80 m./E
23	90.0	1.10 m./N
24	0.0	0.40 m./S
25	No structure	—
26	90.0	0.90 m./E
27–31	No structures	—
32	135.0	0.50 m./S
33	27.0	0.75 m./W
34	28.0	1.25 m./S
35	13.0	0.25 m./N
36	3.0	2.00 m./W
37	17.0	0.50 m./N
38	120.0	1.50 m./S
39	88.0	0.60 m./S
40	12.0	1.80 m./S
41	102.0	0.20 m./S
42	2.5	0.20 m./E
43	86.0	0.20 m./N
44	114.0	1.20 m./N
45	0.0	0.50 m./E
46	80.0	1.00 m./E
47	160.0	1.50 m./S

Table 9-1, *cont'd.*

Structure	Estimated Orientation (Magnetic Degrees East of North)	Elevation & Side Viewed
48	8.0	3.00 m./E
49	94.0	1.00 m./S
50	2.0	1.50 m./E
51	82.0	0.50 m./E
52	6.0	0.50 m./E
53	103.0	3.00 m./N
54	98.0	2.50 m./S
55	8.0	1.50 m./W
56	175.0	0.15 m./W
57	94.0	0.50 m./S
58	102.0	1.25 m./S
59	9.0	1.50 m./S
60	0.0	0.15 m./N
61	113.0	1.50 m./N
62	5.0	2.00 m./E
63	0.0	3.00 m./E
64	93.0	0.50 m./S
65	109.0	3.50 m./S
66	6.0	1.00 m./W
67	6.0	0.30 m./W
68	84.0	0.70 m./N
69	79.0	1.20 m./S
70	71.0	0.15 m./N
71	110.0	2.50 m./N
72	35.0	0.20 m./E
73	7.5	3.50 m./E
74	29.0	2.00 m./S
75	98.0	1.70 m./S
76	110.0	0.60 m./E
77	12.0	1.50 m./W
78	100.0	0.70 m./E
79	0.0	0.15 m./W
80	98.0	0.80 m./W
81	171.0	0.80 m./W
82	122.0	1.00 m./S
83	11.0	1.50 m./E
84	93.0	0.70 m./E
85	2.0	1.00 m./E
86	106.0	1.00 m./E
87	25.0	0.70 m./E
88	75.0	1.50 m./S
89	92.0	2.00 m./E
90	13.0	1.00 m./E

Table 9-1, *cont'd.*

Structure	Estimated Orientation (Magnetic Degrees East of North)	Elevation & Side Viewed
91	No structure	—
92	97.0	1.00 m./S
93	1.0	1.30 m./E
94	138.0	1.00 m./E
95	No structure	—
96	95.0	1.00 m./N
97	93.0	0.50 m./N
98	88.0	0.25 m./W
99	90.0	1.40 m./N
100	0.0	0.40 m./W
101	92.0	0.40 m./W
102	95.0	0.30 m./E
103	92.0	1.80 m./N
104	90.0	1.00 m./W
105	3.0	0.40 m./N
106	0.0	1.00 m./W
107	178.0	0.50 m./W
108	179.0	1.00 m./S
109	2.0	1.50 m./W
110	176.0	1.00 m./S
111	83.0	1.40 m./S
112	86.0	0.40 m./S
113	176.0	0.70 m./W
114	16.0	1.20 m./S
115	94.0	1.00 m./S
116	102.0	1.00 m./N
117	35.0	0.60 m./E
118	9.0	0.40 m./E
119	92.0	0.50 m./E
120	10.0	2.20 m./W
121	10.0	1.50 m./S
122	9.0	2.50 m./W
123	172.0	0.40 m./E
124	9.0	1.00 m./E

Note: Mound group platform or plaza heights are excluded from the elevation figures.

tion rise above the swamp of 2 to 3 meters. The angle of the escarpment south of PS is roughly 12 degrees east of north, while the
meander course of the river averages about 22 degrees east of north.
At the south end of PS the escarpment breaks course to 347 degrees
east of north paralleling the depression.

Throughout the length of Kokeal, the escarpment is broken by
three channels (or natural reentrants) of low ground, oriented east-
west. These channels divide the site, as low areas were avoided for
habitation. The central channel enters the site at a point near the
south end of PS. The low ground of the "plain" below the escarpment opposite this channel is apparently devoid of structures. This
zone was the least examined in survey due to the extreme density
of its vegetation. It is probable that this low zone is periodically
flooded, which may account for both the dense growth and the absence of habitation.

Another example of topographic influence on settlement is
found at the north end of the site. Structures 107 through 109 sur-
round a small depression (an *aguada*?) which may have been modified. This depression is shown on the site map with squared corners. Although no wall masonry was visible within the depression,
the corner angles are sharp and clear.

Similarly, structure 104 is a very low platform on the edge of
the escarpment. Although badly disturbed by recent plowing, an
expansive zone south of the structure is covered with surface scatter, including ceramics, lithic artifacts, and fragments of hard limestone and plaster. The plaster and limestone scatter suggests a
relatively large, flat paved area. The eastern and northern boundaries of the "paved" zone are defined by elevated platform sides,
while the southern edge blends into the natural contour of a reentrant channel. The western boundary is not defined as it blends
into the higher ground level.

Smaller-scale modifications of the terrain are associated with
structures 34 and 35 and 16 and 57.

DITCHES

At a number of locales, long, linear features, reminiscent of canals,
were noted at the habitation limits on the eastern side of Kokeal.
These "ditches" are aligned 1 to 2 degrees east of north and thus do
not parallel either the course of the river or the orientation of a
small pocket of swamp within an eastward bow of the river (fig.
4-4). They were noted only beyond the southern extremity of PS,
even though the settlement extends further north, adjacent to PS.
Although these fragments of swales align in a north-south direc-

tion over a distance of 600 meters, the gaps (unsurveyable due to dense secondary growth) between the noted fragments are too great to allow us to assume continuity. The longest of these gaps coincides with the location of the widest natural reentrant channel, a circumstance that would make the continuation of a natural cross-cutting ditch at right angles rather doubtful. The possibility is raised that the ditch could be artificial. The segment of ditch located closest to a habitation structure does not follow the edge of high ground, as might be expected were it natural in origin. East of this ditch and away from the habitation zone, the ground continues to undulate with high and low contours, all oriented on the same north-south angle. Whether these swales and their separating ridges are natural formations caused by the hydrology peculiar to the area or whether they are remnant canals has not been determined. In either case, the westernmost ditch (fig. 9-2) *does* limit the habitation zone of Kokeal, south of the depression limits.

SETTLEMENT DESCRIPTION

A minor ceremonial precinct is located at the southern end of the escarpment, where the terrain drops off to the south and east. This precinct is comprised of two raised platforms or small acropolises which support a number of structures. A level open space to the north of the larger acropolis is bounded on all sides by structures. To the west of this spacious "plaza," structures 118 through 123 also appear by their form to be ceremonial, particularly structure 122, a pyramidal platform which has been severely damaged by looters' excavations. This group west of the plaza marks the westernmost limit of the site.

The two acropolises provide enclosed spaces of restricted access. Acropolis A, the larger, supports structures 63 through 72. Of these, structures 63 and 65 are pyramidal and rise substantially above the platform surface (2.5 to 3 meters in elevation). Other structures on the acropolis are very low platforms less than 1 meter in elevation. Qualitative differences could not be defined or examined during the limited investigation.

A large looters' excavation has been made at the summit of structure 65, measuring 1.5 meters in diameter and 6 meters deep. The side walls of the excavation did not reveal any evidence of a burial or cache, although the pit was located on the central axis of the mound. Other looters' excavations were found on the exterior slopes of structures 64 and 66. The most extensive looting activity had been devoted to structure 63, where a trench 2 meters wide and 6 meters deep had been cut through the structure to the south of the central axis. This excavation clearly had encountered a small chamber, probably a tomb. Fragments of lithic and ceramic artifacts were strewn in the bottom of the trench. A second looters' trench penetrating the rear of the structure on the central axis failed to reveal any evidence of ceremonial inclusions.

The orientations of the structures of acropolis A are not regular; they are not parallel and do not form right angles to each other. Whether this lack of regularity of orientation indicates different dates of construction or is due to some other factor has not been determined. However, excavation into one surface structure (Late Classic) and at one locale into the greater supporting platform (probably Late Preclassic) does show a considerable time range, which may in fact relate to the nonuniformity in structure orientation (chap. 10).[5]

A connected "walkway" joins the south end of structure 63 of acropolis A to the north end of structure 77 of acropolis B. The main platform of the second acropolis is raised approximately 0.5 meter above the surrounding terrain on the north side. Structures associated with acropolis B are numbered 73 through 79. Of these, 73 and 75 are tall and pyramidal. Structure orientation is more regular than on acropolis A, with the four-sided configuration common in the Maya lowlands, except for the presence of structure 74, which closes the northwest corner of the group at a noncardinal angle. The plaza formed by the surrounding structures is open at the northeast and southeast corners, setting structure 77 apart from the rest of the group. Structure 79 is a low, round platform near the center of the plaza, recalling many such round platforms in similar plaza locations in southern Quintana Roo, Mexico (Harrison 1981).

A test excavation in structure 77 (chap. 10) revealed a complex series of architectural components, with the probability of a Late Classic base to which a number of additions and alterations had been made. The elongate and proportionately low shape suggests that structure 77 functioned as an elite residence. If so, it is the largest of several structures of this suspected function in the two acropolises.

To the east of these elevated platforms are four groups of structures. The east, west, and south groups consist of multiple structures with patios.

The two-structure patio is common at Kokeal, occurring in at least two distinctive arrangements. The patios formed by structures 12 and 36 and by structures 13 and 14 have buildings on their western and southern sides only, closing the southwestern corner of the patio. The same arrangement is formed by structures 16 and 57, further north, and possibly also by structures 32 and 33. In the two latter cases, a raised-patio platform was not noted. The alternate two-structure pattern is comprised of opposed structures at the ends of a long patio; examples are structures 46 and 47, 87 and 88, 92 and 93, 101 and 117, and possibly 18 and 19. It has been observed that dual house-cum-patio arrangements are a rural peasant configuration at peripheral Tikal in the Petén.

A large patio or plaza to the northeast of the ceremonial precinct reflects the pattern of the southern acropolises. This patio is raised above the surrounding terrain, although not enough (less than 2 meters) to classify it as an acropolis. The supported structures are numbered 8, 9, 10, 11, 17, and 37. Of these, structure 8 rises most prominently above the surrounding terrain and has a complex configuration. Its location at the southwest corner of the plaza parallels the locations of pyramidal structures 63 and 73, suggesting its function as an oratory or small temple (a family shrine?).

A series of mounds and mound groups is clustered at the edge of the elevated escarpment or terrace previously described. These include structures 38, 39, 40 through 45, 46 and 47, and 48 through 52, all located between the ceremonial precinct and the first crossing reentrant channel to the north. Only structure 40 was tested. The low ground separating the escarpment and the swamp is scattered with a number of structures. Here, structures 1 and 56 form a patio pair but differ from other such pairs in the relative mass of the two mounds supported by the platform. Structure 1 is relatively tall and spans the west end of the platform, while structure 56 is elevated only a few centimeters above the northeast corner of the platform. Compared to other structures tested, structure 1 yielded more evidence of ceremonial activities and fine ceramic wares both from incidental construction fill and from cache inclusions (chap. 10).

West of this patio is a platform group that can best be described as a small acropolis approximating the size of acropolis B to the southwest. Structure 7 forms the east side of this group and is the dominant feature of the platform. Excavation indicated that this structure was probably not supported by the acropolis platform but predates construction of the platform on the west side. However, this interpretation is based on scant knowledge of the stratigraphy west of structure 7 (chap. 10). Structures 53, 54, and 55 complete the group.

Structures 2 and 3 lie south of the low acropolis described above. Their form suggests large houses comparable to structures

4, 5, and 6. It is assumed that individual structures (i.e., nonpatio groups) are associated with an "ambient space" on at least one side, even though such a space is not defined on the surface in the form of a raised platform. Buried paved surfaces north of structure 3 and south of structure 6 support this assumption.

Structures 16, 24, and 60 are drawn in dashed lines because they represent a type of feature dubbed "ghost structures" in the 1979 season. Such "structures" are represented on the surface by a mixed scatter of white limestone and plaster fragments as well as artifactual material, but they have little or no vertical elevation. Quite clearly, other such ghost structures could have gone undetected by the survey due to vegetation cover. The three examples noted on the map were discovered only because of fresh plowing and the total absence of vegetation during the months of April and May. Conditions of total ground exposure which permitted the observation of such obliterated structures occurred in limited portions of the survey area.

In the northern sector of the site, despite the natural drainage channels, the generally higher ground of the escarpment continues. Structures located on the upper terrace in this sector include 59, 62, 102, and 104. The ancient community is divided into discernible north and south groups by one of the characteristic drainage channels, in this case by the one which separates structures 59 and 60. This broad reentrant blends with the lower plain exactly opposite the southern tip of PS. This segment of the swamp-edged plain is all but devoid of occupation remains. As noted earlier, two mounds were seen here but could not be relocated during the formal mapping.

A habitation group central to the site, located between structures 58 and 117, shows the greatest variety in structure pattern. Here there occur single structures, two patterns of two-structure groups, and two examples of three-sided patios. The two structures which rise tallest above the surrounding terrain are 83 and 90.

A group in the extreme northwestern sector of the site is also isolated by a natural drainage channel. The use of contour modifications in the northern sector has already been mentioned. Structures 103 and 108, which are pyramidal, suggest a function as oratories. Outside of the main ceremonial precinct, there are seven such structures taller than the habitation mounds which may represent minor ceremonial functions.

Structure 80 is not interpreted as a habitation structure because of its linear form, orientation, and proximity to the swamp; it probably is a relic field. It is included and numbered on the map to illustrate the proximity of agricultural activity to the settlement. RF site 1 lies approximately 500 meters to the north of structure 114. This site is the closest tested zone of raised fields to Kokeal.

THE SURROUNDING TERRAIN
Three transects extending away from Kokeal were examined. The southernmost transect, 400 meters wide, extended due west to the northern highway, a distance of about 1 kilometer, from a base between structures 44 and 78. The area of the transect, about 0.4 square kilometer, is void of any construction activity that can be detected on the surface. The northern transect also extended west from a base line between a reentrant contour south of structure 103 and for a distance of 400 meters to the north. The western limit of this second transect was also at the northern highway, still a distance of about 1 kilometer. Here, four poorly defined mounds are present in the southeastern quadrant of the transect. With the exception of these unverified features, the two transects showed little to no occupation west of the structures along the edge of the escarpment.

A third transect followed the edge of the swamp depression for 1 kilometer north of structure 114; this sporadically covered a width of 400 meters east-west. In the immediate vicinity of RF site 1, two ghost structures are identified by a surface scatter of artifacts and limestone fragments. A short distance north of these is one mound that may be habitational. However, the decline in mound occurrence is dramatic north of structure 114. There are a few scattered and isolated structures, but the pattern of community density does not extend north of structure 114. To the west of the third transect, north of Kokeal, other mounds were noted on the terrace edge—a group of three structures. The overall pattern is one of a remarkably well defined and dense community, located at one of the terminus points of the depression complex.

YO TUMBEN
South of the acropolises of Kokeal are several larger structures which have not been included with the enumerated mounds on the Kokeal map. These structures have been given a separate status with the name of Yo Tumben (Yo, "on" or "overlooking"; Tumben, "new"). The distance between these larger structures and acropolis B of Kokeal is not great (about 300 meters), but several features indicate that Yo Tumben may have been distinct from Kokeal, chronologically and/or functionally. The structures of that portion of the group which were superficially examined are of a scale mas-

sive in comparison with those of Kokeal. They occupy the highest terrain in the immediate area, a topographic feature named Indian Hill.

In addition to these differences in structural and spatial scale, ceramic evidence from the northern platform group of Yo Tumben is suggestive of a chronological distinction. Surface material collected over a large plaza was predominantly Late Preclassic, and fill from one test excavation was exclusively dated to this period.[6] The possibility arises that the structure of this group, overlooking the New River rather than the swamp, may date to no later in occupation than the Late Preclassic. As indicated in the following chapters, the Kokeal zone shows first signs of major occupation during the Late Preclassic. Abandonment of a southern zone of a much larger Late Preclassic settlement may be the feature which separates Yo Tumben from the portion of the settlement adjacent to PS and identified as Kokeal.

Although Yo Tumben has not been surveyed, stereo aerial photographs show major construction as far south as 1.3 kilometers from acropolis B of Kokeal as well as from the edge of the New River to the northern highway. The significance of Late Preclassic development in the area remains to be investigated and is stimulated by reports of early development at Cuello (Hammond 1977) and Cerros (Friedel 1979).

COMMENTS
The settlement program has mapped in detail and initially examined (chaps. 10 to 12) one site, Kokeal, which appears to be directly related to the fields along the southern portion of PS. The settlement is dense, and ceramic dating illustrates two expansions of development at the site: one in the Late Preclassic, the other in the Late Classic period (chaps. 10 and 11). Kokeal is restricted to the depression rimlands on the extreme southwest side of PS, with clear limits on the west and north. To the south, paralleling the New River and separated from Kokeal by a natural reentrant channel, structures are present in a different pattern. This zone, designated Yo Tumben, may warrant a separate status from Kokeal for the reasons enumerated above. Indeed, Kokeal itself may represent a functionally special type of site, an argument elaborated in chapter 13.

Definitive statements concerning the nature of the settlement and population associated with the littoral of the Pulltrouser depression cannot now be made, because a complete survey of that littoral was not possible in 1979. It is noted with certainty that, at least on the west side of PS, settlement is discontinuous. In addition to Kokeal (and Yo Tumben), two other loci of settlement have been noted on the littoral of the depression complex. The area of these two other sites is unknown and will be the subject of future surveys.

NOTES

1. The purpose of this chapter is solely to characterize the settlement of the site of Kokeal, with particular emphasis on the relationships between settlement and terrain. Its main function is to provide an explanation of the map in figure 9-2. Any further analysis or detailed archaeological description other than that presented in the following chapters will await a subsequent publication encompassing a broader zone of the Pulltrouser Swamp settlement.

2. The settlement study was seriously impeded by the switch in study locations from Mexico to Belize. Intensive settlement surveys in the original Quintana Roo study area by the Uaymil Project (Harrison 1972, 1981) had provided a firm foundation for the proposed settlement work there. The switch to Belize forced the project to expend considerable effort in surveying with less time for excavating or investigating refined settlement problems.

3. The original survey work was performed under the supervision of B. L. Turner before my arrival in the field. A survey grid was established by Nancy Ettlinger, who instigated the initial examination of PS. Some structures were identified and excavations were begun to insure that at least nineteen structures were tested.

4. The detailed map of Kokeal and a portion of Yo Tumben were recorded in the field at a scale of 1 : 500 and reduced to the publishable scale of 1 : 2,000. This map was further reduced and superimposed on the greater Pulltrouser map.

5. The evidence for a correlation between the orientations of structures and their dates does not derive solely from the site of Kokeal or this season's investigations. The evidence from Kokeal of such a correlation is slender but corroborative of evidence elsewhere. In brief, the indications to date are that structures having an orientation of either axis of 0 to 6 degrees east of north *tend to be* of Late Classic date or later. Structures having an axis significantly greater than these angles (east of north) *tend to be* of earlier date, notably Early Classic or earlier. To my knowledge, the correlation of progressive shifts of angle with advancing time, achieving near-perfect magnetic orientation by the ninth century A.D., has not been actively tested, although the evidence for it is continuously increasing. Of course, every site produces some apparent excep-

tions, and because of these no "rules" or even patterns have been established in the literature.

6. Ettlinger (chap. 10) notes that some construction at structure 77 at Kokeal may date to the Preclassic also. Excavations in one test pit were terminated in a fill of probable Preclassic age. The materials above this fill, however, demonstrated construction after that period.

10. The Excavations at Southern Kokeal

NANCY ETTLINGER

Operation II, the settlement excavations at southern Kokeal, included nine suboperations that tested probable house structures (subops. 1, 3, 4, and 6), areas associated with house structures (subops. 2 and 5), an earth mound in the residential zone (subop. 7), the platform of acropolis A (subop. 63), and a probable palace structure on acropolis B (subop. 77).

These excavations were conducted for the purpose of constructing a relative chronology of the settlement thought to be associated with the raised fields at Pulltrouser Swamp by virtue of proximity. Diagnostic ceramics analyzed by Fry (chap. 11) provided the basis for chronological assessments, supported by several radiocarbon dates.

The probable residential zone at southern Kokeal extends east and north of the acropolis precinct toward the swamp (fig. 9-2). The north and south extensions of Kokeal, as shown on the settlement map, indicate the approximate community boundaries, although the unexplored settlement of Yo Tumben may possibly represent part of the Kokeal settlement (chap. 9). It is perhaps significant that the Kokeal residential area can be represented by community boundaries, since a recent symposium on lowland Maya settlements (Ashmore 1981; Peter Harrison, personal communication) found problems involved in the definition of community boundaries due to the prevalence of continuous settlement. Whether continuous settlement implies an absence of conventionally conceptualized community boundaries or whether such settlement is continuous spatially but not temporally is a problem that can be resolved only by intensive survey and test excavation procedures.

Operation II was placed in an intensively surveyed area, where test excavations revealed ceramically datable structures ranging from the Early Classic through the Terminal Classic periods. In other constructions, strata dated to the Preclassic and Protoclassic periods were found in the context of platform fill. A Late Preclassic stratum was found beneath an Early Classic phase in the fill of acropolis A, but since this excavation was not taken to sterile sascab the dating of the platform to the Late Preclassic is inconclusive. Similarly, a test excavation in structure 77 (a possible palace structure) on acropolis B dated the structure to the Late or Terminal Classic period. Beneath the construction of these dates was a stratum containing predominantly Late Preclassic ceramics. The significance of this Preclassic stratum was not determined, nor was this excavation taken to sterile sascab. Therefore, at this point, conclusively dated settlement construction ranges from the Early Classic through the Terminal Classic. Preclassic middens are present elsewhere in pits carved into the bedrock (subops. 2 and 3), and they date to the Late Preclassic period or earlier. Although Preclassic construction fill is represented, the stratigraphic data are not sufficiently complete to demonstrate that this exemplifies house construction in the purest sense of interpretation. Such Preclassic strata contained within structures were found only at southern Kokeal in the precinct of the two acropolis platforms. It should be further noted that the excavated sample from the site is relatively small; therefore, the presence of the datable strata in the acropolis platforms is more likely to indicate construction at this date than to suggest an absence of it. Also, one test pit located at the adjacent complex of Yo Tumben produced a Late Preclassic assemblage, strengthening the evidence for a Preclassic architectural complex at the extreme southern end of the settlement (chap. 9).

With the exception of suboperations 7 and 63, the suboperations probably represent or are associated with residential structures, although substantial direct evidence cannot be provided at this point. Botanical, ceramic, and lithic data from the present samples must be used with caution in ascertaining the function of structures. Botanical remains that might be expected on house floors have apparently not been preserved in abundance. Despite the retrieval of flotation samples from each stratigraphic level of excavation, relatively few plant remains were found (table 6-1). The wood samples recovered, as Miksicek notes (chap. 6), may represent the remains of firewood, but this evidence does not necessarily signify a residential function. While ceramic data on shape classes would be useful in ascribing structure function (i.e., it is expected that plates and other dishes occur in association with houses), the samples of pure deposits of this kind (table 11-1) pertain to only two structures. One of these samples (structure 4) was retrieved from a limited excavation. However, the other structure (structure 1) is well represented by household ceramic ware. In terms of lithic data, household-oriented and multiple-purpose tools are not singularly associated with the excavated structures. Manos and metates, small though the sample may be, are better represented on the acropolis than in the postulated common residential zone, although this observation may reflect the sampling technique. All tool types, including hoes, celts, axes, and adzes (chap. 12), are fairly evenly represented in most of the structures. Fragmented specimens predominated in most cases, as would be expected from secondary depositions of construction fill, which constituted the bulk of the excavations.

SURVEY AND EXCAVATION PROCEDURES

All excavated structures were situated in cane fields, except for the acropolis structures and one probable habitation structure that was located in a narrow wooded strip between two cane fields. The entire survey area was located within a fairly continuous farming zone, which included maize fields, mixed gardens, orchards, and, predominantly, cane fields. The majority of the structures have most likely been disturbed either by looters or by farmers. Looting was by far most evident on the acropolises. Much of the wooded area lying between cane fields may well have been utilized agriculturally in the recent past, as indicated by successional species. Deep plowing for cane production has disturbed the upper cultural strata, including remnants of floors and platforms. Moreover, plowing of the fields has blurred the shape of the mounds and removed a significant portion of the constructions. It is conceivable that the actual dimensions of the structures are somewhat misrepresented on the surface, since disturbance factors may have distorted the original size of the mounds. However, the excavation units were not large enough to ascertain the complete floor space of any one structure.

The excavation units were generally 2 by 2 meters, with the exception of three trench excavations. The originally planned technique involved placing 2-by-2-meter test pits on the flanks of each mound in roughly the same relative location. The purpose of this procedure was to gather comparative data on construction activity, to recover datable caches, and to test a portion of the midden abutting the construction. However, the severe disturbance of the area posed problems of structural definition that frustrated this sampling plan. Procedures were consequently changed during the course of the settlement survey and excavation to accommodate field realities.

Standard procedure entailed excavation by stratigraphic level, using the northwest stake of each excavation unit as a datum. Factors such as differential soil drying often masked variations in cultural strata marked by soils of slightly different textures and/or colors. In such cases, arbitrary levels were created to minimize any possible mixing of the strata. Section drawings and final interpretations were made after termination of the excavation and after all soils had dried. Grids (usually 10 by 10 centimeters) were placed on the unit walls to facilitate section drawing. When the stratigraphy was not complex, 20-by-20-centimeter grids were used. The next sections of this chapter detail the stratigraphic records of the excavated structures in the settlement survey.

The term "construction level" in this chapter has been used to equate with "floor," not with "fill." As the term is meant to equate with "fill" in other chapters, the different usage must be noted here. In each case, the dimensions given are those of the surface configuration of a mound, into or near which the excavation has been made. The suboperation number is the same as the mound number. For this reason, suboperation (excavation) numbers are not continuous.

SUBOPERATION 1

Dimensions: 30 meters north-south, 17.5 meters east-west, 0.6 meter high from west side.

Orientation: 1.5 degrees east of north.

Datum: Northwest stake, 2-by-2-meter unit.

Structure 1 is a relatively large mound in the middle of a cane field. Deep plowing has significantly reduced the original height. Although the humus is generally underlaid by a level of gray clay-like soil which is distinguishable in color and texture from the levels of fill beneath it, the accumulated soil and the fill are not distinguishable in structure 1 because of cane farming and other disturbance of the strata. Recent disturbance, apparent up to 80 centimeters below datum, is manifest in poorly preserved construction as well as in burned lithic and ceramic artifacts. Burn scars on the artifacts are most likely a recent phenomenon, probably associated with the burning of the fields and the subsequent churning of the soils. Fry has noted that a number of the ceramics have post-breakage burn scars. Fire-popped lithic debris occurs in the same levels as do the burned ceramics.

Structure 1 was the first structure to be excavated. A 2-by-2-meter unit was placed on the flank of the mound with the expectation of exposing both construction fill and a portion of midden. Structure stratigraphy was exposed; caches were recovered; and midden was not present.

Stratigraphy.   Gray claylike soil, which is probably a mixture of accumulated soil and fill, underlies the humus and extends downward for approximately 1 meter (fig. 10-1). Two construction components are present within this level. The later construction level occurs variably between 25 and 60 centimeters below datum and appears in section view as a discontinuous row of sascab fragments. This construction level appeared horizontally continuous in plan view in portions of the excavation unit, primarily within the southeast quadrant. The earlier construction level, occurring variably between 50 and 75 centimeters below datum, is apparent in section view only along the south and east walls. Its state of preservation is much worse than that of the upper construction level. It appeared continuous in plan view only in scattered areas of the southeast quadrant of the excavation unit.

At 1 meter below datum a dark organic soil is present, extending vertically for approximately 20 centimeters. This level represents a buried topsoil. Below the buried topsoil lies a natural deposit of marine mollusks overlying the bedrock. The bedrock is unconsolidated limestone that appears iron-stained in some areas. Areas of partially consolidated calcium carbonate appear within the bedrock, indicative of decomposed mollusks (Alan Covich, personal communication).

Three caches were retrieved from the northeast quadrant in fill associated with the earlier construction level. These caches, found in association with one another, included a limestone figurine that appeared battered on the distal end (fig. 10-2), used and unused chert celts (chap. 12), and a ceramic bowl filled with shells of the freshwater clam *Nephronaias* (Covich, personal communication) (fig. 11-4).

Two features remain unexplained. In the southwest corner of the excavation unit a lens of moist light gray clay, measuring 40 by 55 by 10 centimeters, overlaid the buried soil. The stratum of buried topsoil is 15 centimeters thick immediately below the lens of gray clay; furthermore, the topsoil is 10 centimeters deeper here than elsewhere in the excavation unit. The regularity of the dimen-

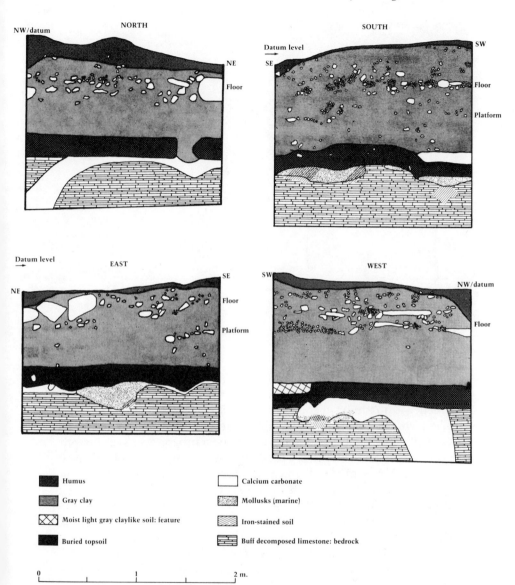

Fig. 10-1. Suboperation 1, structure 1, Kokeal. Excavation profiles.

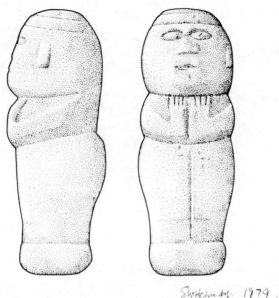

Shaheim toh 1979.

Fig. 10-2. Figurine from structure 1, Kokeal. Drawn to scale.

sions of this feature implies that it is not natural. The second unexplained feature is an intrusion into the buried topsoil in the
northeast quadrant of the excavation unit.

The Ceramic Record.   Although structure 1 has clearly been disturbed, there nevertheless appears to be a progressive stratigraphic
sequence in the ceramics. Preclassic (including a possible Swasey
or López Mamom sherd) and Early, Late, and Terminal Classic (but
mainly Late Classic) sherds are present above the earlier construction level. Within the fill, below the earlier construction surface,
the latest sherds are Late Classic. It is from this cultural level that
the caches were retrieved. Toward the base of the fill, in the earlier
construction level and just above the buried soil, the latest sherds
are early Late Classic, mixed with Early Classic and Preclassic
sherds. It is at this point that the quantity of sherds decreases and
continues to decrease through the buried soil level. The level containing mollusks, between the buried soil and the bedrock, yielded
two small body sherds that were poorly preserved but appeared to
be Late Preclassic. The final or lowest lot, within the limestone,
was culturally sterile.

The later construction level is most likely Terminal Classic,
the earlier construction level Late Classic. Harrison has suggested

that the Terminal Classic component is represented by a floor, situated above a Late Classic platform.

SUBOPERATION 2

Dimensions: 19 meters north-south, 16 meters east-west, 1.1 meters high from east side.
Orientation: 30 degrees east of north.
Datum: Northwest stake, 2-by-2-meter unit.

Structure 2, on the north edge of a cane field, appeared amorphous in form and had evidently been lowered by farming. A 2-by-2-meter test pit was placed on the flank of the structure at approximately the same slope (20 degrees) as the test pit in structure 1. The excavation of structure 2 did not, however, reveal any house construction. The lowering and lateral spreading of the original construction resulting from farming obscured the structural configuration prior to excavation. The likelihood of obtaining identical portions of structures for testing was reduced by differential postoccupational spreading of the structures. Nevertheless, the choice of flank locations for excavation still seemed the best available approach for encountering both structural stratigraphy and a midden sample with a single excavation.

Stratigraphy.   A level of gray claylike soil was encountered directly below the humus (fig. 10-3). Concentrations of small pieces of sascab were also present, particularly in the northernmost area of the northwest quadrant. This concentration of sascab pieces is probably associated with the structure to the immediate north of suboperation 2. A large amount of lithic and ceramic material was recovered from this level, including a number of fragments from several vessels and large fragments of chipped chert. This stratum may represent a trash deposit that built up and leveled the ground surface prior to the construction of the building.

This first cultural level is underlaid by a level of light gray compacted soil puddled with sascab. The level is discontinuous in the northeast and northwest corners of the excavation unit, indicating a probable mixing of the upper and lower strata. This second level appears to have been intruded in the southeast quadrant by a light gray compacted soil that is not puddled with sascab and that slopes downward, forming a V shape. The soil within this V represents a second infilling stage of a pit that was carved into the bedrock. The first infilling stage is represented by a brown soil. The pit extends eastward beyond the limits of the excavation.

Another pit was found in the western half of the excavation

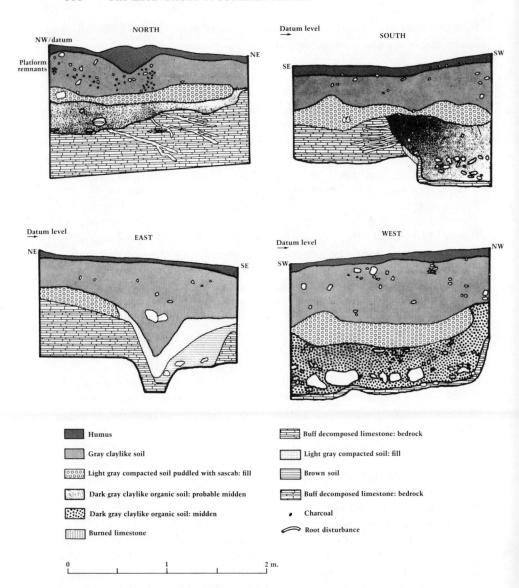

Fig. 10-3. Suboperation 2, structure 2, Kokeal. Excavation profiles.

unit, not contiguous with the eastern pit but at approximately the same level. The west pit extends westward beyond the limits of the excavation. It is filled with dark gray claylike soil that is highly organic and is most likely midden. The interface of the limestone and the midden in the west pit appears burned. Evidently, the function of the west pit was associated with burning activity.

Pieces of burned wood and burned limestone occur in association with a row of fairly large white limestone chunks just above the base of the west pit, within the midden fill. Since no traces of burning were apparent on these white limestone chunks, it may be inferred that the midden was secondarily deposited and that the midden and the pit are not temporally associated.

Several lines of evidence suggest that the east and west pits are not natural features and may have been created or used for different purposes. The angular cuts into an otherwise smooth surface of the sascab indicate human disturbance (fig. 10-4). The west pit shows signs of burning while the east pit does not. The shapes and axes of the pits also differ. Finally, the midden fill of the west pit produced a large amount of artifacts in comparison to the paucity of materials recovered from the east pit.

The Ceramic Record.   Early through Late Preclassic ceramics were recovered from the soil matrices infilling both pits. The east pit appears to postdate the west pit, since the light gray compacted fill of the former intrudes into the fill that overlies the latter. Two Late Classic sherds were recovered from the midden fill of the west pit (110 to 130 centimeters below datum). Since all ceramics except these two sherds were Preclassic at this level and below, it is reasonable to infer that the Late Classic sherds were intruded from higher levels. Radiocarbon dates (table 10-1) support this view. Rodent activity as well as root disturbance could account for the intrusion, particularly in light of the fact that sealed contexts are not present. The first two levels of fill, including the light gray compacted soil puddled with sascab, contained Early, Middle, and Late Preclassic sherds as well as Protoclassic, Early Classic, and early Late Classic sherds.

SUBOPERATION 3

Dimensions: 19 meters north-south, 15.5 meters east-west, 1.2 meters high from north side.

Orientation: 95 degrees east of north.

Datum: Northwest stake, unit 1 (2 by 2 meters);
northwest stake, unit 2 (2 by 2 meters); northwest stake, unit 2, used for unit 3 (4 by 1 meters).

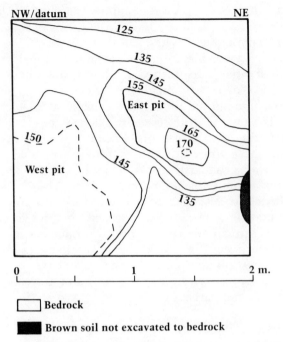

Fig. 10-4. Suboperation 2, structure 2, Kokeal. Contour of bedrock in centimeters below datum.

Structure 3 is situated on the south edge of the same cane field as structure 2. Two 2-by-2-meter pits were established—unit 1 on the north flank of the structure on a 20 degree slope, unit 2 on the crest of the mound, in line with the first test pit. After both these test pits were excavated, a 4-by-1-meter trench (unit 3) was set up that connected the first two test pits. This trench was excavated by natural stratigraphy for the purposes of revealing a broad and continuous profile of the mound construction.

The first test pit, placed outside the structure proper, was situated above the remnants of a plaza or paved ambient space north from the structure. The second test pit was placed on the northeast edge of the structure. Excavation revealed house construction on the west and north sides of the unit and a retaining wall on the south and east sides. The trench revealed the eastern limits of the house construction, two large flagstones marking the entrance to the house, and remnants of stairs and the plaza.

Table 10-1. Radiocarbon Dates of Materials from Southern Kokeal

Suboperation	Provenience	Material	Tree Ring–Corrected Date	Uncorrected Date (Libby Half-Life)	Laboratory & Sample No.
2	110–130 cm. below datum, in midden	Charcoal		1970 ± 50 b.p. (20 ± 50 b.c.)	Cambridge[a] Q-3119
2	110–130 cm. below datum, in midden	Charcoal		1896 ± 45 b.p. (a.d. 60 ± 45)	Cambridge Q-3120
2	137 cm. below datum, in midden	Charcoal		1935 ± 55 b.p. (35 ± 55 b.c.)	Cambridge Q-3118
3	130 cm. below datum, between midden phases	Charcoal (floated)	2137 B.P. (187 B.C.)	2100 ± 167 b.p. (150 b.c.)	SMU[b] 841
7	360 cm. below datum, in buried soil	Charcoal (floated)	2155 B.P.[c] (205 B.C.)	2116 ± 351 b.p. (166 b.c.)	SMU 840

[a] Godwin Laboratory, Cambridge University, by V. R. Switsur.

[b] Radiocarbon Laboratory, Southern Methodist University, by Herb Haas. The dates here have been recalculated by the laboratory and differ slightly from those initially reported (Turner and Harrison 1981).

[c] Large error factor due to the small size of the sample.

Stratigraphy.   Structure 3 faces north, opening onto a plaza. The excavation revealed humus underlaid by rubble masonry within a gray claylike fill matrix (figs. 10-5 to 10-7). This fill is associated with the house construction and the retaining wall. The surface of the retaining wall is at the base level of the house construction.

A platform of light gray compacted soil fill lies directly below the house construction. This level opens onto flat stones marking the surface of a supportive supplementary platform. Remnants of stairs are present to the immediate north of the flat stones, as indicated by three fairly large chunks of white limestone at progressively lower elevations. The base of the lowest stone is level with the plaza, which has been severely damaged by farming and appears as a row of fragments of hard white sascab. The stairs are underlaid by a fill that is apparently mixed with soil from above, suggesting disturbance and poor preservation. A posthole was observed in the northeast corner of unit 1 just below the level of the plaza.

A midden deposit of dark claylike organic soil lies directly underneath the house platform and extends northward, abutting the fill underneath the stairs. This is a second phase of midden deposition and lies directly above a first midden phase that infills a pit that had been carved into the bedrock. The first midden phase is also composed of a dark claylike organic soil, although the soil in the first phase is much darker than that in the second. This color difference was not discernible until after the soils had dried, following termination of the excavation.

The first midden deposit includes small pieces of charcoal and a small amount of burned soil. That burning occurred *in situ* is not certain; secondary deposition is possible, particularly since only a thin layer appears burned. An extension of the first midden phase at its surface level underlies the plaza floor. The south and east section drawings of unit 2 (fig. 10-7) illustrate that in some areas the ground was completely scraped to bedrock, leaving no topsoil.

The excavation included only a sample of the pit which continued westward beyond the limits of the excavation units. The pit appears to be circular in cross section and shaped somewhat like a shallow bowl with a contracted base. The small posthole which had been cut into the bedrock is situated diagonal to the pit.

The function of this pit remains unexplained. Several possibilities can be ruled out. It seems unlikely that the pit functioned in association with burning activities, since the evidence for burning does not occur at the interface of the first midden phase and the bedrock. The burning apparent in the midden fill is situated

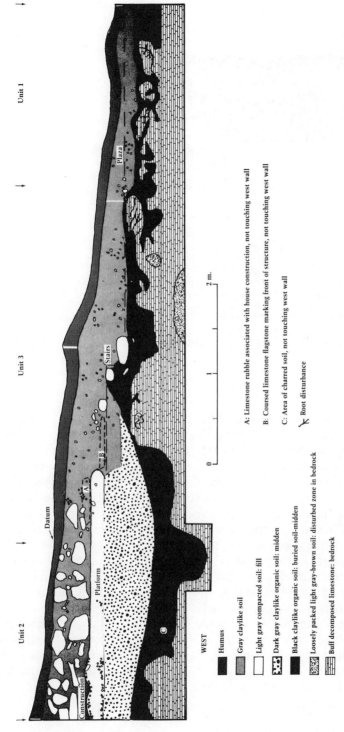

WEST

■ Humus

▨ Gray claylike soil

□ Light gray compacted soil: fill

▨ Dark gray claylike organic soil: midden

■ Black claylike organic soil: buried soil-midden

▨ Loosely packed light gray-brown soil: disturbed zone in bedrock

▨ Buff decomposed limestone: bedrock

A: Limestone rubble associated with house construction, not touching west wall

B: Coursed limestone flagstone marking front of structure, not touching west wall

C: Area of charred soil, not touching west wall

⅄ Root disturbance

Fig. 10-5. Suboperation 3, structure 3, Kokeal. Excavation profile, units 1 to 3.

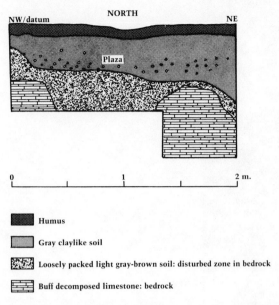

Fig. 10-6. Suboperation 3, structure 3, Kokeal. Excavation profile, unit 1.

not in the basal portion of the pit but in a small area in the shallow basin and is therefore presumed to be a secondary deposit. Consequently, it seems unlikely that the pit functioned as a kiln, a sweatbath, or a curing facility. Its shape precludes storage, unless it was covered with a lid of perishable material. That the pit was intended to hold water is unlikely, considering its relatively small size and the apparent lack of preparation to prevent seepage into the bedrock. Finally, that this feature represents a portion of a canal is unlikely, since it terminates roughly at the northwest and southwest corners of excavation unit 2 and appears to be circular in shape.

The bedrock underlying structure 3 was not culturally sterile. Isolated pockets of light gray-brown soil intruded into the bedrock surface, even on the bottom of the midden-filled pit. A small pocket of seeds, one specimen identified as that of a panicoid grass (chap. 6), was retrieved from one such bedrock-sascab intrusion. Noncultural disturbance, such as rodent activity, seems a plausible explanation for these isolated pockets, particularly because humanmade lines cut into the bedrock are not apparent other than in association with the pit.

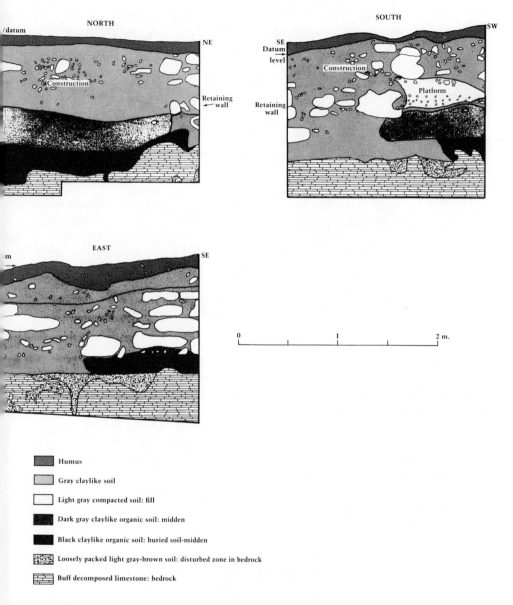

Fig. 10-7. Suboperation 3, structure 3, Kokeal. Excavation profiles, unit 2.

The Ceramic Record.   Middle and Late Preclassic ceramics and
Protoclassic ceramics were recovered from the first midden phase.
Charcoal recovered from the interface of the two midden phases
dates to the Late Preclassic (table 10-1). The predominance of Preclassic ceramics and the radiocarbon date from the associated charcoal date the first midden phase to this period, even though a few
Early Classic sherds were contained in this stratum. The presence
of these Early Classic sherds can be explained as the result of noncultural disturbance, as in the case of the Preclassic fill in suboperation 2. Indications of secondary deposition (i.e., no burning at
the bedrock-fill interface) signify that the date of the fill is not necessarily the same as that of the pit excavation under structure 3.
Near contemporaneity of the bedrock excavation with Preclassic
fill of the same excavation is accepted for suboperation 2, which is
located near suboperation 3. On the balance, a Late Preclassic date
for the bedrock intrusions in suboperations 2 and 3 may be the
most consistent interpretation.

The second midden phase is temporally associated with the
construction level under the house construction and with the house
construction as well. Structure 3 and this second midden phase
date to the Early Classic period. The second midden deposit most
likely functioned as a leveling mechanism prior to construction.

Few Late Classic sherds are associated with construction activities. They were recovered from mixed strata, specifically where
the strata were mixed with the level of soil accumulation directly
below the humus. Since it is known that Late Classic people occupied the area, it is expected that Late Classic sherds would be
present in the upper levels below the present humus. However,
where Late Classic ceramics were found, Early Classic sherds
predominated.

SUBOPERATION 4

Dimensions: 10.75 meters north-south, 17.5 meters east-west,
1.1 meters high from east side.

Orientation: 98 degrees east of north.

Datum: Northwest stake, 2-by-2-meter unit.

Structure 4 is situated in a cane field at the base of the northeast
corner of acropolis A. A 2-by-2-meter test pit was placed on the
west flank of the mound, near the crest; the crest itself has been
lowered by farming. Alterations in the excavation strategy near the
end of the season halted continuation of work on this as well as
other suboperations in favor of tests in the acropolis zone and ex-

pansion of suboperations already well under way. Thus, excavation in structure 4 was terminated at a level just below the humus on the surface of limestone rubble, the present upper limits of structural remains. Ceramics recovered from the surface of structure 4 were Late Classic; ceramics from the one excavated level included predominantly Terminal Classic sherds, some early Late Classic sherds, and some Late Preclassic sherds.

SUBOPERATION 5

Dimensions: 9 meters north-south, 14.5 meters east-west,
                   1 meter high from north side.
Orientation: 102 degrees east of north.
Datum: Northwest stake, 2-by-2-meter unit.

Structure 5 is located at the southeast edge of the same cane field as structure 4, at the northeast corner of the base of acropolis A. Half of structure 5 is in the cane field; the other half is overgrown with the trees and other vegetation that cover the acropolis. The test pit was set on the north flank of the structure at approximately a 20 degree slope above the surrounding terrain. Its placement was a matter of practicality, based on the cycle of cane growth and on the permission to excavate given by two separate property owners. The test pit was placed just outside of the structure, abutting the platform. The ceramic retrieval was relatively poor.
Stratigraphy.   The humus is underlaid by a level of gray claylike soil that is probably a mixture of topsoil and construction fill. The south face of the unit exhibited pieces of broken sascab extending vertically for approximately 30 centimeters that most likely represent remnants of the platform of structure 5. Sherds are present below the platform surface (approximately 30 centimeters below datum), but they decrease steadily below this level. Iron-stained and green-stained clays occur approximately 65 centimeters below datum, implying fluctuations of the water table. The green staining is a result of reducing conditions in the iron-stained zone (Janice Darch, personal communication). Soft white limestone lies below the zone of discolored soil. No evidence of burning was observed.
The Ceramic Record.   Middle and Late Preclassic and Early and Late Classic ceramics were retrieved throughout the excavation. The sascab was culturally sterile.

SUBOPERATION 6

Dimensions: 13 meters north-south, 20.5 meters east-west,
                   1 meter high from south side.

Orientation: 99 degrees east of north.
Datum: Northwest stake, unit 1 (2 by 2 meters);
                   northwest stake, unit 1, used for unit 2 (2 by .5
                   meters extending east from unit 1).

Structure 6 is located in a narrow wooded strip between two
cane fields, near the northeast corner of acropolis A. A 2-by-2-
meter test pit (unit 1) was placed on the south flank of the mound.
The exposure of a bundle burial on the west edge of this test pit led
to the creation of a 50-centimeter extension eastward (unit 2) so
that the burial could be completely exposed; the bones from the
burial were collected for dating purposes. Units 1 and 2 together
covered 2.5 by 2 meters.

Stratigraphy.   Six discontinuous construction levels were observed
(figs. 10-8 to 10-11). Whether some of these construction levels (ab-
breviated as CL in the figures) represent platforms and some represent floors remains uncertain, given the limited area exposed. The
lack of sealed contexts and the mixed ceramic record preclude inferences regarding relative chronology and structural associations.
The first, third, fifth, and sixth construction levels are composed
of white sascab. The fourth is buff-colored sascab which appears
scorched. The second is also composed of buff sascab, although evidence of burning is not apparent.

Level 6, the first construction level to be encountered, has
been poorly preserved; it was identified by a row of small white
sascab chunks within a gray claylike matrix below the humus.
This soil matrix, most likely a mixture of fill and soil accumulation, extends vertically down to the surface of the fourth construction level. The sixth construction level occurs at the same depth as
the base of what appeared to be a structural divider: an east-west
line of limestone rocks in the northern portion of unit 1 and a
north-south line of rocks in unit 2 adjacent to the northwest corner
of unit 1. This "divider," approximately 30 centimeters deep, is
probably contemporaneous with the sixth and final construction
level.

The second level to be encountered, construction level 5, has
also been poorly preserved, although its condition is better than
that of the one above. The fourth construction level has been relatively well preserved, particularly in the northeast corner of the
excavation. The soil matrix of the fourth level is lighter in color
and more compact than the fill above. The third, second, and first
construction levels are composed of a gray claylike fill, similar to
the fill above level 4. The third and second construction levels ap-

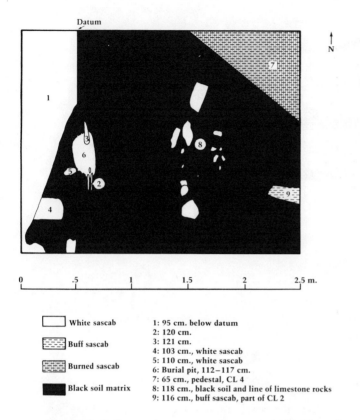

Datum

N

0   .5   1   1.5   2   2.5 m.

☐ White sascab
▨ Buff sascab
▨ Burned sascab
■ Black soil matrix

1: 95 cm. below datum
2: 120 cm.
3: 121 cm.
4: 103 cm., white sascab
5: 110 cm., white sascab
6: Burial pit, 112–117 cm.
7: 65 cm., pedestal, CL 4
8: 118 cm., black soil and line of limestone rocks
9: 116 cm., buff sascab, part of CL 2

Fig. 10-8. Suboperation 6, structure 6, Kokeal. Plan of units 1 and 2, showing lots 502 to 506.

pear to be in much the same condition as the fifth level, except that the second level is buff-colored. The first construction level, white sascab, has been preserved only along a small portion of the north limit of unit 1.

A bundle burial was found underneath an overturned Santana Tepeu decorated bowl at the western limit of unit 1, at the base of the first construction level. The burial is Late Classic and intrusive; the construction levels above the burial were clearly trenched for this purpose. The burial was embedded in black organic soil. Burning at the level of the burial and in its immediate vicinity was indicated by burned ceramics and pieces of burned limestone. A north-south line of limestone rocks was encountered at the level of the burial about 70 centimeters east of it, perhaps indicating the east limit of the burial pit; the area to the west of the north-south

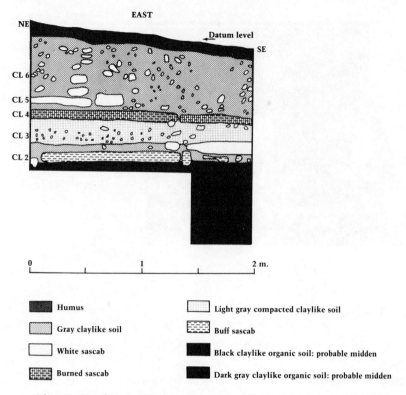

Fig. 10-9. Suboperation 6, structure 6, Kokeal. Excavation profile, unit 1.

line of rocks was pedestaled (the west section of figure 10-10 represents a composite section drawing).

Time constraints limited further excavation to only the southeast corner of unit 1. The dark organic soil that contained the burial is 20 centimeters thick, terminating at 140 centimeters below datum. At 140 centimeters a second organic soil deposit was distinguished by its slightly lighter color. These two organic deposits probably represent two phases of midden deposition. The color difference was apparent only after the soils had dried for several days after termination of the excavation. The excavation proceeded by arbitrary levels, since these two strata appeared as one stratum of great depth. Isolated ceramic samples were recovered from each of the strata. The excavation was terminated arbitrarily at 184 centimeters below datum, within the first midden deposit.

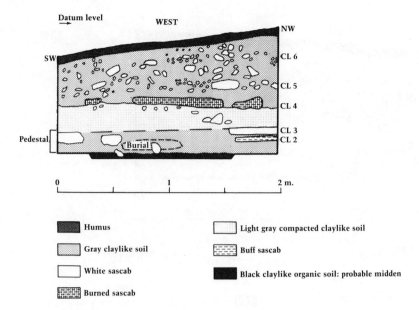

Fig. 10-10. Suboperation 6, structure 6, Kokeal. Excavation profile, unit 2. The burial, located off-section, is embedded in black organic soil.

The stratigraphy of structure 6 suggests that two middens were deposited, upon which a structure was later built and subsequently modified several times. In the Late Classic period a burial was placed underneath the earliest floor, intruded into the later modifications. The association of the burial with a particular construction phase remains unknown.

The Ceramic Record. The ceramic record includes Late Preclassic and Early, Late, and Terminal Classic sherds from the surface through the level of the Late Classic intrusive burial. The second phase of midden deposition is represented by Early and Late Classic ceramics; the first phase of midden deposition is represented exclusively by Late Preclassic ceramics.

SUBOPERATION 7

Dimensions: Approximately 34 meters north-south, 20 meters east-west, 3 meters high from east side, 0.6 meter high from west side.

Orientation: 1 degree east of north.

Datum: Northwest stake, unit 1 (trench, 8.6 by 1.5 meters); northwest stake, unit 2 (2.4 by 1.5 meters).

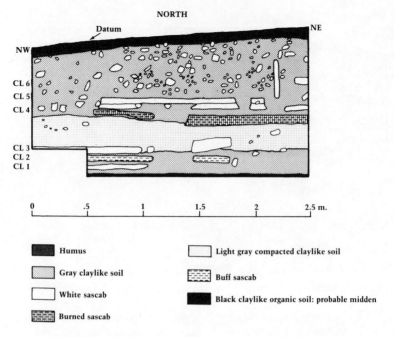

Fig. 10-11. Suboperation 6, structure 6, Kokeal. Excavation profile, units 1 and 2, composite.

Structure 7 is an earth mound situated west of structure 1, just outside the edge of the cane field. Disturbance has occurred in the form of modern construction activities on top of this artificial hill. The current landowner found a small wood house at the summit of structure 7 when he bought the land. He subsequently razed the house and built another.

A trench 8.6 by 1.5 meters (unit 1) was placed along the apparent central axis of the east face of the mound, extending from the highest feasible point (the east edge of the house) to the base of the mound (fig. 10-12). The actual summit of the mound is approximately 1 meter west of the trench datum (northwest stake). A step method of excavation was used down the face of the mound.

The west side of the mound opens onto what appeared to be a platform, at a level 50.5 centimeters below the datum of the trench. To test the constructional and temporal relationship between the earth mound and the west platform, a test pit 2.4 by 1.5 meters (unit 2) was placed on the west side of the house in line with the

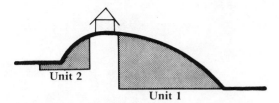

Fig. 10-12. Structure 7, Kokeal. Units 1 and 2.

trench on the east face (fig. 10-12). The midpoint on the east-west line of the test pit was situated where the slope of the earth mound appeared to end and where the platform appeared to begin.

Disturbance resulting from the modern construction activities was evident both in the trench and in the second excavation unit on the west face of structure 7. Historic material was recovered down to 30 centimeters below the ground surface. Postholes were present in both the excavation units just below the humus; these holes most likely represent historic construction. It is quite possible that a perishable structure was built at the summit of the earth mound in prehistoric times, although evidence to this effect was not apparent.

Stratigraphy.   Construction of the earth mound involved episodes of piling dirt from the surrounding terrain. The cultural stratigraphy of unit 1 (fig. 10-13) is most likely limited to one stratum; the fill lenses reflect a chronological sequence not of horizons but of episodes within one construction phase. All fill lenses represent unsealed contexts. Presumably, the black soil lenses indicate prehistoric soils and the lighter lenses represent natural levels below the topsoil. The general sequence of the soil lenses is a function of reverse natural stratigraphy corresponding to initial through terminal construction episodes. The entire trench was excavated to 260 centimeters below datum. Below this level, two small units at the west and east ends of the trench, 1.25 and 1.65 meters long respectively, were excavated a further 1.25 meters down to the buried topsoil upon which the mound was built.

The results of the unit 2 excavation (fig. 10-14) appear to support the interpretation that a platform had been constructed behind the earth mound and abutting it. The humus is underlaid by an accumulation of gray claylike soil. An iron-enriched fill lens underlies this level of soil accumulation, but only in the east portion of the excavation unit. This lens is identical to the fill lens at the

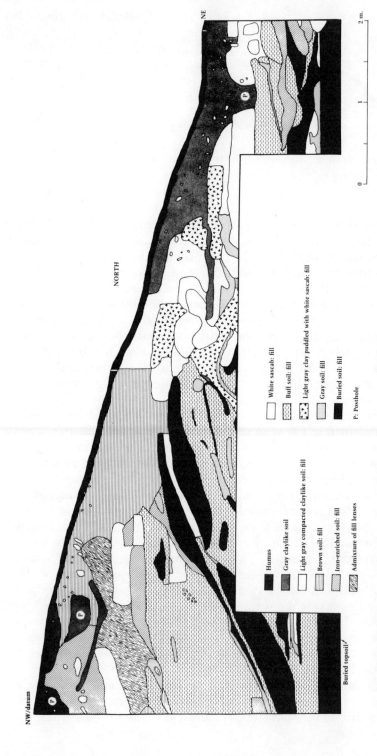

Fig. 10-13. Suboperation 7, structure 7, Kokeal. Excavation profile, unit 1.

same level in the trench excavation on the east face of structure 7. The iron-enriched fill in unit 2 is probably associated with the earth mound construction. A level of light gray compacted claylike fill with large limestone inclusions is present in the west portion of the excavation unit, at the same level as the iron-enriched fill. This gray compacted soil most likely represents construction fill associated with the platform abutting the earth mound. Alternatively, it may be argued that the gray fill represents another fill lens associated with the earth mound. This latter interpretation does not, however, account for the level appearance of the area just 50.5 centimeters below the datum of the trench, on the west face of structure 7.

The Ceramic Record.   The earth mound probably dates to the Late Classic period. Late Preclassic, Early and Late Classic sherds, and a few possible Early Preclassic (Swasey) ceramics were retrieved from the trench, including the buried topsoil. Ceramics from the unit 2 excavation include Late Preclassic and Early and Late Classic sherds, plus one Terminal Classic sherd. If it is accepted that a platform was constructed later than and abutting the earth mound, then three chronological interpretations are possible. First, since a Terminal Classic sherd was found within the iron-enriched fill thought to be associated with the earth mound, a Terminal Classic date can be ascribed to the earth mound and to the platform. In such a case, the platform would represent a structural modification in the Terminal Classic period. Second, since the contexts are un-

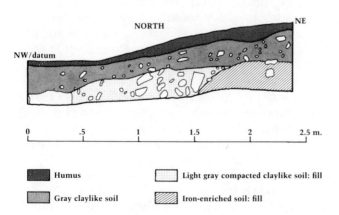

Fig. 10-14. Suboperation 7, structure 7, Kokeal. Excavation profile, unit 2.

sealed and disturbance is apparent, it may be reasoned that the Terminal Classic sherd is not in its true context. In such a case, it could be argued that the platform is Terminal Classic and that the earth mound is a Late Classic construction. Finally, it could be argued that the Terminal Classic sherd is associated with neither the platform nor the earth mound and that it represents an artifact of the Terminal Classic occupation of the area. In such a case, the disturbance factor would explain the position of the Terminal Classic sherd, and a Late Classic date could be ascribed to both the earth mound and the platform, with the platform representing a structural modification within the Late Classic period.

SUBOPERATION 63

Structure 63 is a pyramidal mound on the west side of acropolis A, the northern platform of the ceremonial precinct. Suboperation 63 is an excavation measuring 1.5 by 1.5 meters into the acropolis platform immediately east of (in front of) structure 63 (because of the location, the usual dimensions and so on are not applicable here). The purpose of this excavation was to establish a relative chronology of the construction of the platform of acropolis A.
Stratigraphy.   A level of gray claylike soil accumulation lies below the humus (fig. 10-15). This stratum is underlaid by a level of very light (white to light gray) compacted fill. Remnants of two construction levels, levels 3 and 2, probably earlier platform surfaces, are present in the upper half of this compacted fill level. The construction levels appear as two rows of discontinuous fragments of white sascab. The surface of the light fill stratum is broken by an intrusion of dark soil in a small area in the central portion of the excavation unit, indicating localized mixing of these two levels.

The corner of a construction unit, probably a platform and possibly associated with an early phase of structure 63, is present in the southwest corner of the excavation below the level of the second fill stratum. This feature extends to the base of the third construction stratum, construction level 1. The buried platform corner is composed of four strata: an iron-enriched soil overlying buff soil with limestone inclusions, followed by buff soil and another layer of buff soil with limestone inclusions. The lowest stratum of the buried feature is the same thickness and level as construction level 1, the earliest known surface of construction. This level is a continuous and well-preserved white sascab, the base of which includes densely packed fist-size chunks of burned limestone. The southwest corner of the excavation unit was pedestaled at the base of the buried corner and remained unexcavated.

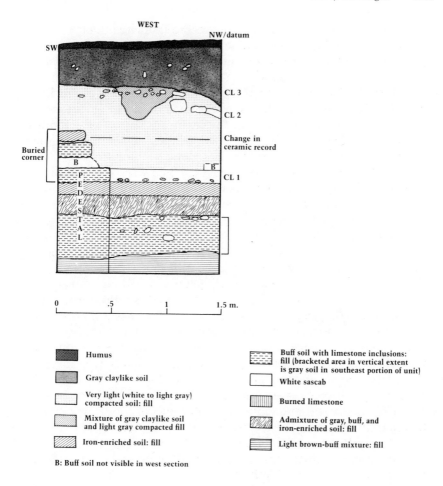

Fig. 10-15. Suboperation 63A, acropolis A, Kokeal. Excavation profile.

Four fill levels were observed below the earliest construction level. The excavation was terminated arbitrarily within the last described fill level due to time constraints. The uppermost fill stratum below construction level I was composed of iron-enriched soil; the second, of an admixture of gray, buff, and iron-enriched soil; the third, of gray soil in the eastern and southern portions of the excavation unit and buff soil with limestone inclusions in the western and northern portions; and the fourth, of a light brown-buff mixture.

The Ceramic Record.   The ceramic record indicates the presence of three components: Late Classic, Early Classic, and Preclassic (predominantly Late Preclassic, although some Middle Preclassic is present). During the excavation, a division in the fill below construction level 2 was discerned in terms of a difference in the degree of soil compaction. Although this division is not apparent in the section view, it does show in the ceramic record. The ceramics retrieved above this division were Late Classic, in addition to some possible Late Preclassic. Late Preclassic and Middle Preclassic (López Mamom) ceramics were recovered below the point of fill division down to the surface of construction level 1. All ceramics within the sascab fill of level 1 itself were Early Classic. Ceramics in the fill levels below construction level 1 itself were exclusively Late Preclassic.

⋅ The earliest construction level dates to the Early Classic period and is underlaid by Late Preclassic fill. The excavation was terminated arbitrarily within the fill below construction level 1 due to time constraints. Although a Late Preclassic floor was not encountered, the exclusive presence of Late Preclassic sherds under a relatively well preserved and continuous Early Classic floor (construction level 1) suggests a Late Preclassic occupation or construction. The Preclassic sherds above the earliest construction level must represent secondary deposition associated with fill. Two construction modifications are indicated during the Late Classic period. The buried corner cannot be dated since no sherds were retrieved from this area. The portions of the unit pertaining to the gray compacted fill between the buff soil in the southwest corner and the buff sascab in the northern portion of the unit (the so-called cut line) yielded Preclassic sherds.

SUBOPERATION 77

Dimensions: 42.75 meters north-south, 19.5 meters east-west, 1.5 meters high from west side.

Orientation: 12 degrees east of north.

Datum: 2 meters east of northeast stake, unit 3, approximately structure summit.

The long, low configuration of structure 77, on the east side of the platform of acropolis B, suggests a palace or range-type structure (Peter Harrison, personal communication). The purpose of the excavation was to obtain a sample of construction activity associated with the south platform. A test pit 1.5 by 1.5 meters was placed at the base of the west flank of the structure with the intention of exposing the edge of the platform. The stratigraphy revealed in this small test pit (unit 1) was sufficiently complex to warrant a 2.5-meter extension east toward the structure summit (unit 2). An apparent extended burial was partially excavated and exposed at approximately 94 centimeters below datum in the northeast corner of the second excavation unit. A third excavation unit was created that extended the second unit 50 centimeters north and 75 centimeters east so that the burial could be completely exposed. Unfortunately, the burial extended eastward beyond the limit of the third excavation unit, and time would not allow for another extension of the excavation. The burial was mapped, photographed, and left in place.

Stratigraphy.   Soil stratigraphy includes humus and accumulated gray claylike soil that is underlaid by two contiguous fill levels of buff soil and light gray compacted soil (fig. 10-16). The gray fill in unit 1 is associated with masonry construction that is apparent on the north and south walls. The absence of masonry in the center of unit 1 is a function of an intrusive pit, which begins at the west end of unit 2 and slopes down into unit 1, continuing beyond the west limit of the unit 1 excavation. The fill of the intrusive pit is distinguished from the structure fill by virtue of its greater degree of compaction and lighter color.

The surfaces of the buff and gray fills to the east of unit 1 occur at approximately the same level. The gray fill is situated in the northern portion of the excavation and is underlaid in units 2 and 3 by white sascab. In the northeast corner of the excavation, a burial has been intruded into the white sascab that underlies the gray fill to an upper-level structure. Fry has suggested that this burial may have been dedicatory to some portion of structure 77. The buff fill is situated in the southern portion of the excavation and slopes downward in a southeast to northwest direction, underlying the gray fill. The excavation continued until the buff level was reached underneath the gray fill in the northwest portion of unit 1. In the southeast corner of the excavation, just to the east of the buff fill, a cornerstone was found below the humus.

The diagonal sloping of the buff fill is suggestive of a mound oriented in a direction different from that of the structure built above it and associated with the gray fill. Possibly two different structural components are present, since different components are often associated with different ranges of orientations (Harrison, personal communication). Alternatively, the buff-colored stratum may

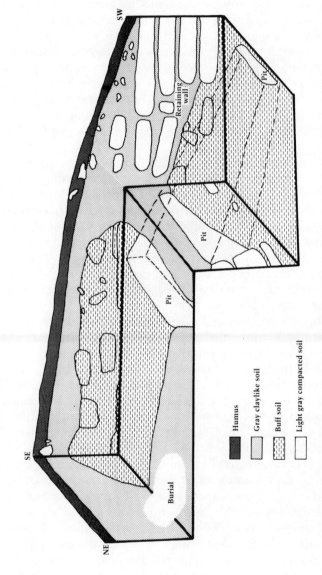

Fig. 10-16. Suboperation 77, acropolis B, Kokeal. Block diagram, no scale. The white sascab in the north portion of units 2 and 3 is not shown.

represent one operation in the construction of a complex platform. The orientation difference of this fill level may be better explained by the expansion of the excavation.

The masonry in unit 1 may have been intended as a retaining wall to buttress the gray and buff fills; the white sascab may represent stairs leading up to a platform which may have supported a perishable structure at the summit. If a perishable structure was present, it was probably associated with the cornerstone found in the southeast corner of the excavation. Third and fourth components (which may be associated, although such an assessment cannot be determined from the limited excavation sample) include the intrusive pit in units 1 and 2 and the intrusive burial in the northeast corner of units 2 and 3.

The Ceramic Record.   The ceramic record includes Late Preclassic through Terminal Classic sherds from almost all the lots, with the exception of a final lot in the buff fill of unit 2 that included only Late Preclassic sherds. The possible earlier component associated with the buff fill is probably Late Preclassic. The later component, associated with the gray fill and white sascab, may be either Late Classic, with Terminal Classic intrusions, or Terminal Classic, with even later intrusions of the same period.

SUMMARY

Operation II, the bulk of the settlement excavations, included nine suboperations involving the testing of structures or areas associated with structures. Suboperations 1, 3, and 6 involved the testing of three different structures. Structure 1 included two construction levels (Terminal and Late Classic); structure 3, one construction level (Early Classic) underlaid by a pit (Late Preclassic or earlier) that had been carved into the bedrock; and structure 6, six construction levels all intruded by a Late Classic burial. The ceramics in structure 6 were mixed in all cultural levels but the last, in which Late Preclassic ceramics exclusively were recovered. Suboperation 4 was near the crest of a mound; this was an incomplete excavation that was terminated after the first level of excavation below the humus zone.

Suboperation 2 included the excavation of two pits (Late Preclassic or earlier) that had been carved into the bedrock; the excavation abutted what is probably the platform of a structure. Suboperation 5 also abutted what appears to have been the platform of a structure (perhaps Late Classic).

Suboperation 7 involved the partial excavation of an earth mound that probably dates to the Late Classic period and may have

had a civic-ceremonial function. What appears to have been a platform, dating perhaps to Terminal Classic times, was partially exposed behind the mound and abutting it.

Suboperations on acropolises A (63) and B (77) entailed the testing of the north platform itself and a structure in the south platform.
The north platform excavation revealed two Late Classic construction levels, underlaid by an Early Classic construction level; the
lowest fill included Late Preclassic ceramics. The structure on the
south platform included a Late Classic component, with probable
Terminal Classic intrusions. Late Preclassic fill or a Late Preclassic
earth mound construction underlies the Late Classic component.

Late Classic and Late Preclassic ceramics were present in all
the excavations; Early Classic ceramics were present in all the excavations except suboperation 4 (table 10-2). In addition to the one
Terminal Classic sherd found in unit 2 of suboperation 7, Terminal
Classic ceramics were present in structures 1, 4, 6, and 77. Protoclassic ceramics occurred above the level of the infilled pits in
structure 2, within the fill of the pit in structure 3, and with other
ceramics in structure 77. Early Preclassic sherds were found in the
lower levels of structures 1, 2, and 7. The possible occurrence of
Swasey sherds in the lower levels of some of the structures has
been noted (chap. 11; table 11-6).

COMMENTS

The ceramics recovered from southern Kokeal probably reflect the
differentially weighted occupations, despite the limited number of
structures that were tested. It is with respect to structural features
that data retrieval is inadequate. Expansion of the excavations and
further testing would be desirable to confirm the tentative statements offered in this chapter and to clarify problematic features.
Neither of the tested areas on the acropolises was excavated to
sterile soil, and only one structure was sampled. Whether Preclassic construction is represented on the acropolises awaits corroborative evidence. The habitation area outlying the acropolis
precinct calls for further excavation, particularly because the disturbance factor rendered structural definition difficult and, consequently, the portions of the structures that were sampled were
dissimilar.

It has been inferred that structures 1 through 6 represented
common houses on the basis of their apparent dimensions and the
absence of any special features indicative of ceremonial functions,
with the possible exception of structure 1. Neither formal stone
coursing nor vaulting was evident in any of the houses; common

Table 10-2. *Structural-Chronological Correlations Based on the Ceramic and Stratigraphic Records*

Presence of Ceramics in Suboperations

Period	1	2	3	4	5	6	7	63	77
Terminal Classic	X			X		X	X		X
Late Classic	X	X	X	X	X	X	X	X	X
Early Classic	X	X	X		X	X	X	X	X
Protoclassic		X	X						X
Late Preclassic	X	X	X	X	X	X	X	X	X
Middle Preclassic	X	X	X		X			X	
Early Preclassic	X	X					X		

Evidence of Datable Construction Activities in Suboperations

Period	1	2[a]	3[b]	4[c]	5	6[d]	7	63	77
Terminal Classic	X						X?		
Late Classic	X				X		X?	X	X?
Early Classic			X					X	
Protoclassic									
Late Preclassic		Pit	Pit					X?	X?
Middle Preclassic									
Early Preclassic									

[a] In suboperation 2, two pits carved into the bedrock may date to the Late Preclassic period or earlier.

[b] In suboperation 3, one pit carved into the bedrock may date to the Late Preclassic period or earlier.

[c] Suboperation 4 was an incomplete excavation.

[d] All strata except the lowest consist of mixed ceramics.

house architecture in the Kokeal environs entailed simple rubble construction over a platform of soil fill or sascab. The earth mound, suboperation 7, has been interpreted as a civic-ceremonial structure serving the immediate residential community. This interpretation is based on the unique character of the construction and the size differential. To date, earth mounds are uncommon features in the Maya lowlands (chap. 13).

The results of the settlement excavations were in some cases intriguing and raise questions which indicate the direction of future excavations. The practice of trenching through buried soil and excavating pits into bedrock is notable. In the case of suboperation

1, the removal of the original topsoil prior to construction is noted. The fact that removal of topsoil was evident in other suboperations suggests that this was not uncommon. It is conceivable that topsoil was removed for the purposes of earth construction. Future expansion of the platform excavation on the acropolis to sterile soil would indicate whether or not topsoil from the habitation area (at the base level of acropolis A) was used to construct the acropolis platform. Whether or not topsoil from the habitation area was used in the construction of the raised fields is another issue. Trench excavations across the postulated plaza areas would be useful in ascertaining the extent to which the topsoil was removed. Moreover, such excavations may shed light on the extent to which pits were excavated into basal sascab.

These pits are morphologically dissimilar to the chultunes and other such features described in the Maya lowlands (e.g., Puleston 1965, 1974). But the excavated sample seems to be located under or near residential structures. Operation II uncovered three morphologically different pits. The function(s) of these pits remains unknown, except that it may be inferred that one pit (the west pit in suboperation 2) was associated with burning activity. Beyond this, more precise associations are questionable. The soil matrices that infilled all three pits were probably not contemporaneous with usage, and therefore the soils and the materials within the soils are of little help in assessing the functions of the pits. Materials were not found embedded in the bedrock in any of the three cases. Whether or not all three pits were constructed and used at the same time is uncertain, although it is likely that all three were excavated sometime in the Preclassic period.

The earliest firmly dated construction activities outside of the acropolis precincts are Early Classic. However, suboperation 6 as well as 63 and 77 in the acropolis precinct have Late Preclassic ceramics either present or predominating. These are not listed as definite indicators of construction in table 10-2 due to some doubt of their relationship to structure date. Earlier ceramics occurred within other fill levels; these most likely represent at least secondary deposition. A possible Late Preclassic earth mound construction is represented as an early component underlying a probable Late Classic palace structure on acropolis B, but it is also possible that this Late Preclassic feature represents fill.

The data raise questions regarding the relatively substantial presence of Late Preclassic ceramics, which underlie Early Classic residential constructions but do not necessarily reflect Late Preclassic residential occupation. Several other lines of evidence are suggestive of a Late Preclassic utilization of the southern Kokeal area. The pits carved into the bedrock at structures 2 and 3 and the apparent removal and utilization of topsoil at structures 1, 2, and 3 are correlated with Late Preclassic times. This evidence is open to several interpretations. It is possible that the bulk of the structures (and thus of the population?) in Preclassic times occurred to the south, near Yo Tumben and outside the excavation zone. Or Preclassic structures may have been leveled beginning in the Early Classic occupation of northern Kokeal. The amount of Preclassic materials found in the fill may be suggestive of this circumstance. These alternative interpretations apply only if the several examples of construction fill with Preclassic content represent secondary deposition. Unfortunately, this point is not certain in any of the several cases.

ACKNOWLEDGMENTS

I thank various members of the project as well as Daniel T. Reff and Christopher Lintz for comments on this chapter. Section drawings and sketches produced in the field were reproduced by James Anderson, University of Oklahoma. Peter Harrison provided data on the dimensions and orientations of the structures.

11. The Ceramics of the Pulltrouser Area: Settlements and Fields

ROBERT E. FRY

THE CERAMIC ANALYSIS PROGRAM: AN OVERVIEW
The ceramic analysis program had as its first priority the development of a ceramic sequence for use in dating the excavated raised
fields, the surface collections, and the excavated structures. Consequently, emphasis was placed on isolating and recognizing distinctive key ceramic types or shape classes rather than on evaluating
and eventually explaining variability among sampled contexts. The
traditional type-variety system of ceramic classification was followed, since this approach is most useful in reconstructing the
cultural-historical sequence and determining external contacts
from relatively limited excavated samples (Gifford 1976). In addition, the type-variety system has been used by most ceramic analysis programs in the immediate area, including the Corozal and
Cuello projects, which had conducted excavations in the same region (Hammond et al. 1979; Pring 1976, 1977a). Since the programs
of our project sampled a variety of depositional contexts, many of
which were not particularly favorable for ceramic preservation (e.g.,
raised fields and adjacent canals), we relied primarily on the better-
grounded ceramic sequence developed by the Corozal and Cuello
projects. This sequence appears to be valid based on the analysis
completed so far, although recently additional complexes and subcomplexes have been created within the broader complexes previously defined. No attribute analyses were performed on the data,
given the limited sampling of contexts and the relatively small collection size. However, analyses of paste and technological characteristics of a sample of the total data set are in progress.

The ceramics were evaluated in the following manner. After a
perusal of the published materials on northern Belize ceramics (Hammond 1976a; Pring 1976, 1977a; Gifford 1976; Bullard 1965), a preliminary examination was made of the largest and best-preserved

collections. Familiarity with the overall Belize sequence and with ceramics from the adjacent Petén (Fry 1969) and southern Quintana Roo (Fry 1973, n.d.) proved most useful, as many of the diagnostic local types and shape classes are also present in both areas.

After an initial overview of the best-preserved ceramic materials from the excavations, detailed evaluations were made of all lots of ceramics from the structure excavations, raised-field excavations, and surface collections. The recorded evaluation provided information on the relative size of each lot, including the number of rim and diagnostic body sherds of the separate vessels used in the evaluation. Other information recorded included the state of preservation, followed by a list of the ceramic complexes represented in the lot, usually with some estimate of the relative proportions of these complexes.

After completion of the evaluations, whole or restorable vessels were reconstructed, drawn, photographed, and described in some detail. Type and variety designations were assigned to these vessels where possible. Rim sherd counts were made of major shape classes for four large lots which appeared to be relatively pure occupation deposits or redeposited middens (table 11-2). No counts of types by lot were made, due to poor preservation and the small quantity of sherds for most operations. Studies indicate that counts of shape classes can provide more significant information than raw type counts of all sherds, as the former provide a better assessment of total vessel counts. Previous studies show that serving vessels have ratios of from 1 : 3 to 1 : 6 of rim to body sherds; monochrome bowls and jars have ratios in the range of from 1 : 6 to 1 : 10; while wide-mouthed coarseware jars tend to have ratios of from 1 : 20 to 1 : 28. Given the small sample size and the limited number of evaluated contexts, no statistical tests were performed on the tabulated data.

THE CERAMIC SEQUENCES AT PULLTROUSER SWAMP AND ADJACENT SETTLEMENT AREAS
The ceramic sequences for northern and central Belize are presented in table 11-1. The sequence developed by the Corozal Project was predominantly utilized because it was based on excavations in a significant number of sites very close to the Pulltrouser Swamp area, including the important site of Cuello (Pring 1977a; Kosakowsky n.d.). The sequence from San Estevan is also given, although in part it has been superseded by the Corozal and Cuello projects' sequence. The San Estevan sequence (Bullard 1965) was based on a relatively small sample, but it is presented here as many of the

diagnostic shapes and attributes found in the raised-field collections and the adjacent settlement of Kokeal are also present in that collection. The site of San Estevan, located only a few kilometers east of Kokeal, may have been one of the major centers for the Pulltrouser Swamp settlement area.

The Corozal Project sequence is a very coarse-grained sequence, especially for the later portions. For example, it is possible to subdivide materials from within complexes as earlier or later, based on comparison of traits with adjacent, more refined sequences such as those for the Belize River Valley (Gifford 1976), Becan, Campeche (Ball 1977), and southern Quintana Roo (Fry 1973). The Santana Tepeu complex would be equivalent to the Tiger Run and earlier Spanish Lookout phases at Barton Ramie and to the Bejuco and Chintok complexes at Becan. The Rancho complex is equivalent to the Xcocom complex at Becan, which shows a decline in polychromes and a dominance of serving forms by reds and blackwares. In addition, monochrome utilitarian bowls and narrow-mouthed jars decline in frequency, while finewares and coarse-wares continue and even increase as at Tikal (Culbert 1973) and Becan. Given the types of excavations conducted and the scale of sampling at Pulltrouser and Kokeal to date, it is not possible at present to create formal subcomplexes, but such patterning was used to specify earlier or later materials within the samples.

In general, Early and Middle Preclassic ceramics were not frequently encountered in the excavations, possibly in part because of the lack of resources for extensive testing of large platform contexts or intrastructure areas. A few sherds found mixed with later Preclassic materials are of Swasey complex origins (Hammond et al. 1979). A few excavation units produced a scattering of materials dating to the López Mamom complex. Again, there were no pure deposits, but some mixture with later materials occurred. López Mamom sherds were identified by their diagnostic attributes of slip color and texture and their paste characteristics. They were found only in occupational deposits in the southern two-thirds of the Kokeal settlement area; none were found north of the large plazuela group, structures 81 to 83 (fig. 9-2).

The earliest pure deposits encountered in raised-field excavations, structural fill contexts, and buried soil horizons were of the Cocos Chicanel complex. The subdivision of Cocos Chicanel into subcomplexes is more difficult in Belize and north central Yucatán than in the Petén due to the greater continuity in forms and shape classes in the former regions. Norman Hammond and Laura Kosakowsky (personal communication) have recently proposed a break-

Table 11-1. *The Ceramic Sequences in Northern and Central Belize*

Date	Period	Corozal Project Ceramic Sequence	Barton Ramie Ceramic Sequence	San Estevan Ceramic Sequence
A.D. 1500	LATE POSTCLASSIC	Waterbank		
A.D. 1300	EARLY POSTCLASSIC		New Town	
A.D. 1100	TERMINAL CLASSIC	Rancho	Late Spanish Lookout	
A.D. 800	LATE CLASSIC	Santana Tepeu	Early Spanish Lookout	Trial Farm
A.D. 600	EARLY CLASSIC	Nuevo Tzakol	Tiger Run	Barklog
A.D. 400			Hermitage	
A.D. 200	PROTOCLASSIC	Freshwater Floral Park	Floral Park	
A.D. / B.C.	LATE PRECLASSIC	Cocos Chicanel — Late	Mount Hope	Vasquez
200 B.C.		Cocos Chicanel — Middle	Barton Creek	
400 B.C.		Cocos Chicanel — Early	Jenny Creek	
600 B.C.	MIDDLE PRECLASSIC	López Mamom		
800 B.C.				
1000 B.C.	EARLY PRECLASSIC	Swasey		
1500 B.C.				
1900 B.C.				

Note: The dates of the periods are cited according to G-M-T correlation. The Corozal Project ceramic sequence is given in Pring 1977a; that for Barton Ramie in Gifford 1976; and that for San Estevan in Bullard 1965.

down of the Cocos Chicanel complex at Cuello into three subcomplexes. The earliest subcomplex runs from 400 to 300 B.C. and is marked by the absence of a locally common type, Xaibe Red. A middle subcomplex or period runs from 300 B.C. to 0 and is marked by the cooccurrence of Sierra Red and Xaibe Red. A later subcomplex, marked by the appearance of triple-slipped monochromes, dichromes, and prepolychromes, runs from 0 to A.D. 250. It was often difficult to assign the Cocos Chicanel material from the Pulltrouser excavations to any of the defined subcomplexes because the sample was small. Since Sierra Red cooccurred with Xaibe Red in a number of contexts, it is quite likely that the majority of the ceramics date to the later two subcomplexes. The absence of dichromes and prepolychromes may result more from sampling problems than from time differences in the collections, especially since there is a fair representation of Freshwater Floral Park materials in the collections. I suspect that each of the two later subcomplexes is equally represented.

There is some representation of the widespread Protoclassic Floral Park horizon in the project collections, especially from the structure 3 excavations. These include Ixcanrío Orange Polychrome and portions of mammiform feet, although no whole specimens have been recovered. Several other structures which span the transition from Late Preclassic to Early Classic may also have Freshwater Floral Park materials. However, the relative scarcity of diagnostics of this complex in the total collections, even where it is well documented, means that some of the ceramics labeled Early Classic (Nuevo Tzakol) or Cocos Chicanel (Late Preclassic) may indeed be part of a Freshwater Floral Park manifestation. Only large-scale excavations would document an intensive occupation in this time period.

The local Early Classic manifestation is represented in small quantities in 80 percent of the excavations and by such activities as cache deposition. The total collection of Nuevo Tzakol materials is small compared to the earlier Cocos Chicanel and Santana Tepeu complexes; however, this may be partly due to the small sample size and the sampling strategy. Cocos Chicanel sherds are abundant in old topsoil deposits under structures and may represent a different pattern of refuse disposal or construction technology (Wilk, Reynolds, and Wilhite n.d.). The Santana Tepeu complex is marked by abundant distribution of refuse adjacent to and in the fill of structures. Thus, Nuevo Tzakol deposits may have been buried under later construction and were less likely to be encountered during the excavations. Diagnostics of both earlier and later Nuevo Tza-

kol are present, but on balance the earlier materials appear to pre-
dominate. However, sampling error cannot be excluded as a cause
of this, given the tendency to encounter Late Classic materials in
midden deposits and only small fill samples for the Early Classic.

Given the small number of Nuevo Tzakol samples, it is difficult to make extensive statements about the complex. There are
some simple Dos Arroyos Orange Polychrome vessels and related
types, but the decoration on these appears to be simpler than that
on comparable specimens from other areas, including other sites
sampled by the Corozal Project. The most exotic items come from
the fill of structure 1, which contained a mixture of materials from
Rancho through Cocos Chicanel (chap. 10). This fill was notable in
that it contained the largest number of exotics and imported rare
items in the whole project sample. The exotics associated with the
Nuevo Tzakol complex included a simple slab foot, perhaps from a
cylindrical tripod vessel, and one sherd of the very rare Baxbachán
Plano-Relief. This plano-relief blackware type with cinnabar rubbed
into the incised decoration is represented by only one other example in the Maya lowlands, a whole vessel from Becan. Joseph Ball
thinks that the Becan cache vessel was originally associated with
a burial. It contained a number of unusual items, including Teoti-
huacán-type jointed figurines. Ball feels that the type has a Guate-
malan highland origin (1977: 101). Similar though not identical
types are represented at Tikal and Altar de Sacrificios, again with
cinnabar rubbed into the design. The combination of attributes of
shape, decoration, and cinnabar incrustation points strongly to origins in a system influenced or dominated by Teotihuacán. The presence of such a rare type with such wide systematic contacts in a
small structure in a very peripheral site is intriguing.

By far the largest quantity of data derives from Late Classic
contexts in middens, structure fill, and one burial. The Santana
Tepeu complex includes both Tepeu I and Tepeu II equivalents;
both seem to be equally represented in the collections. There are
abundant polychromes, especially the regionally popular Azcorra
Buff Polychrome (Ball 1977, n.d.—referred to as Azcorra Ivory Polychrome). This type is also known as Posíto Polychrome because of
its prevalence at that large northern Belize center. This type was
represented by one whole vessel associated with a burial from
structure 6 (fig. 11-1). It is estimated that about 50 percent of the
Late Classic polychromes encountered would fall into this established type. A few types are widespread tradewares, including some
from the Petén or central Yucatán. Although monochrome basins
are not all that common, a few of the specimens from structure 1

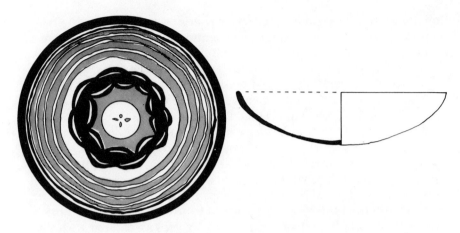

Fig. 11-1. Azcorra Buff Polychrome dish associated with a burial in structure 6. The nine-arc pattern at the base may reflect mortuary symbolism. Red and black on a buff base. Vessel diameter is 32 centimeters. Scale 1/2.

appear to be of Petén export, based on shape and paste attributes. The coarsewares are stylistically unique and appear to be of local production, differing markedly even from the supposedly contemporaneous materials from nearby San Estevan. Santana Tepeu material was found at all excavation units except the structures 40 and 81 test pits. However, a Santana Tepeu midden was located adjacent to structure 83 in the same group, indicating some Santana Tepeu occupation for the plazuela group. Santana Tepeu material was also abundant in surface collections from untested structures.

There is likely a heavy Rancho occupation at Kokeal, as suggested by the decline in the frequency of polychromes from surface lots and by the growing dominance of blackwares, including the Terminal Classic marker Achote Black. One vase with a high annular base is identical to a specimen from the site of Mario Ancona in Quintana Roo (Fry 1973), which was associated with later Classic ceramics. This type, tentatively called Tamnel Incised, may be a horizon marker for the eastern coastal areas and may have some similarities with fine paste ceramics. Its point of origin is not known. In addition, there are a few possible Thin Slate sherds in the collections, although none was sufficiently diagnostic because rim sherds were lacking. Fine paste wares were absent. This circumstance is not unexpected because the type is rare in most of eastern Yucatán and Belize and might well have been missed due to sampling error.

Another indicator of later Late Classic or Terminal Classic occupation is the relatively high frequency of serving forms in monochromes and wide-mouthed coarseware jars compared to monochrome basins and bowls and monochrome narrow-mouthed slipped jars (table 11-2). This shift, also noted at Tikal (Culbert 1973: 86–87) and at Becan (calculated from type-variety counts published in Ball 1977), may be due to shifts in food preparation techniques or to the partial collapse of the pottery production-distribution system. Terminal Classic sherds are abundant at Kokeal, including evidence of association with construction as well as occupation middens. The situation is similar to that recorded at Barton Ramie, with this period representing the latest period of major occupation. The exact extent of the occupation is obscured by the difficulty in separating later Santana Tepeu from Rancho deposits, due to poor preservation and surface destruction of structures by deep plowing.

Finally, it should be mentioned that a few Late Postclassic sherds were found, primarily from surface lots. The largest concentration was associated with structure 81. The majority of the Postclassic finds were associated with a central group of structures, centered on mound 87, called the Comal group. There is no solid evidence of any construction activity associated with the Postclassic occupation. No censer sherds were encountered by the project's excavation or surface collection programs. Historical materials included one fragment of clay pipestem and bottles associated with recent occupation on top of some of the structures.

Table 11-2. *Shape Class Counts for Large, Relatively Pure Deposits of the Santana Tepeu and Rancho Complexes*

| | Santana Tepeu | | Rancho |
Class	Lot 201	Lot 202	Lots 51 & 52
Small & serving wares	69 (47.6%)	43 (53.8%)	69 (38.1%)
Monochrome bowls	26 (17.9%)	8 (10.0%)	27 (14.9%)
Monochrome jars	5 (3.4%)	4 (4.0%)	6 (3.3%)
Wide-mouthed jars	45 (31.0%)	25 (31.2%)	79 (43.6%)
Total	145	80	181

Note: Lot 201 is from suboperation 4 (0 to 50 centimeters); lot 202 is from suboperation 5 (0 to 34 centimeters); lots 51 and 52 are from suboperation 1 (0 to 30 centimeters and 30 to 40 centimeters, respectively).

RAISED-FIELD DATING

Few ceramics were found in the fields, especially at RF site 2, which was a channelized-raised field (tables 11-3 and 11-4). Most ceramics were found in association with surface layers and in the mottled fill zone. The fill sherds were critical in dating the agricultural features. It should be noted that the preponderance of Santana Tepeu sherds were found in excavation units adjacent to canals. Thus, some of the materials may have been deposited not during the initial construction but in the course of mucking operations while the system was in use. A majority of the ceramics encountered were undiagnostic; fluctuating water levels produce poor conditions for preservation. Many sherds had been heavily water-infiltrated and leached. Some were just masses of flaky clay which crumbled easily. However, some did preserve traces of slip. In general, shape and paste were more important in defining ceramic complex affiliations than slip or surface finish.

STRUCTURE DATING

Tables 11-5 and 11-6 summarize the ceramic dating of construction and/or occupation for tested structures. Based on the presence of ceramics, the evidence indicates a significant occupation in the Late Preclassic Cocos Chicanel complex, probably the later facet of Cocos Chicanel. Extensive construction was undertaken on the escarpment above the New River and Pulltrouser Swamp, concentrat-

Table 11-3. *Ceramic Dates for Fields Based on Latest Sherds Found*

Location	Operation-Suboperation-Unit	Latest Sherds in Fill
RF site 1		
Raised field 1	III-1-(1−3)	Santana Tepeu
Raised field 3	III-3-(1−5)	Santana Tepeu
Raised field 4	III-4-(1−4)	Santana Tepeu
RF site 2		
Channelized-raised field 1	III-2-(1−4)	Santana Tepeu
RF site 3		
Channelized-raised field 1	IV-1-(5−8)	Nuevo Tzakol
Raised field 2	IV-1-(9−10)	Cocos Chicanel

Note: Nuevo Tzakol sherds were found in operation III, suboperation 5, a possible canal 160 meters east of mound 7 at Kokeal on low ground between the site and the river.

Table 11-4. *Ceramic Evaluations for Raised-Field Excavations Producing Datable Samples*

Operation-Suboperation-Unit	Ceramic Complexes Represented			
	López Mamom	Cocos Chicanel	Nuevo Tzakol	Santana Tepeu
RF site 1				
III-1-1	?	s	?	
III-1-2	?	x		x
III-1-3		x		
III-1-4		?	?	?
III-1-5		?	x	
III-1-6[a]	?	?	s	?
III-1-7		s	x	?
III-1-8	x	s		
III-3-4			?	x
III-3-5		?	s	
III-4-1			s	x
III-4-2		s	?	
III-4-3		?	?	?
III-4-4	s	s		
III-5-1[b]		?	?	?
III-5-2		s		
III-5-3			s	
III-5-4		?	s	
III-5-5		x	x	
RF site 2				
III-2-2	?	s		
III-2-4		s	x	x
RF site 3				
IV-1-5/6			s	?
IV-1-6	?	s	s	
IV-1-7		?	s	
IV-1-8		s	s	
IV-1-9	?	x		

Note: ? indicates a few sherds probably dating to the specific time period; s indicates scattered sherds with no major occupation or construction; x indicates a significant quantity of sherds and/or a stratigraphically pure construction deposit.

[a] Units 6 to 8 were soil pits associated with Operation III.

[b] This suboperation was a possible canal 160 meters east of mound 7 at Kokeal on low ground between the site and the river.

Table 11-5. *Summary of Settlement Occupation*

Ceramic Complex	Number of Structures Occupied or in Use	Relative Frequency
Waterbank	2	13.3%
Rancho & Santana Tepeu	13	86.7%
Definite Rancho	7	(46.7%)
Definite Santana Tepeu	8	(53.3%)
Nuevo Tzakol	7	46.7%
Freshwater Floral Park	1	6.7%
Cocos Chicanel	7	46.7%
Definite earlier Cocos	2	(13.3%)

Note: The figures indicate some significant activity at a locus, whether it is a construction level of a mounded structure, a midden deposit, or a significant number of sherds indicating activity in the vicinity even if mixed with earlier or later sherds. The figures total more than fifteen—the number of structures tested—since a number of loci were occupied for more than one time span.

ing on areas closer to the river at Kokeal. The large platform of the site of Yo Tumben (chap. 9) apparently dates at least to the Late Preclassic, as may construction levels within the platforms of the acropolis precinct at Kokeal (chap. 10). Many other structures with platform construction dating to the Classic period sit upon what appears to be buried topsoil horizons containing Cocos Chicanel sherds. There would appear to be relative continuity into the Nuevo Tzakol or Early Classic period, with an intervening Freshwater Floral Park manifestation. New platform floors were constructed at the large Kokeal plazas tested, but perhaps not at Yo Tumben.

The peak of occupation and construction of residential structures seems to date to the Late Classic Santana Tepeu period. Most of the mounds have occupation dating to this time span. At least some of the structures on the plazas at Kokeal show activity dating to this time, though the platforms had reached their present bulk in earlier periods. Many of the smaller structures located closer to the swamp appear to have been constructed during the Late Classic, possibly toward the end or into the Terminal Classic. These mounds were lower and more amorphous, often showing no preserved floor or platform surface, though many of these could have been destroyed by later erosion or recent deep plowing for sugarcane production. These structures also appear to be clustered closer together. As indicated, Late Postclassic occupation, possibly mid or later Postclassic, is confined to an area near suboperations 81 to 83

Table 11-6. Ceramic Representation in Tested Structures

Suboperation	Swasey	López Mamom	Cocos Chicanel Earlier	Cocos Chicanel Later	Freshwater Floral Park	Nuevo Tzakol	Santana Tepeu	Rancho	Waterbank
1	?	?	?	s		s	x	x	
2		s	x	?	s	s	x		
3		?	?	s	s	x	x	?	
4				s			x		
5	?	?		s		?	x		
6				s		s	x	x	
7	?			s		s	x	s	
40			x	?			s		s
63				x		x	x	x	
77				?	s	s	s		
81		?		x		x	x	x	x
83						s	x	x	
87						s	?	x	
92				s		s	s	x	
111				s		x	x		

Note: ? indicates a few sherds probably dating to the specific time period; s indicates scattered sherds definitely identified from the specific time period; x indicates a relatively pure occupation or construction lot, a definite construction, or a high frequency of sherds of the specific time period.

in the so-called Comal group. This area also produced one historic clay pipestem.

Surface collections allow us to amplify the pattern determined by the structure excavations. Rancho and Santana Tepeu materials are quite extensive on the surface of mounds. Nuevo Tzakol is relatively rare, while Cocos Chicanel is fairly common, especially in the southern portion of Kokeal. An extensive area of Cocos Chicanel sherd scatter was found in the large flat area—possibly a plaza—north and west of the complex labeled Yo Tumben.

CALIBRATING THE CERAMIC SEQUENCE
The Pulltrouser ceramic sequence follows the Corozal and Cuello projects' ceramic sequence. The latter is calibrated by a large number of radiocarbon dates and is backed by typological and modal links with other well-calibrated sequences from nearby zones and regions. The Pulltrouser excavations did provide some datable samples which in general are in agreement with the established boundaries for complexes. In addition, in cases where lithic types could be cross-dated, based on dated types from excavations at the important lithic workshop sites at Colha (Hester 1979), such dates are compatible with the established sequence.

The structure most thoroughly dated by radiocarbon analysis is structure 2 (table 10-1). The three samples, all from unit 2, range from 1896 to 1970 radiocarbon years using the sample means (20 b.c. to a.d. 60). The associated ceramics from the lots with datable material contain Cocos Chicanel sherds as the latest sherds, plus a few possible López Mamom sherds. The presence of a medial flange bowl sherd in one of the lots indicates a middle or later Cocos Chicanel dating, which is in agreement with the radiocarbon dates. The sample from structure 3 comes at the interface of two midden phases. Ceramics recovered from the first midden phase include López Mamom, Cocos Chicanel, and Freshwater Floral Park diagnostics. The second midden phase included Cocos Chicanel, Freshwater Floral Park, and earlier Nuevo Tzakol sherds. The radiocarbon date of 2100 ± 167 b.p. or 150 b.c. probably reflects the Cocos Chicanel material in the deposit. A datable sample was also recovered from the buried soil under structure 7. This soil contained a mixture of differing complexes, including Cocos Chicanel and Santana Tepeu. The radiocarbon date of 2116 ± 351 b.p. or 166 b.c. could reflect the Cocos Chicanel material.

The radiocarbon dates from the raised-field excavations are even more problematic than those for the structures, due to the poor preservation of ceramics, very small sample sizes, and lack of

sealed contexts (table 4-2). For example, while the ceramics indicate a date of Nuevo Tzakol for the construction of field 1 at RF
site 3, the radiocarbon date of 365 ± 78 b.p. or a.d. 1585 indicates a
Late Postclassic or early colonial date for the deposition of that material (see chap. 4 for explanations). A somewhat more satisfactory
date was produced from the excavated channelized-raised field at
RF site 2. Sherds from the center of the field included material no
later than Cocos Chicanel, while Santana Tepeu sherds were found
near the margins. A radiocarbon sample from unit 1 in that field gave
a date of 1800 ± 150 b.p. or a.d. 150 ± 150, which provides a good
fit with either date. It should be noted that, whenever a series of
units was placed from the center to an edge of a field, the earliest
sherd material was always found in the center and the latest near
the edge.

CULTURAL CONTACTS, INFLUENCES, AND REGIONAL TRADE

Although samples are relatively small, some statements can be
made about cultural influences, contacts, and even exchange. It
must be kept in mind that these statements are tentative; they
should be viewed in light of the results of more intensive excavation programs such as the Cuello and Corozal projects.

The Cocos Chicanel complex is part of the widespread Chicanel sphere. The local variant is marked by a simplicity of forms.
There are two major divisions of the ubiquitous redware. One is
closer to the Petén Sierra Red, having a fairly waxy slip and a strong
color. A regional variant, Xaibe Red, is lighter with a streaky appearance and a drier slip; it tends to have a lighter and brighter color,
though it is not a glossware. Polvero Black is sometimes found, but
no Flor Cream was encountered. There were no dichromes or Usulután wares present in the collections. The striated wares include
the local variant of Sapote Striated, with its horizontal neck striations. One unusual hooked lip waxy dish from a possible canal just
east of Kokeal is very reminiscent of the hooked lip dish which is
diagnostic of the late Cimi facet of the Chuen Chicanel complex at
Tikal. This shape is a late Cocos Chicanel trait in northern Belize.

One type which can be documented as an import is a large
bowl with flaring walls—possibly a cache vessel—uncovered during the excavation of a small "broadside" adjacent to a road cut on
the southeast edge of the Yo Tumben plaza. This very thin-walled
vessel has a fugitive red slip on the interior and the very top of the
exterior wall (fig. 11-2). Almost identical specimens were found in
great frequency with Cocos Chicanel–associated materials at the

site of Laguna Milagros, just northwest of the mouth of the Hondo River. Similar thin-walled types, though without the fugitive red slip, are reported from the site of Cerros on Bahía de Chetumal (Robin Robertson, personal communication). This type, which I have called Laguna Milagros Red, may well have a highly localized distribution along the lower reaches of the New and Hondo rivers and the coastal areas between; it was not encountered at any other sites in Quintana Roo.

The local Floral Park equivalent, the Freshwater Floral Park complex, shares many diagnostic modes, including the first orange polychromes, Ixcanrío Orange Polychrome, which may be imported, and mammiform (probably tetrapod) feet. Again no real exotics such as Usulután wares surface in the local collections. Floral Park horizons are strongly represented in the valleys of the Belize and New rivers and possibly also along the Hondo (Pring 1977b).

The Early Classic Nuevo Tzakol complex fits solidly into the Tzakol sphere, with diagnostics such as a variety of orange polychromes, including Dos Arroyos Orange Polychrome (fig. 11-3). Also represented are Aguila Orange and Balanza Black, two other major components of the Tzakol sphere. The polychromes recovered appear to be simpler in design and execution than the polychromes from larger sites. Monochrome basins and large bowls are also relatively scarce, though this may reflect the contexts sampled. Rare types dating to the later Nuevo Tzakol include the previously described Baxbachán Plano-Relief sherd and a slab foot possibly from a cylindrical tripod vessel.

The Santana Tepeu complex includes a fair representation of polychromes in the serving-shape class, including a few pieces of Saxche Orange Polychrome, a widespread tradeware. The dominant local polychrome is Azcorra Buff Polychrome, which is remarkably uniform in paste and slip colors. The basic shape is a simple round-sided shallow plate or dish (fig. 11-1). Other polychromes are primarily plates or dishes with similar profiles or with small medial ridges. In this regard they are similar to specimens from southern Quintana Roo and Becan as well as Altun Ha, compared to the larger medial flanges prevalent in the Petén. The basal break bowls common in western Belize at San José and Benque Viejo are absent, but there are larger monochrome medial ridge or flange bowls which may be parallel in time—perhaps reflecting influence from northern Yucatán.

Monochrome bowls and basins and narrow-mouthed jars are quite rare, with several of these being possible tradewares from the Petén. Instead wide-mouthed coarseware jars appear to be very prevalent (fig. 11-4), with the dominant types being a relatively short-necked jar with a rolled lip and a medium-necked jar with a medial ridge on the neck. These are quite different from the types reported from San Estevan and may be of highly local manufacture. This pattern is expected from studies of other areas of the Maya lowlands in which pottery production and distribution are confined to areas no more than 6 to 10 kilometers in diameter for this class—an example of supply zone behavior (Fry 1980). Rancho complex dating of some of the occupation area is indicated, although the only evidence for construction comes from several of the smaller mounds, as indicated by the high frequency of blackwares in some lots equivalent to the widespread Terminal Classic marker Achote Black. However, some of the blackwares may be earlier, as Ball has noted persistence of blackwares in his Bejuco and Chintok complexes, which antedated the Terminal Classic–Early Postclassic Xcocom complex.

Other similarities with Becan materials can be seen in the same blackwares and redwares which often seem to be firing variants of one basic type, sharing shape and paste attributes. This includes the common shallow plate or dish, often with a slightly inverted section very near the rim, represented in Corona Red and Molino Black at Becan. Similar types are found in the Pulltrouser collection, including a scalloped lip variant noted at Becan and southern Quintana Roo. Other wares found in both southern Quintana Roo and the Pulltrouser collection include a rare fineware Tamnel Incised vase probably produced at a single production center. This item is also later Late Classic or possibly Terminal Classic. A few possible slateware body sherds were encountered which could be Rancho or Terminal Classic. However, these might just be extreme firing variants of locally produced monochromes. No major collections of slatewares or any fine paste wares were found.

The Postclassic appears to be the later Postclassic Waterbank complex with simple thin redwares and collared-neck coarseware jars. Only a few diagnostic sherds were located, so exact temporal placement and potential cultural influences or trade cannot be documented. No Tulum or Paxcamán redwares were noted in the collections, nor were there any diagnostic later Postclassic foot types such as slipper or scroll feet or trumpet-shaped feet from tripod plates. One comal was found which may be Postclassic or possibly even historic, as it was found directly on the surface.

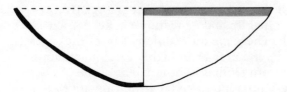

Fig. 11-2. Laguna Milagros Red vessel recovered from the platform of Yo Tumben. There is evidence of "killing" of the vessel at its base. Rim diameter is 39.7 centimeters. Scale 1/2.

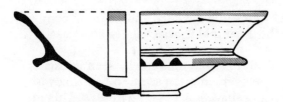

Fig. 11-3. Dos Arroyos Orange Polychrome bowl found adjacent to structure 81. Approximately half a vessel was used as a cache offering. It was heavily scorched on the interior and contained clay embedded with whole and fragmentary human teeth. Rim diameter is 27 centimeters. Scale 1/2.

Fig. 11-4. Miniature striated jar, similar to the full-size Burgos Striated jar recovered as a cache from structure 1. The vessel contained freshwater mussel shells. Rim diameter is 8 centimeters. Vessel height is 9 centimeters. Scale 1/2.

SUMMARY

The ceramics from the Pulltrouser Swamp zone, including the settlement area of Kokeal, are predictable given the location of the zone and its internal structure. As most projects in the area have discovered, it is difficult to find unmixed and undisturbed evidence of Early and Middle Preclassic occupation without deep excavation and extensive sampling. The discovery of a fairly large Cocos Chicanel presence in the zone matches the discoveries of the Corozal Project (Hammond 1976a; Pring 1977a), Bullard's research at San Estevan (Bullard 1965), and Friedel's research at the important site of Cerros at the mouth of the New River (Friedel 1979). The continuing occupation throughout the Classic period is most reminiscent of the sequence at Barton Ramie (Willey et al. 1965). The lack of a significant Postclassic occupation further supports the basically Classic dating proposed by Bullard for the nearby major center of San Estevan.

The ceramics fit solidly into the northern Belize sequences which have been developed. The strongest linkages—as seen in imported items and local serving vessels—are with the northeastern Petén, the coastal sites of Belize, and more distantly with sites in the region from Becan to Lake Bacalar in southern Quintana Roo. These latter links are quite interesting, as this region also includes extensive raised-field systems, as may the Petén (Adams 1980). The boundaries of this zone of more intensive interaction do appear to be close to those described for the contact period *cacicazgo* of Chetumal.

Within the sampled zone, ceramic evidence can be used to mark some degree of internal social differentiation. The greatest number of exotics were produced either from small structures with a possible ritual function, perhaps structure 1 with its unique caches, or from larger plazuela groups such as that including structures 81 to 83. However, much larger samples of occupation debris are necessary to fully confirm this statement.

12. The Lithic Artifacts of the Pulltrouser Area: Settlements and Fields

HARRY J. SHAFER

The primary objective of this chapter is to determine whether functional data can be gained from the lithic artifact analysis that would contribute to the understanding of the development and maintenance of Maya agriculture in wetlands, specifically through association with raised fields. Since the artifact sample was recovered from both field and settlement contexts, diverse uses were expected to be reflected in the lithic collection. However, if stone tools were used in the construction and maintenance of the raised fields and if this activity consumed a significant portion of the population's energy, then such tools should be represented in the assemblage. The analysis was approached with the expectation that specific tools or a tool set related to the general specialization of raised-field construction and maintenance could be identified.

LITHIC STUDIES AND THE MAYA
Only in the last thirty years has the analysis of lithic artifacts been a standard part of prehistoric research in Mesoamerica. This circumstance has largely resulted from the past emphasis placed on the more visible and exotic architectural monuments. Hieroglyphics, sculpture, and ceramics all overshadowed the less impressive lithic artifacts. Attention was first directed at the lithic artifacts in hopes of detecting chronologically significant trends. Although most archaeologists seem to follow this inductive line of inquiry, research designs are beginning to drift away from the previously dominant humanities—art history orientation toward ecologically oriented models of Maya adaptation; consequently, lithic studies are becoming more sophisticated (Sheets 1977).

The growing interest in lithic studies has also been due to an advancement of theory in lithic technology which has taken place over the past two decades, especially in the areas of fracture me-

chanics, experimental studies, and use wear analysis. The use of
trace element and intrasite-intersite analyses for obsidian, a resource restricted to the western highlands, has led to the formu-
lation of models of exchange networks and socioeconomic systems for both the highland and the lowland Maya (Hammond 1972,
1976b; Sidrys 1980; Michels 1976). Chert resources and artifacts
have customarily received little attention, except for descriptive
morphological studies, until recently in the Maya lowlands. Hester
(1976) and Sheets (1977) have reviewed the literature on lithic research in the Maya area, noting its growing emphasis and point-
ing out the lack of a standardized terminology as being a major
problem.

The initial trend in the descriptive and functional terminology
was established by Kidder (1947) in describing the lithics from
Uaxactún. The trend was followed by Willey and colleagues in re-
porting the Belize River Valley lithics (Willey et al. 1965) as well as
the material from Altar de Sacrificios and Seibal (Willey 1972: 1;
1978). The Maya lithic symposium held in Belize in 1976 (Hester
and Hammond 1976) provided a beginning for solving the terminology issue by emphasizing the need for more intensive technological and functional studies in the Maya lowlands. Recent
intensive investigations at Colha in northern Belize under the direction of T. R. Hester (Shafer 1979; Shafer and Hester 1979; Hester, Eaton, and Shafer 1980), stimulated in part, by this symposium,
has provided important information on Maya chert tool production
and craft specialization in this portion of the lowlands. The importance of Colha to understanding lithic technology lies in the massive industrial production of chert tools from Late Preclassic to Early
Postclassic periods and its position as a regional production center.
The entire production sequence and trajectories are represented,
and workshops for each time period have been tested (Shafer 1979;
Shafer and Hester 1979; Roemer 1980; Shafer and Oglesby 1980) and
have yielded a fuller understanding of the formal tools which entered the intrasite and intersite consumption spheres (Hester 1980).

Although interpretations regarding artifact function were made
by Kidder (1947) and others, based on form and visible attributes of
wear, microscopic use wear studies have only recently been conducted on lithics from the Maya lowlands. Comparative data available from Seibal (Wilk 1978), Petroglyph Cave (Shafer, n.d.), and
Cuello (Shafer, Hester, and Kelly n.d.) serve to indicate the excellent potential for technological and functional data that may be
gained through this line of inquiry. It is important, however, to
frame such functional studies within a much broader context that

incorporates form, technology, and sociocultural information. Otherwise, the implications of the findings may not be realized.

Structuring lithic analyses to obtain morphological and technological data is crucial toward identifying the context of the production and distribution of chipped stone tools. Recent archaeological work in Belize has brought to light the influence that the chert-bearing deposits mapped by Wright and associates (1959: fig. X) had on lowland Maya commerce and trade. Chert was not uniformly distributed among the settlements over the lowlands due to several factors. Among these factors were the restricted distribution of lithic raw materials, variations in how these materials were utilized, the degree and magnitude of lithic production, the location and influence of distribution centers, and economic and political demands on the trade networks (Shafer, Hester, and Kelly n.d.). Resources were made available over a large area by the mechanisms of distribution and trade, as indicated by the widespread occurrence of obsidian and jade.

Technological analysis of chipped stone collections will be a principal method of documenting the distribution of materials from the Colha complex, including Colha and similar lithic production sites in northern Belize (Shafer and Hester 1979; Kelly, Valdez, and Hester 1979). A standard taxonomy of chert tools, based on shape alone, will not suffice. Because of the production-consumption patterns that have been observed, the form and, indeed, the function of a tool will often change depending on the distance from the production area and the amount of reduction due to use, retouch, and recycling.

THEORY AND METHODS

A preliminary inspection of the Pulltrouser area lithic collection by Thomas Hester and myself revealed that most of the cherts were virtually inseparable from those that we have observed at Colha. Furthermore, the few recognizable formal chert tools in the collection were identical to those that were produced in Late Preclassic and Late Classic workshops at Colha, particularly the large oval bifaces, tranchet bit tools, and macroblade tools. The chalcedony artifacts constitute a minor resource in the sample. This material was evidently more locally available to the Kokeal population than was chert, based on the frequency of the former in the chipped stone waste and construction fill at nearby Cuello and its absence in the natural outcrops at Colha.

The working hypothesis for the lithic analysis is that the chert artifacts were first introduced into the Pulltrouser consumption sphere as formal tools (fig. 12-1). The chert tools underwent a transformation from the formal tools to their present state through a reduction continuum due to use, retouch, and recycling. If the Pulltrouser lithic collection can be shown to represent an example of the consumption end of the Colha-related production-exchange-consumption system, these findings will contribute significantly both toward the development of a useful lithic taxonomy for this portion of the Maya lowlands and toward our understanding of the socioeconomic context of Colha. By demonstrating that an exchange relationship existed between the two site complexes, it will be possible to link the Pulltrouser raised-field commerce to a broader economic network.

The artifacts were sorted on the basis of observable technological attributes. The initial sorting followed traditional systems for classifying lithic samples, such as grouping into chipped and ground stone categories. The chipped stone sample was further sorted on the basis of how a particular specimen was reduced or retouched for use. For example, if a tool blank was mostly bifaced, thinned, or truncated, special attention is given to these attributes. The original shape of the tool when it was first introduced as a formal tool into the technological system is traced, when possible, to its present form. This observation may seem to be highly subjective, but in fact it is not when the workshop data from Colha are incorporated. The formal tool systems considered are oval biface, tranchet bit, macroblade, and obsidian blade. There are obviously specimens that do not fit into these systems, and these are described under individual headings such as miscellaneous bifaces, miscellaneous unifaces, ground stone artifacts, miscellaneous battered tools, and debitage (debitage is the waste material produced in the manufacture of chipped stone tools). Where possible, debitage of retouch and recycling of tools in specific systems is described under the appropriate system. Debitage relating to more than one system is described under the miscellaneous heading.

All artifacts not classified as debitage were subjected to edge wear analysis. The analysis was carried out using an Olympia binocular zoom microscope with a magnification range of 9× to 75×. The magnification range was sufficient to identify most edge wear attributes which have been described by Ahler (1971, 1979) and Shafer (1973: 86−88, 1979).

Gross information on the kinds of material with which the tools' working edges came into contact can be obtained by examining the edge damage attributes, surface alteration, and general morphology and angle of the working edge. The effective cutting angle

Colha Production	Exchange System	Pulltrouser Consumption

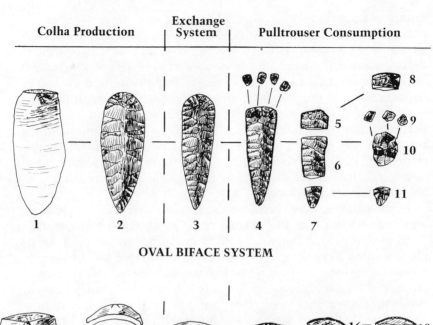

OVAL BIFACE SYSTEM

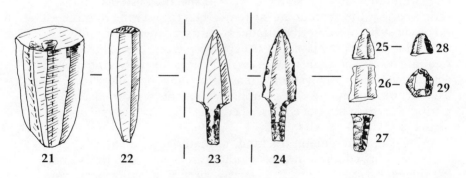

TRANCHET BIT SYSTEM

MACROBLADE SYSTEM

provides certain limitations of the use tasks possible which, in turn, allow for additional clues to use. This, together with the wear pattern information, gives some indication of the nature of the motor habits or use motion (Shafer and Holloway 1979). Abrupt contact of tapered-edge chert tools with relatively hard materials, for example, results in the formation of numerous tiny conelike fractures along the tools' working edges, producing expanding, stepped, and hinged flakes which give the edge an overall battered appearance. Cutting or sawing relatively hard materials with a sharp edge (less than 40 degrees) will quickly yield an edge damaged by randomly removed crescent-shaped or D-shaped microflakes, expanding flakes which terminate in snap or hinge fractures, and a rounding of the edge itself if the contact is intensive. This edge damage pattern is descriptively referred to here as bifacial nicking and smoothing. If the contact is relatively short-term, a sinuous, sawlike edge will result that will be effective until the sharp points of the flake scars become abraded and smoothed. The nature and extent of the edge damage are determined by a number of variables, including the edge angle, duration of use, pattern of motion, angle of pressure, amount of pressure, hardness of tool, hardness of contact materials, and chemistry of both the tool

Fig. 12-1. Lithic production-exchange-consumption model, based on the analysis of Colha (Shafer 1979; Hester 1980) and Pulltrouser lithic assemblages.

Oval biface system: 1, flake blank; 2, biface preform; 3, oval biface (formal tool); 4, retouched oval biface tool and retouch flakes; 5, oval biface distal fragment; 6, oval biface medial fragment; 7, oval biface proximal fragment; 8, 10, 11, second-order tools of recycled oval biface fragments; 9, retouch flakes from recycling oval biface fragment.

Tranchet bit system: 12, flake blank; 13, preform stage representing the formation of the tranchet bit by the removal of the tranchet flake; 14, tranchet bit tool (formal tool); 15, use-scarred tranchet bit tool; 16, tranchet flake from tool rejuvenation; 17, rejuvenated tranchet bit tool; 18, tranchet flake recycled as second-order tool; 19, retouch flake from retouching tranchet bit tool; 20, second-order tool from recycling tranchet bit tool fragment.

Macroblade system: 21, macroblade core; 22, macroblade blank (such blades were also incorporated into the Pulltrouser Swamp assemblage without further modification); 23, stemmed macroblade tool (formal tool); 24, use-scarred macroblade tool; 25, macroblade distal fragment; 26, macroblade medial fragment; 27, macroblade proximal fragment; 28, 29, second-order tools of recycled macroblade fragments.

and the material being worked. See Hayden (1979) and Hayden and Kamminga (1979) for a thorough review of edge wear attributes and their probable causes.

Polish occurs on most tools used against soft materials containing silicates. Witthoft's study (1967) has described possible ways that polish can occur on stone tools. While his hypothesis has been contested, few will deny that polish readily develops on tools used against materials containing opal phytoliths. A very fine polish will be produced by repeated contact against plant materials with a high opaline content, such as grasses (Semenov 1964: 122) or desert succulents (Shafer and Holloway 1979). Kamminga (1979) presents an excellent discussion of phytolith polish and argues that it is probably caused by a chemical interaction between the plant opal, water, and the contact surface of the stone tool. If the contact material is both soft and granular, such as soil, tools may exhibit a combination of edge damage attributes, including rounding, smoothing, polish, grooves, and striations; the grooves and striations will reveal the direction of contact relative to the cutting edge of the tool.

In brief, wear patterns may reveal not only the motion of use of a tool but also information on the nature of the materials that came into contact with the working edge (Keeley 1977). Significant behavioral data may be derived from extensive and intensive edge wear studies, especially when the archaeological context is secure.

Functional assessments are based on the artifact's form, technology, and edge and surface wear patterns. To assess function, implements are usually assigned to one of two tool classes, formal or second-order. Formal tools are those manufactured with a specific design in mind, whereas second-order tools are recycled masses or flakes which are either retouched and used or used without further modification. Formal tools in the Pulltrouser sample often display evidence of hafting and were undoubtedly made with this in mind; these tools include oval biface celts-hoes, tranchet bit tools, thick biface celts, stemmed macroblades, biface picks, and obsidian blades. Second-order tools include retouched or utilized proximal, medial, and distal biface fragments, tranchet flakes, miscellaneous bifaces, miscellaneous unifaces, utilized flakes, and certain recycled obsidian blade fragments. This tool distinction, while partly subjective, was useful in the analysis since it aided in testing the hypothesis that formal tools become transformed through use, retouch, and recyling. Furthermore, it demonstrates that in a zone of poor resources, despite the presence of a formalized lithic production industry in the region, second-order tools from both re-

cycled imported materials and locally obtained resources constitute a major aspect of the stone tool assemblage.

The morphological, functional, and technological observations
will be presented together, followed by a discussion section. The
report is mainly descriptive in nature owing to the need to present
basic lithic observations on the Pulltrouser sample in particular
and on a nonceremonial context in general. Hester (1976) and Sheets
(1977) have aptly pointed out that there is a regrettable paucity of
detailed lithic technology studies in the Maya literature. The implications of the morphological, technological, functional, and distributional findings toward the raised-field study and their relationship to the Colha production area are also presented.

Chipped stone material types are described as being chert,
chalcedony, or obsidian. Cherts are fine-grained, cryptocrystalline
quartz, usually opaque, banded with brown or tan, solid or mottled;
gray is present but is rare in this sample. The cortex is usually a
white to brown hydrated, sometimes slightly chalky surface. Chert
colors will range from gray to reddish brown when burned. These
materials outcrop throughout northern Belize (Wright et al. 1959),
occurring in the form of cobbles and boulders in limestone deposits. Chalcedony is a term used to identify a somewhat coarser cryptocrystalline material which occurs in translucent or semitranslu-
cent nodules. The nodular formation is different from that of the
cherts, and the cortex is a lacelike white hydrated surface. The
hues are white, milky white, cream, ice-blue, or light brown. These
colors change to white or light gray when burned. The chemical composition and crystalline structure are clearly different from those of
chert, although the parent formation is probably in the northern Belize limestones. The common occurrence of chalcedony in the region provided a suitable resource for use in the production of mostly
second-order tools. Few formal tools made from chalcedony have
been found.

The basic techniques of Mesoamerican prismatic blade production from obsidian have been described ethnohistorically (Fletcher
1978; Hester, Jack, and Heizer 1978), experimentally (Crabtree 1968),
and archaeologically (Sheets 1978). This generally specialized craft
was presumably carried on in the vicinity of the obsidian source
outcrops. Since there are no obsidian sources in Belize, these artifacts are regarded as products of interregional exchange networks.
The most likely source areas are El Chayal, Ixtepeque, and San
Martín Jilotepeque in Guatemala (Stross et al. 1976; Sidrys and
Kimberlin n.d.; Hammond 1976b). The obsidian in the Pulltrouser
sample is mostly light to medium gray with dark gray streaks or

bands; a few examples are clear smooth gray, with one being a smoky gray material. Hammond (1976b) has hypothesized that the inland sites in Belize were receiving obsidian via overland trade routes from El Chayal. An earlier version of this model (Hammond 1972) has been questioned by Sidrys and Kimberlin (n.d.) on the basis of trace element studies and the identification of obsidian from lowland Maya sources being traced to the Tajumulco Volcano near Izapa, Mexico.

Proveniences of the artifacts are listed in table 12-1 by operation. The specific provenience of certain artifacts within each operation is discussed in chapter 10. Measurements are presented in the text only for some of the nearly complete specimens; examples of most descriptive categories are illustrated to scale.

OVAL BIFACE SYSTEM

The manufacturing system for the large oval bifaces has been described by Shafer (1979) and Shafer and Oglesby (1980) from four workshops at Colha. The production of these items has been dated to the Late Preclassic. The form is an oval or teardrop outline with a convex wider end tapering to a narrow blunt end which typically has an unfinished appearance. The biface's length is usually about two and a half times its width, and most are expertly thinned. The wider end characteristically displays a finishing retouch that produces an evenly tapered bifacial angle of about 60 to 80 degrees. One complete, unretouched example was recovered at Kokeal (fig. 12-2a).

The sample, with the one exception, consists of fragmentary specimens. These were sorted on the basis of physical appearance as well as how this quality relates to the form of the original biface. For example, one specimen is unretouched and conforms to the original outline; three specimens display distal retouch of a worn, polished bit end; other examples are distal, medial, and proximal fragments of once-large oval bifaces. A model of the relationship of the artifacts to use, retouch, and recycling is shown in figure 12-1 in a hypothesized reduction sequence.

Initial Form.   The specimen displaying an unaltered oval biface form is a banded tan chert from the Colha area (fig. 12-2a). Form and skill of craft are identical to those observed at Late Preclassic workshops at Colha. Wear on this specimen is not obvious immediately, but light blunting and smoothing of the lateral edges with some accompanying polish were observed microscopically. The specimen measures 10.5 centimeters long, 7 centimeters wide, and 2.4 centimeters thick.

Retouched Forms.   All these specimens are of banded tan Colha-like chert. The largest has a retouched distal end and evidence of. abrasive wear in the form of polish and striations parallel to the long axis (fig. 12-2f). These striations and polish also occur on both surfaces. The lateral edges are dulled, smoothed, and polished; striations seen at the edge are perpendicular to the long axis. Edge and surface wear extends most of the length, ending about 3 centimeters from the narrow proximal end. The smallest specimen exhibits a greater degree of modification (fig. 12-2h). The bit end has been extensively retouched and damaged by impact. Surface polish near the bit is accompanied by many striations oriented both parallel to and perpendicular to the long axis. The lateral edges are smoothed and semipolished, with many grooves and striations perpendicular to the edge and to the long axis. A third specimen was broken across the distal end by a bending (snap) fracture, possibly from use impact (fig. 12-2g). The surfaces near the distal end, near and at the lateral edges, are smoothed and polished. The polish is extensive and displays grooves and striations clearly indicative of patterned use motion. The striations at the distal end are parallel to the long axis; those along the lateral edges and the surfaces near the edges are perpendicular (fig. 12-7a). Like the other two examples, the polish on this specimen stops about 3.5 centimeters from the proximal end. Respective dimensions are 15.8, 11.9, and 14.4 centimeters long; 7.3, 5.3, and 5.5 centimeters wide; and 2.2, 2.2, and 2 centimeters thick.

Distal Fragments.   These distal end fragments of extensively used large oval biface tools all display heavily polished surfaces and distal edges (fig. 12-2e). The polish, accompanied by grooves and striations perpendicular to the edge and parallel to the long axis, occurs bifacially (fig. 12-6a). Three specimens were broken by bending (snap) fractures, and one is a thermally fractured piece. None appears to have been recycled and used as a second-order tool.

Medial Fragments.   Each of these artifacts displays evidence of moderate to well-executed bifacial flaking, indicating that they are fragments of once-large bifaces (fig. 12-2i–k). It is possible that some are fragments of large tranchet bit tools. Many display evidence of retouch and recycling since breakage. Sixteen specimens failed to show evidence of wear on either the breaks or the retouched edges. Another seventeen fragments were burned and broken by thermal spalling; twenty-one display retouch subsequent to breakage; and twenty exhibit use wear on broken or retouched edges in the form of smoothing, smoothing and polishing, or smoothing, polishing, and microchipping in the form of nick-

Table 12-1. Provenience and Number of Artifacts

Artifact	No Prov.	Op. IA	Op. II	Op. III	Op. IV	Op. V	Total
Oval biface system							
Initial form			1				1
Retouched forms			3				3
Distal fragments		1	4	1			6
Medial fragments	2	6	42	2	1	10	63
Proximal fragments		6	18			4	28
Distal retouch flakes		4	30	1		18	53
Tranchet bit system							
Tranchet bit tools			4				4
Tranchet flakes	1		3				4
Miscellaneous bifaces							
Biface celts			3				3
Biface pick				1			1
Beveled bit tools		1		1	1	1	4
Miscellaneous thin bifaces			2				2
Miscellaneous pressure-flaked bifaces			2				2
Miscellaneous biface fragments	1	3	25	2	1	2	34
Macroblade system							
Stemmed macroblades		1				1	2
Proximal fragments		1	6				7
Medial fragments		3	15			1	19
Miscellaneous macroblade fragments		1	5			1	7
Blade tool						1	1

Miscellaneous battered tools							
Battered bifaces		3	5				8
Battered nodules	2	7	20	3		2	34
Unifaces & utilized flakes							
Miscellaneous unifaces		2	8	1		2	13
Utilized flakes	1	7	42	2	1	7	60
Obsidian blade system							
Prismatic obsidian blades	1	2	25	1		9	38
Obsidian flakes			2			2	4
Ground stone artifacts							
Celts		1	2				3
Mano fragments			4				4
Metate fragments	1	1	5			1	8
Miscellaneous ground stone			1				1
Total	9	49	280	14	3	62	417

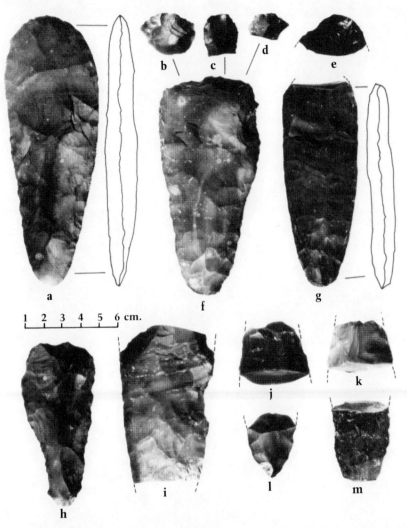

1 2 3 4 5 6 cm.

Fig. 12-2. Examples of the oval biface system: a, initial form; b–d, distal retouch flakes; e, distal fragment; f–h, retouched forms; i–k, medial fragments; l, m, proximal fragments.

ing. Striations were observed on two specimens, indicating a use motion perpendicular to the edge.

Wear motions on others varied. Seven show edge or surface battering scars. The amount of recycled use varied, although most items appeared to have been used with a single motion, such as adzing, chopping, slicing, and so forth, which were probably likely to occur in a context with household activities. Fifty-two examples exhibit edge and surface wear or retouch consistent with that observed on the retouched biface forms described above. This wear is the product of use prior to breakage or recycling. All but three are of chert comparable to that at Colha; the exceptions are two chalcedony specimens and one chert of unknown origin.

Proximal Fragments.   These artifacts are proximal fragments of tapered biface tools (fig. 12-2l, m); the former tools were most likely large oval biface implements, such as hoes or celts, judging from the character and location of the surface and edge wear seen on nineteen specimens. Twenty of these were broken by bending or snap fractures (fig. 12-2l, m). The patterned fracture took place usually 3 to 6 centimeters from the proximal end, and the use wear on most begins just before the break. The fracture pattern and wear strongly hint that these were the hafted ends of biface tools whose use placed a bending stress on the blade. Bending fractures occurred near or at the haft contact. Only eight of the specimens clearly show recycling wear indicative of their use as second-order tools. Five exhibit rounded, smoothed, and slightly polished breaks or retouched edges similar to those observed on the medial fragments described above. Four were fractured by burning. All but two are of chert similar to that occurring at Colha.

Distal Retouch Flakes.   These flakes were removed from the distal portions of biface implements probably used as hoes (fig. 12-2b–d). The faceted exterior surfaces display polish with parallel grooves and striations consistent with the wear observed on the retouched oval biface tools. The striking platforms are multifaceted, often displaying the rounded, smoothed, edge-damaged, and polished implement bit edge. Other flakes were removed from the retouched bit or edges near the distal end of the tool. Most if not all were removed with a hard-hammer technique, based on the prominent conelike fractures (Shafer 1979; Tsirk 1979), and most cannot be regarded as biface thinning flakes. The flakes appear to have been caused by resharpening dulled, damaged, or polished bit tools or by recycling a broken polished bit tool.

Discussion.   The absence of manufacturing debitage such as aborted bifaces and thinning debitage in the Pulltrouser sample indicates that the large oval bifaces were produced elsewhere. Based on the similarity of the cherts, technology, and form, it is suggested that the manufacturing locus for most of the oval bifaces was the Colha area, where that chert and manufacturing industry is well documented (Shafer 1979; Shafer and Hester 1979). This is to say that the implements were incorporated into the Pulltrouser technological system in finished form. The oval biface is suitable for several possible tools, namely, celts as exemplified by the hafted celt from a channelized-field context at San Antonio (Palacio 1976) or hoes or mattocklike tools for ground working. Similar tools were evidently used as celts at Colha (Shafer 1979), while some may have been used as hoes or mattocks in ground working at Cuello (Shafer, Hester, and Kelly n.d.).

These functional interpretations are based on the nature and pattern of the edge damage. Polish observed on the retouched specimens of distal and medial fragments and on the distal retouch flakes described above is consistent with that observed on items interpreted as hoes which I have examined from the Middle Mississippian context in eastern Missouri. Abrasive wear patterns on the Pulltrouser specimens suggest that they were hafted at the narrow end, that the wider distal end was subjected to a consistent impact against a soft, granular substance, and that the implement blade cut into the material several centimeters. Also, that the tools were turned on edge and used in short, chopping strokes against the same material is indicated by the directions of the striations on the lateral edges. In other words, the wear patterns are consistent with their use as ground-working tools. The retouching and the location of the retouch flakes further indicate that tool refurbishing and maintenance took place in and around the households, as would be expected. The breakage patterns, especially those observed on the proximal fragments, further support the contention that the blades were hafted and that the use motion consistently put tensile stress across the blade near the proximal end.

TRANCHET BIT SYSTEM
The tranchet bit tool system has been described by Shafer (1976, 1979) from Colha. These tools are made on large flake blanks which are roughly chipped to a triangular shape. The wider end, which is the bulbar end of the parent flake, was prepared for the tranchet flake removal by unifacially trimming a convex edge and notching one lateral edge so that one end of the notch intersects with the convex edge. This intersection point was dulled and strengthened to serve as the striking platform for the tranchet flake removal.

The flake was removed and, if the operation had been successful, the angle formed by the flake scar and the ventral surface of the parent flake served as the tool's cutting edge. The artifact was then shaped to the desired form. Wear patterns on specimens from Colha and Moho Cay indicate that these tools were evidently used as axes or celts and adzes, depending on the overall size and edge angle.

Tranchet Bit Tools.   These implements (fig. 12-3a, d–f) are generally triangular in outline and were manufactured from large flakes, following the system described above. All are of chert indistinguishable from that at Colha. The working edge was created by the removal of a single flake from across the wider end, which was the bulbar end of the flake blank. The angle created by the flake removal and the intersection with the ventral surface of the flake blank core served as the cutting edge. Wear patterns on the four tools vary, indicating probably more than one use for tranchet bit tools, a finding consistent with observations of like tools in other collections. One specimen exhibits bit edge rounding with light polish extending to both surfaces, suggesting that it was used as an ax (fig. 12-3a). Small hinged flakes were removed from both sides of the bit; the removal of these flakes and the polish are more pronounced on the ventral side, where the grooves resulting from abrasive wear were observed perpendicular to the edge (fig. 12-7c). The edge angle is 65 degrees. Both lateral edges are blunted and coarsely rounded at mid length, creating broad, shallow concavities which may have facilitated hafting.

Another nearly complete specimen displays hinged flakes removed from the ventral side of the bit edge (fig. 12-3d). Slight edge rounding and polish were observed, mostly on the ventral side. The edge damage is consistent with that expected by an adzing motion. The edge angle is 74 degrees.

One example is a recycled tranchet bit implement (fig. 12-3e). The lateral edges have been blunted and retouched; the distal end and the dorsal surface both exhibit extensive battering scars, as if the specimen was used as a hammer in recycling the material.

A fourth tranchet bit specimen is proportionately wider at the distal end than the other specimens; it has a flatter ventral surface and a sharper bit angle (fig. 12-3f). The edge angle is 60 degrees. Edge damage occurs in the form of minute unifacial trimming from the ventral side, edge rounding, and polish. This is evidently a specifically manufactured tool form, as almost identical examples are known from Colha and Cuello, both from Preclassic contexts.

Tranchet Flakes.   Flakes removed to form the tranchet bit, tranchet flakes, have been described by Shafer (1976). They occur liter-

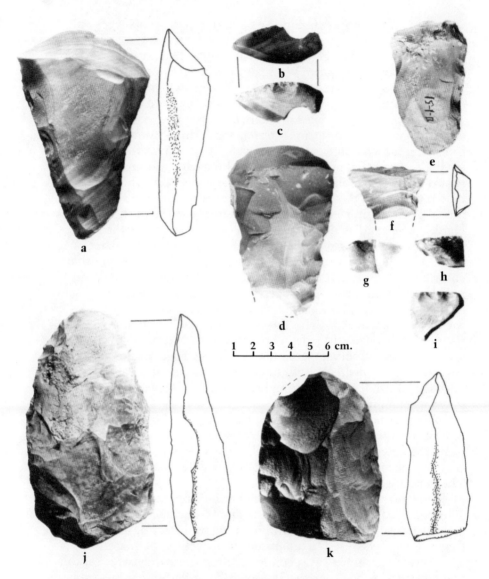

Fig. 12-3. Tranchet bit system and biface tools: a, d–f, tranchet bit tools; b, c (two surfaces of the same flake), g–i, tranchet flakes; j, biface pick; k, biface celt.

ally by the tens of thousands at Late Preclassic workshops at Colha and are debitage in the tranchet bit tool manufacturing system. Their occurrence at Pulltrouser is therefore surprising, considering the absence of workshops here. Two are fragments, but both exhibit subsequent use as utilized flakes, as indicated by the smoothing, microedge damage, and polish along one or both edges (fig. 12-3h, i). One of these also exhibits a polished bit prior to its removal. A third specimen is not a classic example of a tranchet flake but represents an attempt to create a tranchet bit by recycling a biface tool (fig. 12-3g). One specimen is indeed a classic example of a tranchet flake, although it did not carry across the entire bit edge (fig. 12-3b, c). It was removed from the bit edge of an extensively used tranchet bit tool. The tool's bit was polished extensively, and striations perpendicular to the edge can readily be seen on both faces of the bit (fig. 12-6b). The approximate angle of the parent tool bit is 65 degrees.

Discussion.   Tranchet bit tools, like the oval bifaces, were evidently being received by the Pulltrouser farmers in a complete state. The two tranchet rejuvenation flakes, however (fig. 12-3h, i), may suggest that the local flint knappers were sufficiently skilled at this specialized technique to retouch their own tools. The flake illustrated in figure 12-3g may also indicate that these people could manufacture their own tranchet bit tools, given the proper raw materials.

MISCELLANEOUS BIFACES

Specimens described under this heading are tools made in manufacturing systems different from those described above, are fragmentary, or have been retouched to the point that the original state cannot be ascertained.

Biface Celts.   These items are large, heavy, well-made biface celts. The more complete specimen is best described as a truncated base celt designed for heavy cutting (fig. 12-3k). The lateral edges are slightly convex, dulled by coarse edge abrasion. The distal end is convex, originally having a carefully shaped bit, the edge angle of which cannot be determined due to the edge damage. The base has been truncated by a single blow, and the resulting edges have been dulled by direct-impact battering. This form of celt is not uncommon in the collections from Belize, having been observed at Colha, Cuello, and Moho Cay. The proximal truncation was deliberate and may have been done to secure the celt in a socketed or mortised haft. Distal wear on this specimen includes edge rounding, smoothing, and polish; striations perpendicular to the cutting edge attest to its use in a patterned direct-impact motion against firm but not coarse materials.

The remaining two examples are fragments. One has been extensively retouched, and that the recycled artifact was used is evidenced by the light rounding and polish and the retouched edges. The third specimen is a fragment created by a massive snap or bending fracture. There is no evidence of recycling or retouch.

Biface Pick.   This crudely fashioned biface tool displays unusually prominent distal polish (fig. 12-3j). The specimen was made from a large blocky nodule of chert shaped to a tapered biface end. The distal end is rounded and is plano-convex due to unifacial distal retouch. The distal wear includes edge rounding as well as extensive edge and surface polish, accompanied by grooves and striations perpendicular to the edge and parallel to the long axis. The polish is more prominent on the flatter side, suggesting that the tool was used as a hoe or mattock. The proximal end has been deliberately blunted by edge battering, as have the edges near this end. The character and location of the wear patterns certainly suggest use as a digging implement of some kind. The consistency of the polish and striations and their location and orientation strongly hint that the specimen was once hafted perpendicular to the wide axis.

Beveled Bit Tools.   These artifacts exhibit beveled distal ends (fig. 12-4a–d). One specimen is a recycled medial fragment of a bifacial celt or hoe (fig. 12-4a). The wider end exhibits unifacial retouch. Wear on the retouched edge includes rounding and light polish. Another specimen exhibits wear across the beveled end in the form of smoothing, polish, and striations perpendicular to the edge (fig. 12-4d). The wear pattern is consistent with that of an adzlike tool. The specimen was broken by a bending fracture. A third specimen is an elongated beveled tool (fig. 12-4b). The surfaces are polished on the ventral side, and striations were observed perpendicular to this edge. The lateral edges are dulled. Polish and striations are observed on the ventral side of the distal end which are perpendicular to the edge and parallel to the long axis. The distal wear is consistent with that expected from adzing, but the lateral edge wear is difficult to explain. The specimen was broken by a bending fracture. The fourth example is a broken recycled biface tool with a steeply beveled gougelike distal end (fig. 12-4c). The wear is represented by a mere trace of smoothing. It too was broken by a bending fracture. All these implements are of Colha-like chert.

Miscellaneous Thin Bifaces.   One distal fragment is the thinnest biface in the collection (fig. 12-4e). The edges are smoothed and polished, and a trace of surface polish was also observed. The chert

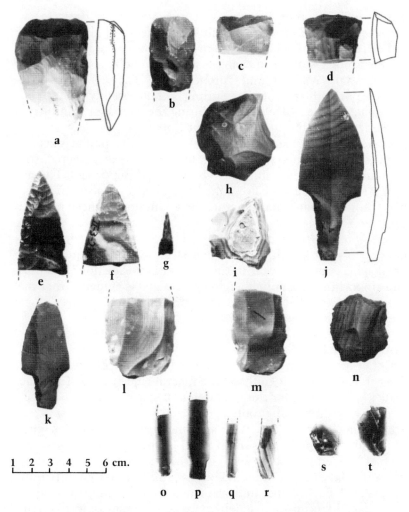

Fig. 12-4. Miscellaneous biface, macroblade, and obsidian artifacts: a–d, beveled bit tools; e, f, thin bifaces; g, pressure-flaked biface; h, i, biface fragments; j, k, stemmed macroblades; l, m, macroblade proximal fragments; n, miscellaneous macroblade fragment; o–r, prismatic obsidian blades; s, t, obsidian flakes.

has a shiny appearance that may be indicative of heat treating; however, I have never seen conclusive evidence of chert annealing in Belize lithics. This specimen may be part of a large, expertly thinned biface similar to examples found in Belize caves (Shafer n.d.; Graham, McNatt, and Gutchen 1980). The second example (fig. 12-4f) exhibits light edge dulling, a trait possibly related to manufacture (i.e., edge abrading during the course of thinning). The chert is similar to that found at Colha.

Miscellaneous Pressure-Flaked Bifaces.   Two small artifacts exhibit evidence of pressure flaking. One of these is a tapered, triangular item with a unifacially chipped base (fig. 12-4g). The other, a thin flake with a pressure-flaked lateral edge, appears to have been broken during manufacture. The function of these items is unknown.

Miscellaneous Biface Fragments.   These artifacts are fragments of biface tools (fig. 12-4h, i). Nine exhibit no wear subsequent to breakage; on others, wear in the form of battering (four specimens) and smoothing and polish (eight specimens) is evidence that the items were recycled and used as second-order tools. Three of the fragments are badly burned.

MACROBLADE SYSTEM

Another production system recognized in the Preclassic and Late Classic workshops at Colha is the macroblade system. The macroblades were blanks for the production of sharp-edged or pointed cutting and/or piercing tools.

Stemmed Macroblades.   Both specimens are macroblades with unifacially chipped stems (fig. 12-4j, k). One is a complete specimen of banded tan Colha-like chert (fig. 12-4j). Slight bifacial nicking is displayed on both lateral edges. Unifacial marginal trimming occurs at the distal end, indicating deliberate shaping. The shaping by unifacial trimming to a deliberate point argues that this item served as a projectile point. The second specimen, also of tan Colha-like chert, was broken during recovery (fig. 12-4k). One of the lateral edges displays unifacial trimming, accompanied by faint edge polish. The opposite (right) edge exhibits bifacial nicking, smoothing, and polish, suggesting that this functioned as a knifelike tool.

Proximal Fragments.   All these specimens were removed from faceted blade cores and have well-prepared, multifaceted striking platforms (fig. 12-4l, m). Only one displays cortex on the striking platform. One example is notched for hafting; the notches are broad, shallow, and unifacially chipped near the proximal end (fig. 12-4m).

Wear occurs in the form of edge nicking, smoothing, and polish on two specimens; coarse nicking on three; and edge smoothing and polish with striations on the edge, indicating sawing motion, on one. One is burned.

Medial Fragments.   These medial fragments of large macroblade implements functioned as sharp-edged cutting tools. Wear patterns are characteristically in the form of edge nicking, smoothing, and polish. Striations perpendicular to the edge are seen on four examples, indicating a cutting motion perpendicular to the edge. This wear is not consistent with scraping, as it occurs bifacially. One specimen had been recycled and utilized as a cutting tool. All are of Colha-like chert.

Miscellaneous Macroblade Fragments.   These artifacts are fragments of macroblade tools. Five are bifacially (fig. 12-4n) or unifacially chipped tapered stems, and two are mostly unifacially trimmed distal fragments. Edge smoothing and rounding are present on four of the fragments, but these conditions may be due to recycling the fragments.

Blade Tool.   This specimen is a chalcedony blade struck from a single-faceted platform core. The lateral edges exhibit microfracturing, smoothing, and light to moderate polish. This was a sharp-edged cutting or sawing tool. The tool measures 7.8 centimeters long, 3 centimeters wide, and 1 centimeter thick.

MISCELLANEOUS BATTERED TOOLS

Battered tools or hammerstones are divided into two groups: those recycled from bifaces and those utilized from chert or chalcedony nodules.

Battered Bifaces.   These artifacts are segments of bifacial implements recycled for use as battering implements, probably because of their mass (fig. 12-5d, e). One is intentionally shaped and was probably hafted. Traces of light surface polish are evident on three specimens and may be the result of haft wear. The remaining specimens are mostly fragments but appear to have been hand-held battering tools. All are of Colha-like chert. The maximum diameter varies from 5.2 to 11.8 centimeters.

Battered Nodules.   These nodules display slight, moderate, or extensive degrees of battering (fig. 12-5f–i). They vary from well-shaped and rounded specimens to amorphous chert or chalcedony nodules exhibiting a few battering marks. Their function varies, probably from hafted hammers—based on the patterned occurrence of the wear—to hand-held, one-time-use examples. Sixteen are of

Fig. 12-5. Ground stone and battered stone artifacts: a, b, cherty limestone celts; c, chalcedony celt; d, e, battered bifaces; f–i, battered nodules (f–h are chert; i is cherty limestone).

chalcedony, two are of cherty limestone, and the remainder are of chert similar to that at Colha. The maximum diameters of complete examples range from 4.7 to 12.1 centimeters.

UNIFACES AND UTILIZED FLAKES
Miscellaneous Unifaces.   These items are not formal tools but, rather, second-order implements or artifacts made from recycling chert and chalcedony. One or more edges are unifacially retouched. Two exhibit burinlike flake removals but show no evidence of use on the resulting facets. Wear patterns, when present, vary from slight edge rounding and polish on the steeper angles to edge dulling by microfracturing and crushing. Four specimens are of chalcedony; the remainder are of Colha-like chert. Lengths range from 3.1 to 5.1 centimeters; widths from 2.5 to 4.5 centimeters, and thicknesses from 1.2 to 9 centimeters.
Utilized Flakes.   These are hard-hammer percussion flakes, flake fragments, or nodules that exhibit edge damage patterns indicative of use as second-order cutting, slicing, adzing, whittling, or possibly even scraping tools. Use edge angles vary from 20 degrees to about 85 degrees. The most common wear features are edge smoothing, rounding, and polish, often accompanied by bifacial microflaking or nicking. Thirty-one specimens are derived from chert cores or recycled chert artifacts, all but two of which are similar to those at the Colha source area. The remainder are milky to light brown chalcedony. Lengths range from 3 to 9.5 centimeters, widths from 2.2 to 5.3 centimeters, and thicknesses from 2 to 23 millimeters.

OBSIDIAN BLADE SYSTEM
Prismatic Obsidian Blades.   These prismatic obsidian blades have all been systematically removed by pressure from prepared polyhedral cores. Twenty-one are proximal fragments (fig. 12-40-r). The striking platforms are all flat (approximately 90 degrees to the flake axis) and display two noticeable attributes of blade-removal preparation: (1) the platform surfaces have been abraded to roughen the surface and prevent the pressure tool from slipping (Crabtree 1968: 457) and (2) the intersection between the platform and the edge of the core has been ground to remove the overhanging platform mass created by the negative bulb of a previously removed blade. This grinding is done to insure that enough material is present beneath the percussor to withstand the force (Crabtree 1968: 463).

Twelve specimens are medial fragments, and four are distal segments. None of the obsidian blade examples is complete, although the longest fragment measures 7.7 centimeters; widths in the sample vary from 0.5 to 1.7 centimeters, and thicknesses range from 1.5 to 3 millimeters.

Wear patterns observable on the obsidian blades indicate use with slicing or sawing motions. One specimen (fig. 12-4o) is notched on each edge at the proximal end; another (fig. 12-4p) is trimmed at the proximal end, presumably for hafting. The trimmed example clearly displays striations parallel to the edge and microedge damage, indicating a slicing or back-and-forth cutting motion (fig. 12-7b). This wear pattern is common on obsidian blade fragments in the sample. Virtually all specimens display random scratches or striations. Many of these scratches are probably fortuitous and may be attributed to postdepositional damage. Others, however, can most certainly be attributed to use as sharp-edged cutting implements or to packaging or handling during use.

Obsidian Flakes.   These are percussion flakes removed from exhausted or abandoned polyhedral blade cores (fig. 12-4s, t). Evidence of either blade facets or ground platforms or both is present on the specimens. Two appear to have been utilized as second-order cutting or slicing tools. The largest specimen measures 3.6 centimeters long, 2.3 centimeters wide, and 0.8 centimeter thick.

No cores were recovered from the Pulltrouser test excavations, nor is there any evidence that blades were actually removed from cores at the site complex, as would be indicated in debitage concentrations and platform rejuvenation flakes. The use of cores as sources of obsidian raw material may indicate that exhausted polyhedral cores were also being traded and used as implements of some kind. The presence of obsidian cores at lowland Maya sites located far from obsidian source areas is not uncommon, although the cores are not numerous.

GROUND STONE ARTIFACTS

The specimens described here are shaped primarily by pecking and grinding. Final shaping may either follow a formal design (as with the celts) or occur through use (as with the manos and metates).

Celts.   Two of these artifacts are of cherty limestone shaped by pecking and grinding (fig. 12-5a, b). Both display a bit at the broader end, convex lateral edges that taper to a pole end, and lenticular cross sections. The bit end on the smaller example is ground to a blunt cutting edge of about 115 degrees. The other specimen does not appear to be finished, as the blunted bit end displays light battering, evidently from shaping; the battering or pecking does not appear to be related to use. The third celt is a burned distal frag-

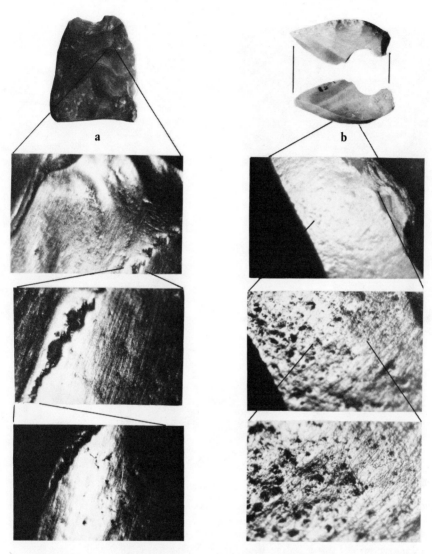

Fig. 12-6. Microphotographs of surface wear on selected tools: a, oval biface distal fragment with 18×, 47.5×, and 75× enlargements of attrition; b, contact surface of the tranchet flake illustrated in figure 12-3b, c, with 9×, 47.5×, and 75× enlargement of surface wear on the tranchet bit tool prior to removal of the flake. Microscopic analysis and photography were accomplished using a Wild M5A stereo microscope with a magnification range of 9× to 75× and outfitted with a Nikon AFM automatic 35-millimeter camera back.

Fig. 12-7. Microphotographs of surface wear on selected tools: a, lateral edge wear on a 47.5× enlargement of the oval biface specimen illustrated in figure 12-2g; b, surface scratches and striations on 18× and 47.5× enlargements of the obsidian blade in figure 12-4p; c, 18× and 47.5× enlargements of attrition displayed on the ventral side of the tranchet bit tool in figure 12-3a. Microscopic analysis and photography were accomplished using a Wild M5A stereo microscope with a magnification range of 9× to 75× and outfitted with a Nikon AFM automatic 35-millimeter camera back.

ment of chalcedony (fig. 12-5c). The two complete specimens are 10.5 and 15.5 centimeters long, 6.4 and 7.5 centimeters wide, and 3.9 and 4.9 centimeters thick.

Mano Fragments.   These artifacts are shaped by battering or pecking and are faceted through abrasive use. All are fragmentary. One is a cherty limestone; the remaining three are of a sedimentary fossiliferous rock from a limestone formation. The stone has many fossil voids or geodes which are partially or completely filled with quartz crystals, giving the stone a vesicular characteristic. This feature, together with the hardness, gives the stone excellent properties for use as a grinding implement.

Metate Fragments.   Seven of the metate fragments are unifacial, that is, displaying a single grinding facet; one is bifacial. Six are of the same fossiliferous limestone material described above for the manos. One is quartzite, and the remaining specimen is a vesicular basalt.

Miscellaneous Ground Stone.   This specimen is a thin, oval, quartzite artifact shaped by chipping and pecking. It exhibits a single grinding facet. The maximum diameter is 10.9 centimeters, and the thickness is 2.6 centimeters.

CHIPPED STONE AND BURNED STONE DEBITAGE

Chipped stone debitage is the residue created from the manufacture or retouch of implements. The sample includes all flakes, flake fragments, spalls, cores, and so forth which do not evidence obvious edge or surface wear subsequent to their removal from a larger piece. The sample was sorted first on the basis of material (chert or chalcedony), except for the excessively burned specimens, which were separated and counted.

The chert and chalcedony flakes were further sorted on the basis of the presence or absence of striking platforms (terminology following Crabtree 1972 and Shafer 1979). Next, bulbar characteristics were used to determine the probable method of detachment (i.e., hard-hammer or soft-hammer percussor), and the platforms were analyzed to determine the degree of core preparation or to gain information on the nature of the core itself (i.e., whether the flake was struck from a biface core, a recycled nodule, or an unprepared nodule). Single-faceted striking platforms, for example, are possibly indicative of flakes struck from the primary reduction of a core or from recycling material masses. Multifaceted striking platform flakes, on the other hand, would expectedly be the result of tool retouch or core preparation for the removal of a specific kind of flake, such as a blade. There are other possibilities, to be sure, and certainly exceptions to these hypothetical patterns. Table 12-2 lists the chipped and burned stone debitage by material, descriptive class, and operation.

The debitage sample from the Pulltrouser site complex is striking in that there is a notable paucity of debitage resulting from primary core reduction. Flakes with cortex platforms occurred only in chalcedony, and flakes retaining some cortex on the exterior surfaces were proportionately more frequent in this material category. Chalcedony occurs primarily in rounded nodules suitable for thick tools and for the acquisition of flakes for second-order tools or for reduction into smaller tools. Bifaces of this material occur in the sample but were relatively small and infrequent. The primary reduction of chalcedony cores may have occurred at Pulltrouser but was not a common practice.

The predominant material in the sample is chert. Furthermore, the virtual absence of primary flaking debitage and manufacturing failures, plus the residue derived from retouching and recycling tools and bifaces, would argue strongly that a high percentage of the chert and chalcedony artifacts were brought to the site as finished tools. These implements, in turn, were retouched and, when exhausted or broken, they were recycled and utilized as raw material for second-order implements. The faceted exterior surfaces of most hard-hammer chert flakes suggest that many of these were removed from the edge of bifacially flaked cores, and the presence of 260 flakes that show smoothing, polish, and striations (not counting the distal retouch flakes described under the oval biface system) is convincing evidence that tool retouch, refurbishing, and recycling were carried out in each of the sampled areas.

In summary, analysis of the chert flakes reveals the following patterns. Virtually all are interior flakes with single-faceted or multifaceted striking platforms and multifaceted dorsal surfaces. The chert varieties fall within the Colha spectrum, with rare exceptions. The flake sample is derived mostly from the reduction of former biface tools by retouching the working end of chert hoes or axes (as evidenced by the distal retouch flakes and flakes struck from the dulled and smoothed lateral edges) or by reducing or recycling tools or tool fragments. This retouching and recycling of flakes from biface tools account for over half of the entire flake sample. Attempts were made to sort flakes that were clearly or probably struck from biface tools, and the category of biface retouch flakes was created in order to demonstrate the occurrence of such specimens in the sample. Most distal retouch and recycling

Table 12-2. *Chipped Stone and Burned Stone Debitage*

Category	Op. IA	Op. II	Op. III	Op. IV	Op. V	Total
Chert						
Hard-hammer flakes						
Single-faceted platform						
With cortex	4	11	2		1	18
Without cortex	13	57	4	3	21	98
Multifaceted platform						
With cortex		6			1	7
Without cortex	11	117	3		23	154
Biface retouch	19	191	9	1	40	260
Soft-hammer flakes	1	7			1	9
Flake fragments	39	283	11	7	8	348
Cores		2	1			3
Chalcedony						
Hard-hammer flakes						
Single-faceted platform						
With cortex	1	15	1	1		18
Without cortex	6	23	2		2	33
Cortex platform	3	6				9
Multifaceted platform						
With cortex	1	4			3	8
Without cortex	3	21	1		5	30
Bipolar cores-flakes		2				2
Fragments	6	69	3	1	2	81
Cores		2				2
Burned chert-chalcedony		720	1		18	739
Total	107	1,536	38	13	125	1,819

retouch were done using a hard hammer; soft-hammer retouch flakes are rare, representing less than 1 percent of the total sample.

DISCUSSION

The principal objective of this study was to conduct a form-function analysis of the lithic artifacts from the Pulltrouser survey and test excavations in order to determine if the data gained would correlate with raised-field maintenance and use. It was also hoped that specific tools or a tool set could be identified that would be related to the technology of wetland fields.

Except for obsidian blades, identifiable formal tools are rare in the sample. This circumstance is more a function of the sample itself, however, rather than of the possibility that formal tools do not constitute a major element of the technology. The majority of the chipped stone sample is composed of broken, retouched, and recycled formal tools and debitage resulting from retouch and recycling. There is ample evidence to indicate that the formal tools were not made at Pulltrouser. First, Pulltrouser is located outside the chert-bearing zone of northern Belize and large nodules of chert are not readily available; second, there is a notable absence of the primary flaking debitage, manufacturing failures, and thinning debitage in the sample which would indicate on-site manufacture; and, third, most of the chert in the sample is inseparable from that observed at Colha, which lies within the chert-bearing zone. In addition, the economic ways in which chert was utilized, retouched, recycled, and cached indicate the relatively high value placed on this material by the Pulltrouser inhabitants.

A major chert tool incorporated in the technology was the large oval biface. The oval bifaces were being used in a chopping motion against soft, abrasive materials. Wear patterns indicate that the bifaces were hafted, and breakage patterns also suggest that the use motion placed a bending stress across the blade near the narrow (proximal) end. The abrasive wear occurs in the form of smoothing and extensive polish, accompanied by striations which are usually visible even without the aid of a microscope. The edge and surface smoothing and polish also indicate that the tool penetrated the contact material consistently for about one-third of its length and occasionally for most of its length. Perhaps the most convincing attribute is the abrasive wear; the edge and surface smoothing, polish, and the grooves, striations, and scratches argue for use against soft, granular material. The mollisols of the raised fields contain varying amounts of quartz and sand grains (chap. 5). Contact material of this texture would be expected to yield the wear patterns observed. It is therefore suggested that many of these tools were the blades for ground-working tools.

One other possible use for these tools which could result in the extensive polish would be against fibrous materials, such as grasses or palms, which contain opal phytoliths. Chert tools used in processing palms readily display a bright polish after extensive use (Kamminga 1979). I doubt, however, that such usage adequately explains the wear on these tools because of the motion of use and the depth of contact implied by the wear patterns, but polish observed on chipped celts may be partly due to chopping palms along with hardwoods.

The recycled fragments of the oval biface tools also indicate not only that chert was economically important as a raw material but that a large number of oval bifaces were being brought to the site and extensively utilized. With the exception of obsidian, other formal tools incorporated into the technology in finished form which were apparently the products of intraregional exchange were tranchet bit tools, macroblades, and obsidian blades. The edge wear suggests that the tranchet bit tools were serving as axes and adzes. Interestingly, tranchet bit tools may have been refurbished by the Pulltrouser flint knappers, as indicated by the two tranchet flakes removed from extensively used tranchet bit tools.

The stemmed macroblade artifacts were used either as projectile points or as hafted knives. The use of macroblade cutting tools, stemmed, notched, and unnotched, may be a trait more common in the Preclassic and Late Classic before obsidian blades were readily available. This hypothesis is based on observations at Colha (Roemer 1980) and may be tested with more detailed contextual data from Pulltrouser. The macroblade tools at Pulltrouser were being used with cutting and slicing motions against relatively soft materials—materials rigid enough to cause microflaking, smoothing, polish, or even rounding on the cutting edge. The primary use of these tools is, however, often masked by edge damage patterns resulting from recycling and retouch of the broken fragments. I suspect that the macroblade artifacts were serving household and general community maintenance needs requiring the use of heavy, sharp-edged cutting or slicing implements. Single-purpose use is not implied by the observed wear patterns. This statement also applies to the prismatic obsidian blades. There is no evidence to argue that these artifacts are exclusively elite status tools; indeed, their general use in household and other maintenance tasks is suggested on the basis of their wear patterns and context.

Two artifacts deserve special mention due to their contextual situation. They are both biface artifacts, a biface pick and an oval biface distal fragment. Both were recovered from the test excavations in the raised fields, in a context that would argue direct association with raised-field activities. Both display extensive distal edge and surface smoothing, polish, and striations documenting the manner and direction of use and the general texture of the contact materials. Based on the wear patterns and context, it is difficult *not* to argue that these artifacts were associated with raised-field maintenance.

Artifacts used in clearing brush or in procuring or working with wood may include the chipped celts, tranchet bit tools, and ground celts. The chipped celts display extensive evidence of use against resistant but not rigid materials. No wear was observed on the ground stone celts.

The remaining tools do not display form or wear patterns other than those which would be expected in general household or community maintenance activities. The second-order recycled biface fragments, retouched biface fragments, and utilized flakes display a variety of edge wear attributes indicating uses in slicing, sawing, chopping, adzing, and battering motions. Fragments with suitable mass were frequently recycled and used as battering tools. Chalcedony was incorporated either as small, thick bifaces for the acquisition of flakes for second-order tools or as nodular masses for battering tools.

Manos and metates were also probably brought to the site in finished form. Most of the manos and metates are of fossiliferous, vesicular limestone. I have observed metates of this material at the other northern Belize sites of Colha, Cuello, and El Pósito. I suspect that this material, like the chalcedony, was being quarried somewhere in the general area. The vesicular basalt metate was clearly an import.

The majority of the occupation at Pulltrouser appears to have taken place from the Late Preclassic (Chicanel) through the Late Classic (Tepeu) ceramic periods (chap. 11). The lithic sample was analyzed as a unit and has not been correlated with the ceramic assemblage. This approach was necessary because the two studies were done apart and independently. On the basis of technological comparison with the ceramically dated workshops at Colha, the majority of the Pulltrouser lithic sample falls generally in the Late Preclassic and Late Classic time span, which is consistent with the general ceramic findings of the project. No Postclassic lithic items were identified among the formal tools; indeed, most formal tools, such as the oval biface implements and tranchet bit tools, would comfortably fall in the Chicanel and Tepeu ceramic periods.

The contrast between the Pulltrouser and Colha lithic assemblage is indeed marked (fig. 12-1). The Colha complex is a regional chert tool production center, as stated earlier, and the functional association of the lithic assemblage clearly reveals that fact. The Pulltrouser complex was in a consumer position with regard to chert tools. The assemblage is diagnostic, given the absence of tool manufacturing debitage and the fact that the chert was imported. These findings are offered as evidence that intraregional exchange or market systems were in operation in Late Preclassic times, if not earlier. Furthermore, regional specialization in the technology is demonstrable at Colha as early as the Late Preclassic, and one cannot help but speculate that Pulltrouser may have been specializing in the raising and exchanging of produce from the wetland fields.

ACKNOWLEDGMENTS

I would like to express my appreciation to those individuals who provided invaluable cooperation and assistance during the course of this lithic study. The editors of this volume have been especially patient and helpful in making the Pulltrouser lithic collection available for study and in allowing me to have total freedom in the analysis and interpretation. Thomas R. Hester, Center for Archaeological Research at the University of Texas at San Antonio, has been my close consultant throughout this study. Originally we had planned to collaborate on the analysis, but other commitments prevented his more direct participation. His consultations have been invaluable, especially since he provided me with complete access to the Colha data.

Robert Murry, Anna J. Taylor, and Erwin Roemer, graduate assistants at Texas A&M University, shared in the laboratory duties of tabulating, measuring, and photographing the specimens. Provenience data on the lithic sample from Kokeal were provided by Nancy Ettlinger.

13. Pulltrouser Swamp and Maya Raised Fields: A Summation

B. L. TURNER II and PETER D. HARRISON

The 1979 Pulltrouser Swamp Project was a pilot study of interdisciplinary scope which succeeded in scratching the surface of the environmental, agricultural, and settlement evidence. The integrative research effort produced several lines of evidence that provide insights into some of the environmental and cultural histories of the depression zone. While continued studies will strengthen, clarify, and alter the evidence, the following overview emerges.

The origins of Pulltrouser Swamp, beyond the broader geological history of the peninsular region, are not known. Its peculiar Y shape and the axis of the depression in relation to that of the New River make fluvial origins of the swamp suspect. The unconsolidated carbonates—limestone or sascab—that underlie the Pulltrouser area may be the product of deep weathering in the past (Darch 1981). The region undoubtedly was affected by sea-level rises which stabilized about 2000 B.P. (High 1975) or, interestingly, about the time that the depression may have been put to agricultural use by the Maya. Environmental conditions in the immediate area previous to this time are not known, but concentrations of gypsum crystals found at depth in the sascab suggest that conditions were once drier. Environmental conditions in the depression zone by or subsequent to the Late Preclassic period (200 B.C.) are uncertain, although the data are suggestive of several possibilities. At the time of the field construction the mainland was probably cleared of forest, as suggested by the pollen from the fields. The depression may have been dominated largely by the marsh association, and the escoba-botan forests were absent or much more restricted in area than they are today. Pollen evidence and the minimal plant remains of swamp forest species seem to corroborate this pattern. The surface water of the depression may have been deeper than it is today and probably maintained a permanent habitat for many species of aquatic mollusks. That the edges of the swamp exhibited seasonally fluctuating water levels is also suggested by the molluscan remains. Any changes in climate in the area that may have occurred subsequent to the field construction are not known, although major rainfall changes would have been required to appreciably alter surface water characteristics.

The Maya manipulated this wetland habitat for hydraulic cultivation perhaps no earlier than 200 B.C. and undoubtedly by Classic times. Channelized fields were carved out of the mainland-depression border by excavating canals into the mainland. A network of canals and raised fields was ultimately constructed over at least 311 hectares of the three arms of the depression and, perhaps, over as much as 668 hectares. The savanna zone of PW, where extreme seasonal water-level changes occur, was apparently not utilized for field cultivation. Raised fields were constructed by removal of the depression solum, excavation of canals into the underlying clays and sascab (or other materials), creation of a fill platform between the canals (mostly material from the canals), and placement of a topsoil on the platforms. The initial evidence indicates that field surfaces constituted about 60 percent of the field network. The hierarchy of canals included at least two canals leading to the New River.

The field-canal system was apparently a complex hydraulic work. Mere drainage of excessive water was neither its sole nor, perhaps, its primary function. Drainage per se would have been impeded by the very shallow slope of the depression and the low discharge of the New River. A more subtle hydraulic scheme was probably accomplished in which water was regulated to canals and, perhaps, to the depression's interior while field surfaces were kept from inundation. A permanent supply of water was apparently available to the fields throughout most years. Year-round cultivation was a distinct possibility in the system. Canal muck may have been used to help maintain fertility of the soils on the fields, as suggested by the remains of water lilies. Also, hoeing or some sort of tillage may have been a major cultivation procedure, as attested by the lithic evidence and, perhaps, by the incorporation of pollen and macrofloral remains in the upper fill zone. Tillage serves several important cultivation purposes associated with raised fields, including soil aeration. The soils of the fields presented no major cultivation problems which the Maya could not have successfully confronted by technological or procedural means. The strongest case for cultivars employed on the fields can be made for maize, although numerous other possibilities exist.

The development of the Pulltrouser field network coincides with the growth of the Maya population and, presumably, with the demand for agricultural production throughout northern Belize. Several habitation sites are located adjacent to the swamp, such as Kokeal. The specifics of the temporal relationships between the population sizes associated with these sites and the development of the depression require refinement. Nevertheless, the southern end of the site of Kokeal shows a Late Preclassic presence with probable construction activity. Such activity is definite by the Early Classic period. Much of this site seems to have been devoted to habitation structures of presumed farmers, as suggested by the lithics found there.

The raised-field system at Pulltrouser was probably abandoned sometime in the Terminal Classic, as was Kokeal, in association with the collapse of the central lowland civilization about A.D. 850. The cultural collapse and depopulation of much of the region would have made the upkeep of the Pulltrouser fields difficult, although agricultural theses (e.g., Boserup 1965) suggest that a lag time may well exist between major decreases in demand for production and the disuse of an agricultural system involving costly inputs. As the demand for agricultural production decreased sufficiently, the remaining population apparently focused on less costly agricultural production in the uplands. The abandoned field surfaces created a new or expanded niche for the escoba-botan forests, which invaded the fields along the exterior segments of the depression in the southern and eastern arms and in the interior of the western arm.

The escoba-botan forests housed several valuable woody species which were logged during colonial times. Perhaps reusing the ancient Maya canals, loggers entered the swamp and collected logwood (*Haematoxylum* species) and other species, effectively reducing their presence there. Logging persisted in the swamp into this century. Subsequently, Pulltrouser has remained virtually unutilized. Local inhabitants hunt and fish in it; the northern neck of PS is the major crossing point from the west side of Pulltrouser to the village of San Estevan on the east side of the New River; and the savanna of PW is used for grazing cattle. Recent swamp modification has involved only the dredging of the channel between PW and PE to facilitate drainage of the cane land to the west. Agronomists with the Belize Sugar Industries have an eye on other swamps in the area, for future drainage for the increasing sugarcane lands.

SPECIFIC ISSUES

The Verification and Distribution of Wetland Fields.   Proof of the existence of raised fields and their distribution beyond riverine circumstances have been major sources of controversy since the report of extensive field systems in southern Quintana Roo and the suggestion that such systems may have existed in the Petén, especially at Tikal (e.g., Turner 1974a; Harrison 1977; Siemens 1978; Puleston 1978; Sanders 1979; Turner and Harrison 1978, 1979, 1981; Adams, Brown, and Culbert 1981). Essentially, the fundamentals of the controversy were established by Puleston's caution that many of the field networks reported from aerial observations or photographs during the 1970s may have been misidentified natural features, such as gilgai or successional hummocks (1978: 234–239). Puleston maintained that depression or *bajo* mounds, particularly those in seasonally inundated-desiccated soils with montmorillonite clays, could be gilgai, and he implied that raised-field cultivation may have been restricted to riverine circumstances only. As noted, riverine lands comprise a small segment of the lowlands in comparison to depressions. Furthermore, subsequent to Puleston's unfortunate death, pedological studies of the riverine fields at Albion Island suggested that the features there may well be channelized, not raised, fields (Antoine, Skarie, and Bloom 1982). Other interpretations of channelized fields come from studies at Barber Creek, near Lamanai (John Lambert, personal communication), and Cerros (Friedel and Scarborough 1982).

The studies at Pulltrouser and at Albion Island indicate that gilgai do not form at either locale, even where conditions are most suitable for them (chap. 5). Soil desiccation is not sufficient to create deep cracking in the solum; indeed, surface cracks occur only in the savanna of PW or on cleared land, not in the escobabotan forests. While 2 : 1 silicate lattice clays are present, the 1 : 1 silicate lattice clays reduce the shrink-swell potential. Furthermore, the project demonstrated conclusively that true raised fields occur at Pulltrouser and are the dominant field type. These fields apparently cover most of the depressions in the immediate area, including the nearby New River zone. The question remains, however, regarding the transferability of these finds to southern Quintana Roo and the Petén, where depression soils apparently maintain a higher clay content (e.g., Turner 1974b). The patterns proposed as fields in these zones invariably occur in *bajo* or swamplike forests, not in savannas, which tend to exhibit severe soil-moisture extremes suitable for the mixing of expansible clays which can lead to gilgai formation. Furthermore, the soils of some of the Quintana

Roo *bajos* are of the same type as those at Pulltrouser, namely,
haplaquolls (Turner 1974b, 1978). Despite these similarities, many
of the Quintana Roo and Petén *bajos* do lose most of their surface
water during the dry season, in contrast to Pulltrouser, and are situated at elevations considerably higher than that of northern Belize.
Some of the *bajos* of Quintana Roo lie 80 meters or more above sea
level, and many of them in the Petén are even higher. Siemens
(1978) has noted that the increase in elevation may have hindered
use of the *bajos* for agriculture, especially with regard to the depth
of the water table.

Turner examined Bajo Morocoy in Quintana Roo in 1973,
1974, and 1979 and found no major surface cracking or ground
heaving in the forest, as was also noted at Bajo de Santa Fe near
Tikal in 1974 and 1975. In 1980 Stephen Gliessman and Turner
inspected the now-cleared sections of Bajo Morocoy during the extreme end of the dry season (see n. 2, chap. 1). Although barren soil
lay exposed directly to the sun, no major cracking or heaving was
observed. Soil pits revealed moist subsurface clays; the water table
(perched?) was found at about 150 centimeters from the surface.
Furthermore, the checkerboard ground and vegetation patterns previously reported there (Turner 1974a; Harrison 1977, 1978; Turner
and Harrison 1978) were confirmed as slightly elevated mounds
and ditches (Gliessman et al. n.d.).

Both channelized and raised fields occur in riverine and depression contexts throughout northern Belize and southern Quintana
Roo. This work complements the recent remote-sensing work (radar imagery) by R. E. W. Adams and colleagues and the Jet Propul-
sion Laboratory, Pasadena, California, which suggests the patterns
of larger canals apparently associated with wetland fields in Belize
and the Petén (Adams 1980).

Habitats Associated with the Fields.   The riverine and depression
studies to date indicate that relic fields in Maya wetlands occur in
zones with relatively permanent but fluctuating water levels and
with seasonal inundation. Today the fields occur in marsh, *bajo*,
and swamp habitats. It is not clear if the forest association in *bajos*
and swamps is a product of the fields. At Pulltrouser it may be,
while elsewhere similar forests cover *bajos* with and without any
apparent patterns of relic fields.

Harrison (1977), following Cooke (1931) and Ricketson and
Ricketson (1937), proposed that *bajos* throughout the central Maya
lowlands were once open, shallow lakes, that these habitats were
used for raised-field agriculture, and that Maya land use practices
adjacent to the field zones led to sedimentation of the lakes. The

evidence to date is equivocal on the issue, which is the subject of continued study. Cowgill and Hutchinson (1963: 30) argued that they could find no evidence that Bajo de Santa Fe was once an open body of water, although their evidence was taken from the edge of that *bajo*, where water fluctuations would be expected. The Pull-trouser data have not resolved the question, but the molluscan remains suggest that permanency of water was a characteristic of the swamp. Accelerated colluviation during Maya times at Lakes Yaxha and Sacnab, Petén, has been demonstrated by Deevey and colleagues (1979). Evidence of this effect has not yet been found at Pulltrouser, although a systematic search for it was not attempted in 1979. It is apparent that the potential for sedimentation by colluvial processes in *bajos* or depressions throughout the area varies enormously. Those depressions in the more rugged interior segments of the central lowlands typically are bordered by reasonably steep slopes, although the drainage basins are not large. In contrast, depressions in the eastern periphery zone are surrounded by minimal slopes. Numerous depressions, however, are subject to sedimentation by aquatic processes, and Pulltrouser and other wetlands may have been filled by such processes. The precise conditions in the depressions of the central Maya lowlands at the time of the field construction and land use impact in them undoubtedly varied in relation to the specifics of each case. More concrete assessments for Pulltrouser and elsewhere in the Maya area await additional data from a larger sample.

Explanations of Wetland Use.   Numerous forms of wetland cultivation, particularly the use of raised fields, have been interpreted as evidence of high input and output agriculture. Population pressure or pressure on production has often been used to explain the employment of major raised-field technology (Denevan 1970; Turner 1974a; Denevan and Turner 1974; Brookfield 1962; Sanders, Parsons, and Stanley 1979). These explanations follow stress or pressure theses of agricultural growth influenced by the works of Boserup (1965) and others (e.g., Brookfield 1972). The fundamental basis of these themes is that traditional farmers display a coherent economic rationale within the constraints imposed on them. This rationality involves an emphasis on the minimization of effort and risk (e.g., Sanders, Parsons, and Stanley 1979; Turner 1980, n.d.a, n.d.d) and an understanding that increases in output can be achieved only by increases in input, under typical circumstances. Given this reasoning, farmers are seen as reluctant to increase output unless forced to do so by coercion or need (population growth) or by a change in production objectives. A strong relationship probably existed in the past between local (regional) pressures on production and the input and output qualities of the cultivation systems. Hence, the documentation of elaborate systems of intensive agriculture is typically interpreted as indicating that population densities in the immediate or larger area were reasonably high.

A population trend, with local spatial and temporal variances, apparently existed in the central Maya lowlands in which populations grew through Late Preclassic times, perhaps stabilized, and expanded again in Classic times (Culbert 1973; Adams 1977). Undoubtedly, the central lowlands and their eastern periphery were well inhabited during the Late Classic (e.g., Bullard 1965; Haviland 1969, 1970, 1972; Willey et al. 1965; Dahlin 1977; Turner 1976; Hammond 1974a; Ashmore 1981). Population densities projected for various sites and zones (although recognition of the problems of these projections is necessary) suggest that the central Maya lowlands had sufficient demand for production to make high-input wetland manipulation an economically viable activity.[1]

A major question concerns the source of the demand relative to the zones of wetland production and the abilities to transport foods long distances. Siemens (1978, 1982) suggests that foods from the raised fields of the eastern periphery were geared toward supplying the Petén zone to the west through a series of river and canal networks. The distance between the northern Belize zone of wetland fields and the central Petén (focusing on Tikal) is about 150 kilometers. This distance probably borders on that which is energetically efficient to transport food by human portage (i.e., the energy of transport does not exceed the energy of the food being transported). However, the Hondo River provides an avenue to the edge of the Petén, and a system of canals (Siemens 1978; Thompson 1974) could make the postulated trade energetically feasible. The question remains regarding the existence of such canal systems and/or the engineering capabilities of the Maya to connect the higher central Petén with the Hondo River. Siemens (1978) suggests that the route could have been achieved by use of discontinuous water routes across *bajos*.

Clarification of the source-of-demand issue requires further demographic evidence from the environs adjacent to field zones and from the eastern periphery zone in general. Northern Belize contains a large number of known and probable sites (as attested by Kokeal and Yo Tumben). The demand for agricultural production stemming from these local and/or intraregional sites could have been considerable. Pulltrouser, for example, is immediately surrounded by at least three small sites, and Nohmul, Cuello, and San

Estevan are located no farther than 7 or 8 kilometers from various arms of the depression (fig. 9-1). Furthermore, the Pulltrouser-Kokeal people had contact with or obtained goods from chert-bearing zones (Colha?), pine zones, and the larger northern Belize area and beyond. While production in the fields may have been linked to long-distance trade (the Petén and elsewhere), the initial indications are that such trade need not be invoked as an explanation for the rise of wetland agriculture in the area. Demand on a local or intraregional level may have been sufficient to warrant wetland use. An alternative explanation involves specialized production (see the section on crops below).

The Sequence of Agricultural Development.   The sequence of agricultural development in the central Maya lowlands, strongly associated with the issue of the causes of development, has been discussed elsewhere (Turner and Harrison 1978). One perspective suggests that the Maya principally expanded across the uplands, especially the mollisol-dominated zones, before any major effort was extended to wetland manipulation (Sanders 1973; Turner 1974a, n.d.c). The rationale for this interpretation follows modifications of the pressure or stress theses, which incorporate variables of land quality and crop types (Brookfield 1972; Turner, Hanham, and Portararo 1977; Sanders, Parsons, and Stanley 1979).

The central Maya lowlands are not homogeneous with regard to constraints on cultivation; they maintain numerable micro- and macrolevel habitats for farming (Sanders 1977; Turner 1978). Nevertheless, a broad distinction can be made between well-drained (uplands) and inundated (wetlands) lands in that the latter require considerable modifications before major or permanent cultivation can be pursued. As noted above, farmers are reluctant to expend the effort to make these modifications unless they are needed or unless less costly alternatives are not available. The well-drained uplands, especially those dominated by mollisols and other limestone-enriched soils, are high-quality environs for cultivation (Sanchez and Buol 1975; Wright et al. 1959), especially for the array of presumed Maya staples (Turner and Miksicek n.d.). The costs of manipulating these lands are thought to be considerably less than the costs of producing channelized and raised fields. Hence, it is expected that agriculture would have developed and expanded first in the uplands until the demand became sufficient to warrant the use of wetlands. The population data indicate that such demand emerged throughout much of the central lowlands perhaps by the Late Preclassic and certainly by Classic times.

The specific sequence of wetland uses, particularly in depres-

sions, is not certain. Siemens (1982) suggests that the margins of
the wetlands may have been utilized first in a *marceño* type of
cultivation. This practice, as reported in Tabasco (Orozoco-Segovia
and Gliessman n.d.), involves the cultivation of quickly maturing
crops along the margins of swamps and rivers as the waters recede
during the dry seasons. A similar practice is reported for the Petén
(Cowgill 1962). Siemens (1982) postulates an adjustment from *marceño* to channelized-field and, ultimately, raised-field agriculture as
the need arose, with an emphasis on dry season "security cropping"
to supplement production from wet season cultivation on the uplands. This interpretation is logical for certain types of fields and
for the origins of wetland use. However, once the high construction
costs were undertaken, it seems doubtful that a dry season crop
alone would have been justified (Turner n.d.d). Indeed, it seems
highly probable that, once major wetland alterations took place,
the wetland systems would have sustained intensive, permanent
cultivation for a variety of purposes.

The Pulltrouser data tend to support the view that wetland
cultivation developed after dryland cultivation was in use. The ceramics found in the fields at Pulltrouser date to the Late Preclassic
through Late Classic periods. Neighboring Kokeal shows a strong
Late Preclassic presence and occupation through the Late Classic.
The a.d. 150 ± 150 radiocarbon date from a channelized-raised field
supports the ceramic dating, suggesting depression edge usage by or
subsequent to that time (table 4-2). The other two radiocarbon
dates from the fields were from samples which were suspect for
various reasons. The Postclassic date was obtained from a sample
taken from a field adjacent to the major pathway across the swamp
to the main canal used by loggers to transfer materials from PE into
PS and the New River. Also, local inhabitants burn the marsh during the dry season to facilitate hunting and fishing. The other date
involved a well-preserved trunk (mahogany family) which may
have succumbed to logging activity during this century. While
more dating of all kinds is needed, the evidence supports the use of
the fields sometime within the Late Preclassic and Classic periods.

This interpretation seems to conflict with the argument that
the Maya entered the lowlands along riverine (wetland) routes, emphasizing wetland (channelized and raised fields) cultivation (Puleston and Puleston 1971). Support of the riverine view relies on a radiocarbon date, 1110 b.c. ± 110 (1400 B.C.), from a post or stake
taken from a canal adjacent to a channelized field (Puleston 1977a,
1978). The Early Preclassic use of wetlands for major raised-field
agriculture does not necessarily follow the logic of farming behav-

ior discussed above, because it implies that labor-intensive or high-cost and, perhaps, inefficient (in terms of initial inputs compared to outputs) wetland agriculture was chosen over the lower-cost, extensive, and efficient upland systems of cultivation which were apparently available at that time. In other words, the "wetlands first" thesis implies that Maya farmers disregarded the principle of least cost and effort which has been demonstrated among other traditional cultivators.

Several explanations for the wetlands first thesis can be postulated (Turner and Harrison 1978: 358–359). First, production demand may have been much greater during Early Preclassic times than has been presumed, especially in northern Belize. The evidence from nearby Cuello indicates agriculture in the area at this time, and various other sites, including those adjacent to or on Albion Island, may yet reveal a substantial Early Preclassic occupation. But this evidence may only push back in time the dryland-to-wetland theme, supporting the use of wetland fields as a consequence of the depletion of drylands by Early Preclassic times. Second, the early use of wetlands at Albion Island may reflect local circumstances of land restriction, either by coercion or by choice. There is no evidence to support the coercion theme, such as confinement of people to the island by a hostile force. The choice theme could involve the emphasis of cultivars requiring soil-moisture conditions associated with wetland fields, such as cacao (Hammond 1974b; Dahlin 1979). However, this theme is not yet supported by the excavation and other evidence (see the section on crops). Third, as suggested by Siemens (1982), channelized fields along riverine lands may have been the forerunners of raised fields, and as such they may have been experimented with during the Early Preclassic, particularly as a technology for security (dry season) crops. This rationale is reasonable, but it also calls for either evidence of early pressures sufficient to have required the necessary input or a demonstration that this input was not excessive.

A fourth explanation involves the possible reinterpretation of the dated post from Albion Island and its association with the fields there. The fields apparently contained Classic ceramics (Puleston 1977a). Although possible, it seems highly unlikely that Early Preclassic ceramics would not be found in fields which were constructed at that time. Interestingly, the initial settlement survey indicated occupational dominance from the Late Preclassic through Late Classic periods on the island (Dahlin 1977). Is it possible that the dated post is associated with a ditch or canal which was originally constructed for a purpose other than cultivation? This question may be clarified by the recent work on the island by Mary Pohl.

At this time, the best evidence which can be marshaled indicates Late Preclassic-Classic or later development of major wetland agriculture throughout the eastern periphery zone, particularly in nonriverine habitats, although local temporal variations may have occurred. The numerous channelized and raised fields at Pulltrouser seem to date to no earlier than the Late Preclassic. The later development of wetlands may also be supported by the evidence at Bajo Morocoy. Photographs of surface ceramics found there were examined by Robert Fry, who suggests that the material appears to be Classic in age.

Field Functions.   Data from which the major functions of the various Maya wetland-field systems may be determined are limited, and assessments of functions have relied primarily on comparisons with extant raised- and drained-field technologies elsewhere. Unfortunately, such comparisons have been impeded by the limited knowledge of Maya field morphologies and of environmental conditions during field use (not to mention the paucity of detailed studies of the extant systems). Comparisons have centered on two primary functions: drainage and drainage-irrigation. The former function involves an emphasis on the removal of standing water from the wetland depression. This feat, typically accomplished through the use of ditches or canals to drain water "somewhere else," requires some slope in order to move the water. The second function, drainage-irrigation, usually involves the control of water to designated areas (canals) within the wetland and the manipulation of water levels within the canals in association with field surfaces or rooting zones. In this case, drainage per se is not sought, but control of water through space and time is attempted. Such hydraulic manipulation is perhaps more adequately referred to as drainage-irrigation. Use of the term raised field is inadequate because it does not necessarily denote a hydraulic function (Denevan and Turner 1974).

It is important to note that, throughout much of the riverine lands and most of the depressions in the eastern periphery zone of the central Maya lowlands, a drainage technology alone was impractical because of the almost imperceptible gradients involved. There were literally no places to drain water into, especially in the wet season. Regulation of water to designated spaces and to field surfaces was not only a feasible procedure, but it would be rewarding in terms of potential cultivation practices, especially the apparent ability to cultivate through the dry season.

Support of this argument for the Pulltrouser fields can be drawn from several sources. The raised fields found there are morphologically classified as monolevel platforms, types generally associated with permanent water retention in canals, as in the chinampa system of highland Mexico. Even today only the more shallow and infilled canals adjacent to the mainlands at Pulltrouser desiccate. Furthermore, observation of fields along the New and Hondo rivers, including many on Albion Island, reveals considerable water retention in the infilled canals. The remains of water lilies and some types of gastropods found in the Pulltrouser fields could be explained by the presence of relatively deep water in the canals previous to infilling. Finally, the location of the fields in the depression suggests an association with zones of permanent but fluctuating water. The wet-dry savanna portions of PW, those zones seemingly most suitable for pure drainage procedures, apparently were not utilized for field construction. Indeed, the initial environmental data suggest that the Pulltrouser fields were constructed within an environment not unlike that in which the chinampa system was created (Armillas 1971).

Finally, it should be noted that raised fields are used for a number of agricultural purposes (Denevan and Turner 1974) and that their functions in the central Maya lowlands may have varied with local circumstances. Nevertheless, at Pulltrouser the evidence suggests that a drainage-irrigation function was employed and that this may have been true for fields located in similar habitats throughout the area. These observations do not negate the contention that channelized fields of a principally drainage function existed in appropriate locales.

Crops.   Considerable interest has been invested in the issue of the suite of cultivars utilized on Maya raised and channelized fields (Turner and Miksicek n.d.). Such interest has been invoked partly as a response to understanding the development of the systems throughout the eastern periphery zone. For example, use of the agricultural circumstances provided by the fields for a suitable specialty crop could explain the early development and ultimate spatial extent of the technology. In this regard, it has been postulated that the fields may be related to the production of cacao (*Theobroma* species), a cultigen of immense importance to Mesoamerican peoples (Millon 1955). Hammond (1974b) postulated a cacao-field theme, drawn from the ethnohistoric and historic evidence of cacao production in the northern Belize–Bahía de Chetumal area. Dahlin (1979) provided support, particularly with regard to the suitability of the wetland fields for cultivation of the finicky species, which requires stable moisture and shade conditions. Puleston

(1977a) challenged this view with the evidence from Albion Island. Fossil pollen of maize and possibly cotton and amaranth was found in the canals adjacent to the fields. To our knowledge, pollen within the fields was not found or not reported. Hammond (1978: 27–28) reported that the lack of cacao pollen in field associations was not proof of its nonuse, because this insect-pollinated species does not produce much pollen and preservation of its remains in canals would be suspect.

The Pulltrouser Swamp Project tackled this issue in several ways. Much of the excavation material was examined by hand; numerous samples were floated for plant remains; and pollen samples were taken for study. The latter two procedures proved fruitful in producing some evidence of possible cultivars. However, no macrofossils or pollen of cacao were recovered. Only a few fragments of cacao were found, located in the fill of the earth mound (structure 7) at Kokeal. Hammond (personal communication) has suggested that cacao remains may have been used as a mulch, masking its presence because of the recycling of the material. Cacao husks make a good mulch, particularly when burned.[2] However, it is difficult to envision a processing system so efficient that evidence of a cultivar's use would escape detection, particularly the remains of the roots in the fields. While a larger sample size is needed for verification, the initial evidence from Pulltrouser does not support the growth of cacao on the fields.

The best evidence for a cultivar associated with the fields is for maize (*Zea mays*). Less support can be advanced for cotton (*Gossypium*), amaranth (*Amaranthus*), and, perhaps, a Euphorbiaceae (chaya?). Maize pollen was found in limited quantities in the fields, and a carbonized maize fragment was uncovered as well. While these materials may have been deposited during field construction, it is possible that they represent the remains of the past cultivation of maize on the fields. Wiseman (chap. 7) cautions that the *Gossypium*-type pollen could represent any number of wild species. Of these two possible crops, the evidence for *Gossypium* is stronger when plant macrofossil data from the lowlands are considered. To date, no macrofossil remains of grain amaranth have been found in the lowlands (Turner and Miksicek n.d.). Furthermore, *Amaranthus*-type pollen is ubiquitous throughout the lowlands as the product of weedy plants of that genus. Finally, several roots of a Euphorbiaceae were found in flotation samples from the fields. A possibility exists that these roots could be of chaya (*Cnidoscolus* subspecies), but they could also represent weedy, successional species (chap. 6).

The Pulltrouser evidence appears consistent with the fossil pollen

data from Albion Island, where maize and perhaps cotton and amaranth pollen was found in association with field zones. However,
further work is needed to support the maize argument and to provide precise identifications of the other possible cultivars. Finally,
the agricultural habitat created by the fields is suitable for a large
number of crops, particularly if procedures to combat soluble salt
buildups are utilized. Studies in Tabasco have demonstrated that a
number of cultivars can produce well on the fields (Maier 1979;
Gliessman, Espinoza, and Alarcón 1978).[3]

Construction and Production.   Evidence from highland New Guinea
demonstrates that complex networks of raised fields can be constructed with stone tools and baskets, items utilized by the Maya.
But, while it is evident that the Maya fields were constructed with
relatively simple tools, the sequence and plan of construction remain unclear. The field and canal network at Pulltrouser may have
developed incrementally from the edges of the depression inward
or may have been constructed in mass as part of a predesigned,
large-scale scheme. The hierarchical canal network would seem
difficult to produce without a master plan. Furthermore, given the
discussion on presumed field functions, the system may not have
worked properly without total implementation. For example, the
use of only ditches along the depression edges to create channelized fields may have facilitated the seasonal drop in water level
there, providing a drier cropping surface earlier in the dry season.
However, the amount of land involved using only this technology
would have been small, because the low grade of the depression
would not have facilitated the drainage of water. Unfortunately,
dating of individual fields is not yet sufficiently refined to allow
a chronological assessment of construction.

Regardless of the sequence of development, the field complex
at Pulltrouser was no small undertaking. Estimates of construction
time for the 311-hectare zone of well-defined fields range from 710
to 3,266 workyears (table 13-1). Unfortunately, we cannot be sure of
the error in such estimates, because construction rates vary enormously with physical and economic circumstances. For example,
depending on the field type and construction rates, a wetland system could have been constructed in anywhere from 833 to over
3,833 workdays per hectare (Turner n.d.d; also see Puleston 1977b).
The 710 to 3,266 estimates are lower than those previously given
(Turner and Harrison 1981), due to expanded analyses and compu-
tation refinements.

The productivity of the field-canal network in terms of cultivation only (not considering possible aquatic foods) is speculative; at

Table 13-1. *Estimates of Construction Time and Labor for the Wetland System at Pulltrouser Swamp*

Item of Calculation	High Rate of Work	Low Rate of Work
Total volume of fields & canals[a]	3,110,000.0 m.^{3}	3,110,000.0 m.^{3}
Construction rates[b] (workdays/10,000 m.^{3})	833.0	3,833.0
Total workdays	259,063.0	1,192,063.0
Total workyears	710.0	3,266.0
Years of construction with		
100 workers	7.1	32.7
1,000 workers	0.7	3.3

[a] Assumes field height and canal depth to average 1 meter.
[b] Based on the construction rates derived from Turner (n.d.d).

best only estimates can be ventured. The reasons for this circumstance are numerous. To derive relatively accurate production figures requires knowledge of cultivars, cultivation procedures (e.g., weeding, mucking, or crop rotation), harvests per year, length of fallow, and so forth.[4] Obviously, much of this information can never be known for ancient agricultural systems, and analogies must be utilized to establish estimates.

Sanders (1976: 147, table 10) estimates that after 100 B.C. in the Basin of Mexico chinampa cultivation of maize could yield about 3,000 kilograms per hectare (presumably one harvest per year) and support about 19 people per hectare (family composition).[5] Use of these figures produces a conservative estimate of over 3,500 people supported by the 311-hectare zone at Pulltrouser (table 13-2).

These estimates should be considered with caution but as conservative. Sanders' data are from the highland zone, and their accuracy for the lowlands is not known.[6] However, the production figures for chinampas are apparently based on one harvest of maize per year (also see Denevan 1982). We note that it is feasible to double crop (producing two harvests per year) at Pulltrouser (contemporary chinampas are under constant production with only short fallow periods). Conservatively guessing that a second harvest would produce an additional 1,500 kilograms per hectare of maize or maize-equivalent foods (perhaps beans, root crops, and so forth), we estimate that the population figures would rise to over five thousand at Pulltrouser. Again, this figure must be viewed with caution, as information on production and on soil, pest, and other

Table 13-2. *Productivity of Raised-Field Maize Cultivation and Population Supported*

Item of Calculation	311-Ha. Zone
Number of people supported per hectare with one harvest[a]	19
Cultivated surface area of the fields[b]	187 ha.
Total population supported with one harvest	3,553
Number of people supported per hectare with two harvests[c]	28
Total population supported with two harvests	5,236

[a] Sanders 1976: 147; Parsons 1976.

[b] Based on field calculations that approximately 60 percent of the field-canal zone is field surface.

[c] Based on the assumption that the use of double cropping would minimally produce a harvest equal to one-half of that produced by the first harvest.

conditions affecting the fields under double cropping is not known. Finally, it must be recognized that cultivation in the Pulltrouser area was not limited to the depression. Much of the surrounding uplands is comprised of high-quality agricultural land which could have produced well under a variety of cropping systems. Much of this area is prime cane land today.

Settlement Distribution and Population.   Major controversial issues dealing with the association of settlement distribution and wetland fields have not yet developed, largely because the subject is so new. Harrison (1977) observed that sites in south central Quintana Roo tend to be located adjacent to *bajos*, and Adams (1980) has provided a somewhat similar argument for segments of the Petén. Unfortunately, quantitative comparisons of site locations by site situations (habitats) have not been produced over sufficiently large segments of the lowlands, so verification of the observations cannot be made. Green (1973) suggests that sites in northern Belize are located on prime agricultural soils. While this assessment may be true—there is an apparent clustering of sites in limestone-enriched soils (Wright et al. 1959)—it must be noted that Belize is replete with high-quality agricultural soils and water sources.

Since the 1979 Pulltrouser settlement work was limited in scope for various reasons (chap. 9), a relatively complete settlement survey of the immediate Pulltrouser complex was not attempted, nor was a survey of settlement distribution away from the depression made to assess the issues outlined above. However, the settlement work did establish that at least three sites are located adjacent to the depression and that at least one, Kokeal, has definable limits in the sense that it is bounded by zones to the west and north in which virtually no or, at best, few habitation structures exist. This suggests that settlement was not continuous around the depression but was, perhaps, clustered.

The population adjacent to Pulltrouser may have been substantial, as indicated by the number of structures at Kokeal and by the assumption that the other known sites (and perhaps those as yet undiscovered) are equivalent to or larger than Kokeal in size. Kokeal contains 117 structures of varying sizes within a zone of 1.08 square kilometers (table 13-3), providing a density of structures of about 108 per square kilometer. The total zone "sampled" in the Kokeal area was 4.48 square kilometers, however. This larger area was examined by means of *brechas* which revealed a small number of mounds to the northwest of the site, and other small structures may exist in the area missed by the *brechas* (chap. 9). For the most part, however, the number of structures appears to drop off dramatically outside the 1.08-square-kilometer zone, and for our purpose the larger zone is considered vacant in terms of structures. Considering the larger zone as devoid of structures produces a density of 26.1 structures per square kilometer.

Of the 117 structures, 23 have been classified as probably civic-ceremonial in function on the basis of size, proportion, and location within groupings.[7] This figure represents 20 percent of all the structures. Of the net remaining structures, 94 in number, 10 percent have been eliminated to account for other nonresidential functions (a procedure which may be unnecessary but is used as a precaution), leaving 85 house structures. Utilizing the traditional and, perhaps, conservative (e.g., Hellmuth 1977) figure of 5.6 occupants per house structure produces varying population estimates of 476, 428, and 357, depending on a consideration of total, 90 percent, and 75 percent simultaneous occupancy, respectively. The density of population within Kokeal would have been about 440, 396, and 330 people per square kilometer for the three estimates.

It is noted that the population estimates for Kokeal fall far below the number of people possibly supported by production from the raised fields at Pulltrouser. Furthermore, the population at Kokeal was probably too small to have maintained the field system, assuming that most of it was operative at one time. This interpretation suggests that the other known sites probably maintained rather large populations and/or that sites yet to be found rimmed the depression. For example, immediately south of Kokeal, the large site of Yo Tumben fronts the New River. The relationship

Table 13-3. *Structures and Population Estimates for Kokeal*

Feature & Area of Settlement	Total No.	Density (Km.²)
Number of structures	117	
At 1.08 km.²[a]		108.3
At 4.48 km.²[b]		26.1
Number of nonresidential structures[c]	32	
At 1.08 km.²		29.6
At 4.48 km.²		7.1
Number of residential structures	85	
At 1.08 km.²		78.7
At 4.48 km.²		19.0
Population estimate if all structures are occupied simultaneously[d]	476	
At 1.08 km.²		440.7
At 4.48 km.²		106.3
Population estimate if 90% of the structures are occupied simultaneously	428	
At 1.08 km.²		396.3
At 4.48 km.²		95.5
Population estimate if 75% of the structures are occupied simultaneously	357	
At 1.08 km.²		330.6
At 4.48 km.²		79.7

[a] Area encompassed by Kokeal.

[b] Area sampled by *brechas* which suggested nominal structures outside of Kokeal.

[c] Figure includes twenty-three structures indicative of a civic-ceremonial function and nine structures (10 percent of residential types) as an estimate of small structures used for purposes other than habitation.

[d] The tradition of 5.6 people per residential structure is used.

of Yo Tumben to Kokeal and Pulltrouser is not known, although the massive and, perhaps, earlier construction at Yo Tumben may indicate a functional or chronological division from Kokeal.

The Dating of Kokeal.   The dating of settlements associated with wetland-field zones is critical in that various theoretical issues, such as field development, are linked to settlement characteristics. For example, the proposed Early Preclassic use of fields at Albion Island predates the evidence of major habitation on the island, prompting a nonstress or nonpopulation explanation of field use. Interestingly, if major field use is proposed at dates preceding major habitation, where did the labor force necessary to construct and maintain the fields come from?

In this regard, the dating of Kokeal and the adjacent fields demonstrates that the field system may date anywhere from the Late Preclassic through the Late Classic. It is expected that Kokeal should display signs of major occupancy by Late Preclassic times. The site exhibits two major periods of rapid expansion of habitation, as interpreted by the number of ceramics found: Late Preclassic and Late Classic. The limited excavations at Kokeal uncovered several construction levels with pure Preclassic content, low in the stratigraphic sequence, but none of these was ultimately traced to bedrock and so may remain unconfirmed. However, the architectural and ceramic evidence strongly indicates a Late Preclassic presence at Kokeal. A number of circumstances can explain the construction-ceramic relationship found (chap. 10), one of which is the small sample size involved.

All lines of evidence demonstrate occupation of the site from the Early Classic through the Late Classic. The number of ceramics suggests an increase in activity in the Late Preclassic. The Postclassic occupation was slim; a few ceramics of that period were found in surface contexts. For the most part, however, Kokeal does not appear to have been a major center of activity at that time; it had succumbed to the larger pattern of population decline and site abandonment associated with the collapse of the Classic Maya in the central lowlands.

Architecture and Site Status.   Kokeal displays several construction characteristics that distinguish it from small sites elsewhere in the central Maya lowlands, especially in the interior ridgeland zone along the Tikal-Becan corridor. For example, one structure (structure 7) is a large mound constructed of earth (fig. 9-2; chap. 10), a construction method reported in the Olmec–Gulf coast area at an earlier period (Coe 1977). In addition, none of the platforms at Kokeal supported buildings with masonry walls or vaulted roofs, even though these are found at nearby San Estevan and Nohmul. The only parallels which can be found for this type of short-cut construction in the Maya area are associated with the Postclassic and have been interpreted as cost-control mechanisms, for whatever reasons that they may have emerged (Rathje 1975).

The cost-control mechanisms in architecture reported elsewhere are chronologically earlier or later than the construction found at Kokeal. For this reason, it is postulated that Kokeal may represent a unique site of special status or a class of such sites common to the locality or even to the Maya lowlands in general. Precisely what this status was is a matter for conjecture. Perhaps Kokeal was basically a farming (peasant?) community, as suggested by the lithic remains of agricultural tools which had been consistently recycled. This argument suggests that Kokeal was composed largely of a class of occupants which differed from those at Nohmul and other sites more elaborately constructed. The function of Kokeal and its internal composition of sites adjacent to Pulltrouser Swamp are subjects of further study.

The Collapse of the Classic Maya.   Cooke (1931) and the Ricketsons (1937) proposed that the collapse of the Maya culture and the ultimate depopulation of the central lowlands may have been linked to the desiccation of depressions—*bajos* were once lakes which were infilled. Harrison (1977) developed a more elaborate hypothesis in which local food production was predicated on raised-field cultivation in these depressions. Land use practices adjacent to these locales led to sedimentation and infilling of the raised-field zones, not unlike the colluviation processes described for Lakes Yaxha and Sacnab (Deevey et al. 1979). Yet another theme has been suggested by Turner (1974a; also see Willey and Shimkin 1973), in which it is proposed that, if there were an initial agricultural cause of the collapse, it may be more attributable to disease and/or pest problems brought on by the monocropping associated with intensive systems of agriculture. A recent argument favoring such a circumstance has been presented by Brewbaker (1979), who suggests that sustained failure of maize production in the central and southern lowlands may have resulted from a maize mosaic virus instigated by the movement of the corn plant hopper (*Peregrinus maidis*) into the lowlands. Crop failure would have been most disastrous in large-scale monocropping systems, especially where cultivation was conducted year-round (on raised fields?).

The Pulltrouser data do not lend much insight into any of these proposed collapse factors. As yet no evidence of major sedimentation has been found in the raised-field zone which cannot be accounted for by local erosion of the fields themselves or by the accumulation of organic detritus, but this observation is the subject of further study. In contrast to the eastern periphery zone, however, the depressions of the Petén are commonly ringed by steep slopes (Siemens 1978), such that their potential for colluviation and infilling was greater than in the eastern periphery zone. The better preservation of ancient wetland systems in the eastern periphery zone and in the Candelaria zone of Campeche may be related to the sedimentation issue.

Substantiation of monocropping disasters may be more difficult to achieve by direct evidence and must draw support from indirect lines of study, such as spatial-temporal patterns of collapse and abandonment. Recent attempts to utilize this approach have suggested that agricultural disasters per se may not have been prime movers in the collapse-depopulation phenomenon but that class-conflict theory and increasing regional fractionalism may better describe the data sets (Hamblin and Pitcher 1980; Bove 1981).

The problem with any explanation of the collapse based on a single or prime cause is the inability to verify the presumed cause-and-effect relationships. For example, does a sedimented depression with fields represent farmers' mismanagement of the cultivation system or sociopolitical disruption of the farmers' activities? Unfortunately, chronological controls are typically insufficient to handle the problem. An alternative approach involves casting an explanation in terms of multiple interactive variables (systemic approach), which are exceedingly difficult to demonstrate beyond the macro-level of data support. Regardless of these issues, we favor agricultural collapse and depopulation in the region as a response to any number of prime collapse causes, although the disruption of agricultural activities would have undoubtedly increased the impact of the other events. Finally, agricultural causes of the collapse, if they existed, probably were not associated with long-term problems such as soil fertility or persistent indigenous diseases, because traditional farmers tend to develop mechanisms to lessen their impact. If such mechanisms are not developed, then high levels of agricultural production are rarely achieved and, presumably, the Maya would have never developed as they did. Farmers are most vulnerable to unpredictable, "big bang impact" perturbations, such as the introduction of a new crop disease (Turner n.d.a).

FINAL COMMENTS
The use of wetlands, specifically depressions, by the ancient Maya has wide-ranging implications for a variety of issues specific to lowland civilization and for numerous theories dealing with ecological, economical, and sociopolitical issues in prehistory. We have discussed those issues specific to the Maya for which we think the data are sufficient to warrant some insights. For example, the Pulltrouser evidence suggests a temporal relationship between the broader growth of population and culture in the central lowlands and the movement to major wetland cultivation. This relationship is interpreted as supporting the broader theories of traditional farming behavior and land use patterns. Unfortunately, the data dealing with wetland systems of cultivation in the lowlands are as yet sufficient only to allow speculation on many major theoretical issues. Some of these issues include the fit of wetland raised

fields into the hydraulic typology, the managerial controls associated with the systems, and the implications of these issues for sociopolitical development. Nevertheless, the evidence continues to
mount that the Maya were on a par with other early civilizations in
terms of agrotechnology. Whether or not this evidence adds strength
to theories of sociopolitical development that emphasize agrotech-
nological controls is the subject of future work.

The 1979 Pulltrouser Swamp Project has provided a good base
of departure from which to clarify and expand various data and interpretations. Ongoing and future work will emphasize further data
collection from the fields at Pulltrouser and nearby depressions, detailed ecological work on past and present conditions at Pulltrouser, including a coring of the central part of the depression, complete
surveying of the settlements surrounding the swamp complex, increased excavations at the various settlements, and comparisons
with settlement patterns outside the swamp zone. While this pilot
project has firmly established the validity and nature of ancient
Maya agriculture and agrotechnology in depression-type habitats,
the significance of the finds to the course of Maya prehistory remains to be investigated. This study has only been able to touch on
the questions of chronology, productivity, and population related
to wetland and raised-field use. It is expected that further work
at Pulltrouser Swamp will elucidate these questions.[8]

NOTES
1. Although the initial construction inputs for channelization
and field raising vary by habitat and purpose of use, there is no
doubt that construction costs were high by absolute or relative
measures (Denevan 1982; Turner n.d.d).
2. Experiments in constructing and cultivating raised fields
have begun in earnest in the lowlands of Tabasco and Veracruz,
Mexico. The first such project was the Balancán-Tenosique Project
in Tabasco (Gómez-Pompa and Venegas 1976; Maier 1979; Gómez-
Pompa et al. 1982), followed by experiments at the Colegio Superior
de Agricultura Tropical, H. Cárdenas, Tabasco (Gliessman, Espinoza, and Alarcón 1978), and by the Camellones Chontales (Tabasco) Project and the La Mancha (Veracruz) Project (Gómez-Pompa
et al. 1982). For a discussion of these and other studies, refer to
the references. The cacao husk experiments were observed by the
authors and discussed with Arturo Gómez-Pompa and Stephen
Gliessman.
3. In addition to the more likely cultivars projected for raised
fields in chapter 7, the various experiments elsewhere have sug-

gested good production results from rice, chiles, yucca, sugarcane, and numerous vegetables (Maier 1979).

4. An intensive output (high production per unit area and time) would require substantial inputs, especially fertility-sustaining mechanisms. Several mechanisms and procedures were probably utilized to sustain fertility, including the use of aquatic plants. For example, water hyacinths (*Eichhornia crassipes*) can produce as much as 900 kilograms per hectare of dry matter per day (National Academy of Sciences 1976).

5. The contemporary production figure for chinampas is higher than the figure used here. For example, maize yields range from 6,000 to 8,000 kilograms per hectare (Maier 1979:75).

6. While various cultivation experiments have been undertaken (n. 2), few production figures have yet been published. Those figures available should be used cautiously, because the techniques of constructing the fields were experimental and cultivation procedures were not thoroughly understood. Also, the creation of the fields provides only the medium for cultivation, while yields are also a response to specific procedures and crops. Gliessman, Espinoza, and Alarcón (1978: 17) report that the monocultivation of maize by mechanized means at the Chontales Project initially resulted in a poor production of about 1,500 kilograms per hectare. This figure deserves comment. The *camellones* or raised fields at this project were constructed by mechanized means and by engineers with no experience in the system that they were creating (Gómez-Pompa et al. 1982). The results were huge fields somewhat like the polders of the Netherlands in which thick, gray, and nutrient-poor clays from below the swamp solum were dredged, inverted, and dumped to make the fields. These clays became part of the field solum for cultivation. Furthermore, the fields were sufficiently large to inhibit capillary action of water to the rooting zone in the middle. Much of the initial energy of the project was devoted to overcoming the technical errors. Subsequent problems in production are principally associated with sociomanagerial issues, not unlike those reported for the Uxpanapa (Veracruz) Project (Ewell and Poleman 1980).

7. The structures classified as probably not habitation structures per se are 7, 8, 14, 19, 36, 40, 47, 48, 58, 63, 65, 73, 74, 80, 83, 85, 88, 99, 103, 108, 120, 121, and 122.

8. During the final stages of publication of this book, a brief but important update of the work on wetland fields adjacent to the Río Hondo at Albion Island was released (Bloom et al. 1983). This

report, which reexamined two "fields" and two canals originally studied by Puleston (1977a), has significant implications for the findings and interpretations offered in this book about the fields at Pulltrouser Swamp and in the Maya lowlands in general.

The new study finds evidence of a canal cut through high organic carbon clay and clay with peat bands and into banded and sapric peat. The resulting profile gives the appearance of a channelized field with no major "raising." Over this field and canal were several meters of nutrient-deficient marl and clay which, on the surface, gives the appearance of a raised field. However, because of the composition of this material and the absence of agricultural indicators (pollens and macrofossils), the conclusion was that it represents natural sediments created by rises in sea level and, hence, the level of the Río Hondo during the Preclassic period. Charcoal of maize taken from the peat into which the canal was cut produced an uncorrected radiocarbon date of 670 b.c. in the Middle Preclassic. The information provided indicates that a channelized field had been created, presumably during the Preclassic, because of the need for drainage as water levels rose. Ultimately the field-canal was abandoned due to inundation, and the clay-marl material was deposited over it. Determination of why the deposition has a surface morphology of "raised fields" and canals remains under investigation.

While channelized fields occur at Pulltrouser, their profiles and those of the raised fields differ from those established at Albion Island. Most significantly, the canals at Pulltrouser are cut into "marl." A raised-field profile from bottom to top includes the "marl" base of swamp, a thin buried organic layer, a clay-carborate-gypsiferous layer, and a solum. The clay-carbonate-gypsiferous zone (or fill) occurs only in the fields and has agricultural indicators. In other words, the Pulltrouser raised fields do not display a profile indicative of "buried" channelized fields. Differences in field morphologies should be expected, given that the Albion Island fields are riverine and those at Pulltrouser are in a depression.

Use of drained fields along the Hondo sometime during the Preclassic is consistent with the interpretations given in this text about the possible chronologies of the Maya wetland use. Unfortunately, we still do not have a date directly from the cropping surface of a field at Albion Island. The date reported in the new study, attributed to material taken from the peat zone below the channelized field, thus may represent some sort of activity previous to the construction of the canal or the use of the field.

Two interpretations fit with those from Pulltrouser. First, the best evidence indicates that maize was an associated cultivar with the Albion Island fields; second, the pollen evidence on these fields suggests that considerable clearance of the upland forest had taken place. If the Albion Island fields are Middle Preclassic in origin, then the uplands were also heavily altered by that time. The same type of relationship at Pulltrouser supports the proposition that wetland cultivation, no matter how early in date, did not precede major agriculture in drylands. The precise type of dryland agriculture in use at the time that wetlands were manipulated cannot be established with certainty.

References

Adam, David P. n.d. Report on Pollen Analysis of a Tikal Chultun. On file with T. P. Culbert, University of Arizona.

Adams, R. E. W., ed. 1977. *The Origins of Maya Civilization*. Albuquerque: University of New Mexico Press.

———. 1980. Swamps, Canals and the Locations of Ancient Maya Cities. *Antiquity* 54: 206–214.

———, W. E. Brown, Jr., and T. Patrick Culbert. 1981. Radar Mapping, Archaeology, and Ancient Maya Land Use. *Science* 213: 1457–1463.

Ahenkorah, Yaw. 1970. Potassium Supplying Power of Some Soils of Ghana Cropped to Cacao. *Soil Science* 109: 127–135.

Ahler, S. 1971. Projectile Point Form and Function at Rodgers Shelter, Missouri. *Missouri Archaeological Society Research Series* 8.

———. 1979. Functional Analysis of Nonobsidian Chipped Stone Artifacts: Terms, Variables, and Quantification. In *Lithic Use-Wear Analysis*, B. Hayden, ed., pp. 301–302. New York: Academic Press.

Aho, J. 1978. Freshwater Snail Populations and the Equilibrium Theory of Island Biogcography, I: A Case Study in Southern Finland. *Annals Zoologica Fennici* 15: 146–154.

Andrews, E. Wyllys, IV. 1969. *The Archaeological Use and Distributions of Mollusca in the Maya Lowlands*. Middle American Research Institute Publication 34, Tulane University. New Orleans.

Antoine, P. P., R. L. Skarie, and P. R. Bloom. 1982. The Origin of Raised Fields near San Antonio, Belize: An Alternative Hypothesis. In *Maya Subsistence: Studies in Memory of Dennis E. Puleston*, K. Flannery, ed., pp. 227–236. New York: Academic Press.

Armillas, Pedro. 1971. Gardens on Swamps. *Science* 174: 653–661.

Ashmore, Wendy, ed. 1981. *Lowland Maya Settlement Pattern*. Albuquerque: University of New Mexico Press.

Baer, Phillip, and William R. Merrifield. 1971. Two Studies on the Lacandones of Mexico. *Summer Institute of Linguistics Publication* 33. Norman: University of Oklahoma.

Baerreis, David A. 1973. Gastropods and Archaeology. In *Variations in An-

thropology, D. W. Lathrop and J. Douglas, eds., pp. 48–53. Urbana, Ill.: Illinois Archaeology Survey.

Ball, Joseph W. 1977. *The Archaeological Ceramics of Becan, Campeche, Mexico*. Middle American Research Institute, Publication 43, Tulane University. New Orleans.

———. n.d. Polychrome Pottery and Regional Exchange in the Early Classic Northern Maya Lowland. Paper presented at the 43rd annual meeting of the Society for American Archaeology, Tucson, 1978.

Basch, Paul F. 1959. Land Mollusca of the Tikal National Park, Guatemala. *Occasional Papers of the Museum of Zoology, University of Michigan* 612: 1–15.

Belisle, Joseph, Said Musa, and Assad Shoman, eds. 1977. *Journal of Belizean Affairs* 5, Special Issue: The Río Hondo Project and Investigations of the Maya of Northern Belize.

Benya, Edward S. J. 1979a. Forestry in Belize, Part I: Beginnings of Modern Forestry and Agriculture, 1921–1954. *Belizean Studies* 7: 16–28.

———. 1979b. Forestry in Belize, Part II: Modern Times and Transition. *Belizean Studies* 7:13–28.

Bequaert, Joseph C. 1957. Land and Freshwater Mollusks of the Selva Lacandona, Chiapas, Mexico. *Bulletin of the Museum of Comparative Zoology, Harvard University* 116: 204–227.

——— and William J. Clench. 1933. The Non-Marine Mollusks of Yucatán. *Carnegie Institution of Washington Publication* 431: 525–545. Washington, D.C.

——— and ———. 1936. A Second Contribution to the Molluscan Fauna of Yucatán. *Carnegie Institution of Washington Publication* 457: 61–75. Washington, D.C.

——— and ———. 1938. A Third Contribution to the Molluscan Fauna of Yucatán. *Carnegie Institution of Washington Publication* 491: 257–260. Washington, D.C.

Black, C. A. 1965. *Methods of Soil Analysis*. Agronomy 9. Madison: American Society of Agronomy.

Bloom, A. L. 1971. Glacial-Eustatic and Isostatic Controls of Sea Level since the Last Glaciation. In *Late Cenozoic Glacial Ages*, K. K. Turekian, ed., pp. 355–379. New Haven: Yale University Press.

Bloom, Paul R., Mary Pohl, Cynthia Buttleman, Frederick Wiseman, Alan Covich, Charles Miksicek, Joseph Ball, and Julie Stein. 1983. Prehistoric Maya Wetland Agriculture and the Alluvial Soils near San Antonio, Río Hondo, Belize. *Nature* 301: 417–419.

Boserup, Ester. 1965. *The Conditions of Agricultural Growth*. Chicago: Aldine.

Boss, Kenneth J., and Juan J. Parodiz. 1977. Paleospecies of Neotropical Ampullariids and Notes on Other Fossil Non-Marine South American Gastropods. *Annals of the Carnegie Museum of Natural History* 46: 107–127.

Bove, Frederick J. 1981. Trend Surface Analysis and the Lowland Classic Maya Collapse. *American Antiquity* 46: 93–112.

Boyer, J. 1972. Soil Potassium. In *Soils of the Humid Tropics*, M. Drosdoff, ed., pp. 102–135. Washington, D.C.: National Academy of Sciences.

Bradbury, J. Platt, and Dennis E. Puleston, n.d. The Use of Pollen Analysis in Investigations of Prehistoric Agriculture. Paper presented at the 75th annual meeting of the Association of American Anthropologists, Mexico City, 1974.

Branson, Bradley A., and Clarence J. McCoy, Jr. 1963. Gastropods of the 1961 University of Colorado Museum Expedition in Mexico. *Nautilus* 76: 101–108.

Brewbaker, James L. 1979. Diseases of Maize in the Wet Lowland Tropics and the Collapse of the Classic Maya Civilization. *Economic Botany* 33: 101–118.

British Honduras Land and Survey Department. 1939. *Atlas of British Honduras*.

Brookfield, Harold C. 1962. Local Study and Comparative Method: An Example from Central New Guinea. *Annals of the Association of American Geographers* 52: 242–254.

———. 1972. Intensification and Disintensification in Pacific Agriculture: A Theoretical Approach. *Pacific Viewpoint* 13: 30–48.

Brown, Paul, and Aaron Podolefsky. 1976. Population Density, Agricultural Intensity, Land Tenure, and Group Size in the New Guinea Highlands. *Ethnology* 15: 211–238.

Browne, Robert A. 1981. Lakes as Islands: Biogeographic Distribution, Turnover Rates, and Species Composition in the Lakes of Central New York. *Journal of Biogeography* 8: 75–83.

Bullard, William R., Jr. 1960. Maya Settlement Pattern in Northeastern Petén, Guatemala. *American Antiquity* 25: 355–372.

———. 1965. *Stratigraphic Excavations at San Estevan, Northern British Honduras*. Royal Ontario Museum, Occasional Papers in Art and Archaeology 9. Toronto.

Buol, S. W., F. D. Hole, and R. J. McCracken. 1973. *Soil Genesis and Classification*. Ames: Iowa State University Press.

Burky, Albert J. 1974. Growth and Biomass Production of an Amphibious Snail, *Pomacea urceus* (Müller), from the Venezuelan Savannah. *Proceedings of the Malacological Society, London* 41: 127–144.

Buterlin, J., and F. Bonet. 1963. Mapas geológicos de la peninsula de Yucatán. *Ingeniería hidráulica en México*. Mexico City.

Charter, C. F. 1941. *A Reconnaissance Survey of the Soils of British Honduras North of the Central Metamorphic and Igneous Massif*. Trinidad: Government Press of Trinidad.

Clench, William J., and Ruth D. Turner. 1956. The Family Melongenidae in the Western Atlantic. *Johnsonia* 3: 161–181.

Coe, Michael D. 1977. Olmec and Maya: A Study in Relationships. In *The Origins of Maya Civilization*, R. E. W. Adams, ed., pp. 183–195. Albuquerque: University of New Mexico Press.

——— and Kent V. Flannery. 1967. *Early Cultures and Human Ecology in South Coastal Guatemala*. Washington, D.C.: Smithsonian Press.

Cooke, C. W. 1931. Why the Mayan Cities in the Petén District Were Abandoned. *Journal of the Washington Academy of Science* 21: 283–287.

Covich, Alan P. 1976. Recent Changes in Molluscan Species Diversity of a Large Tropical Lake (Lago de Petén, Guatemala). *Limnology and Oceanography* 21: 51–59.

———. 1978. A Reassessment of Ecological Stability in the Maya Area: Evidence from Lake Studies of Early Agricultural Impacts on Biotic Communities. In *Pre-Hispanic Maya Agriculture*, P. D. Harrison and B. L. Turner II, eds., pp. 145–155. Albuquerque: University of New Mexico Press.

——— and Minze Stuiver. 1974. Changes in Oxygen 18 as a Measure of Long-Term Fluctuations in Tropical Lake Levels and Molluscan Populations. *Limnology and Oceanography* 19: 682–691.

Cowgill, George L. 1975. On Causes and Consequences of Ancient and Modern Population Change. *American Anthropologist* 77: 505–585.

Cowgill, Ursula M. 1962. An Agricultural Study of the Southern Maya Lowlands. *American Anthropologist* 64: 273–286.

——— and G. Evelyn Hutchinson. 1963. El Bajo de Santa Fe. *Transactions of the American Philosophical Society* 53: 1–51.

——— and ———. 1966. La Aguada de Santa Ana Vieja: The History of a Pond in Guatemala. *Archiv für Hydrobiologie* 62: 335–372.

———, ———, A. A. Racek, Clyde E. Goulden, Ruth Patrick, and Matsuo Tsukada. 1966. *The History of Laguna de Petenxil: A Small Lake in Northern Guatemala*. Memoirs of the Connecticut Academy of Sciences 17.

Crabtree, D. E. 1968. Mesoamerican Polyhedral Cores and Prismatic Blades. *American Antiquity* 33: 446–478.

———. 1972. An Introduction to Flintworking. *Occasional Papers of the Idaho State University Museum* 28.

Culbert, T. Patrick, ed. 1973. The Maya Downfall at Tikal. In *The Classic Maya Collapse*, T. P. Culbert, ed., pp. 63–92. Albuquerque: University of New Mexico Press.

Dahlin, Bruce H. 1977. The Initiation of the Albion Island Settlement Pattern Survey. *Journal of Belizean Affairs* 5: 44–51.

———. 1979. Cropping Cash in the Protoclassic: A Cultural Impact Statement. In *Maya Archaeology and Ethnohistory*, N. Hammond and G. R. Willey, eds., pp. 21–37. Austin: University of Texas Press.

Darch, Janice P. 1981. The Characteristics and Origins of Sascab in Northern Belize, Central America. *Zeitschrift für Geomorphologie N.F.* 25: 400–419.

Deevey, E. S., D. S. Rice, P. M. Rice, H. H. Vaughan, Mark Brenner, and M. S. Flannery. 1979. Maya Urbanism: Impact on a Tropical Karst Environment. *Science* 206: 298–306.

Denevan, William M. 1970. Aboriginal Drained-Field Cultivation in the Americas. *Science* 169: 647–654.

———. 1980. Latin America. In *World Systems of Traditional Resource Management*, G. A. Klee, ed., pp. 217–244. New York: Halstead Press.

———. 1982. Hydraulic Agriculture in the American Tropics: Forms, Measures, and Recent Research. In *Maya Subsistence: Studies in Memory of Dennis E. Puleston*, K. Flannery, ed., pp. 181–203. New York: Academic Press.

——— and B. L. Turner II. 1974. Forms, Functions and Associations of Raised-Field Agriculture in the Old World Tropics. *Journal of Tropical Geography* 39: 24–33.

Directorate of Overseas Surveys. 1958. *British Honduras Monthly Rainfall (Map)*. London.

Dixon, C. G. 1956. *The Geology of Southern British Honduras, with Notes on Adjacent Areas*. Belize City: Her Majesty's Stationery Office.

Duffield, L. 1970. Vertisols and Their Implications for Archaeological Research. *American Anthropologist* 72: 1055–1062.

Edelman, C. H., and R. Brinkman. 1962. Physiography of Gilgai Soils. *Journal of Soil Science* 94: 336–370.

Emery, K. O. 1969. The Continental Shelves. *Scientific American* 221: 106–122.

Evans, John G. 1972. *Land Snails in Archaeology*. London: Seminar Press.

Ewell, Peter T., and Thomas T. Poleman. 1980. *Uxpanapa: Agricultural Development in the Mexican Tropics*. New York: Pergamon.

Faegri, K., and J. Iversen. 1975. *Textbook of Pollen Analysis*. 2nd ed. New York: Hafner Press.

Feldman, Lawrence H. 1978. Seibal and the Mollusks of the Usumacinta Valley. In *Excavations at Seibal, Department of Petén, Guatemala*, G. R. Willey, ed., pp. 166–167. Memoirs of the Peabody Museum 14. Cambridge, Mass.

Fish, Susan K. n.d. Palynology of Edzna and Aguacatal: Environment and Economy. Paper presented at the 43rd annual meeting of the Society for American Archaeology, Tucson, 1978.

Fletcher, C. 1978. Torquemada's Description of Aztec Obsidian Working. In *Archaeological Studies of Mesoamerican Obsidian*, T. R. Hester, ed., pp. 24–27. New Mexico: Ballena Press.

Flores, G. 1952. Geology of Northern British Honduras. *American Association of Petroleum Geologists Bulletin* 36: 404–409.

Folan, W. J. 1978. Cobá, Quintana Roo, Mexico: An Analysis of a Pre-Hispanic and Contemporary Source of Sascab. *American Antiquity* 43: 79–85.

Friedel, David A. 1979. Culture Areas and Interaction Spheres: Contrasting Approaches to the Emergence of Civilization in the Maya Lowlands. *American Antiquity* 44: 36–54.

——— and Vernon Scarborough. 1982. Subsistence, Trade and Development of the Coastal Maya. In *Maya Subsistence: Studies in Memory of Dennis E. Puleston*, K. Flannery, ed., pp. 131–155. New York: Academic Press.

Fry, Robert E. 1969. Ceramics and Settlement in the Periphery of Tikal, Guatemala. Ph.D. dissertation, University of Arizona. Ann Arbor: University Microfilms.

———. 1973. The Archaeology of Southern Quintana Roo: Ceramics. *Atti del XL Congresso Internazionale degli Americanisti:* 487–493. Genoa: Tilgher.

———. 1980. Models of Exchange for Major Shape Classes of Lowland Maya Pottery. In *Models and Methods in Regional Exchange,* R. Fry, ed., pp. 3–18. *Society of American Archaeology Papers* 1. Washington, D.C.

———. n.d. Settlement Systems in Southern Quintana Roo, Mexico. Paper presented at the 41st International Congress of Americanists, Mexico City, 1974.

Furley, Peter A. 1968. The University of Edinburgh British Honduras–Yucatán Expedition. *Geographical Journal* 134: 38–54.

———. 1975. The Significance of the Cohune Palm, *Orbignya cohune* (Mart.) Dahlgren, on the Nature and the Development of Soil Profiles. *Biotropica* 7: 32–36.

——— and A. J. Crosbie. 1974. *Geography of Belize.* London: Collins.

——— and W. W. Newey. 1979. Variations in Plant Communities with Topography over Tropical Limestone Soils. *Journal of Biogeography* 6: 1–15.

Global Atmospheric Research Project. 1975. *Understanding Climatic Change.* Washington, D.C.: National Academy of Sciences.

Gasser, J. K. R., and C. Bloomfield. 1955. The Mobilization of Phosphate in Waterlogged Soils. *Journal of Soil Science* 6: 219–232.

Gifford, James. 1976. *Prehistoric Pottery Analysis and the Ceramics of Barton Ramie in the Belize Valley.* Memoirs of the Peabody Museum 18. Cambridge, Mass.

Gliessman, Stephen R., Roberto García Espinoza, and Moisés Amador Alarcón. 1978. *Módulo de producción diversificado.* H. Cárdenas, Tabasco, Mexico: Colegio Superior de Agricultura Tropical, Secretaría de Agricultura y Recursos Hidráulicos.

———, B. L. Turner II, F. J. Rosado May, and M. Amador Alarcón. n.d. Ancient Raised-Field Agriculture in the Maya Lowlands of Southeastern Mexico. In *Drained Fields: History and Potential,* J. P. Darch and R. Smith, eds. British Archaeological Reports, Oxford University, Oxford (in press).

Gómez-Pompa, Arturo, Héctor Luis Morales, Epifanio Jiménez, and Julio Jiménez. 1982. Experiences in Traditional Hydraulic Agriculture. In *Maya Subsistence: Studies in Memory of Dennis E. Puleston,* K. Flannery, ed., pp. 327–342. New York: Academic Press.

———, and Raúl Venegas. 1976. La chinampa tropical. *Informa* 5. Xalapa, Mexico: Instituto Nacional de Investigaciones sobre Recursos Bióticos.

Goodrich, Calsin, and Henry van der Schalie. 1937. Mollusca of Petén and North Alta Vera Paz, Guatemala. *Miscellaneous Publications of the Museum of Zoology, University of Michigan* 34: 1–50.

Graf, A. B. 1973. *Exotica.* 8th ed. East Rutherford, N.J.: Roehrs.

Graham, Elizabeth, Logan McNatt, and Mark A. Gutchen. 1980. Excavations in Footprint Cave, Caves Branch, Belize. *Journal of Field Archaeology* 7: 154–172.

Green, Ernestine L. 1973. Locational Analysis of Prehistoric Maya Sites in Northern British Honduras. *American Antiquity* 38: 279–293.

Guedes, Lucia Maria L. A., A. M. C. Fiori, and C. O. da C. Dienfenbach. 1981. Biomass Estimation from Weight and Linear Parameter in the Apple Snail, *Ampullaria canaliculata* (Gastropoda: Prosobranchia). *Comparative Biochemistry and Physiology* 68A: 285–288.

Haas, Fritz, and Alan Solem. 1960. Non-Marine Mollusks from British Honduras. *Nautilus* 73: 129–131.

Hallsworth, E. C., Gwen K. Robinson, and F. R. Gibson. 1955. Studies in Pedogenesis in the New South Wales, VII: The Gilgai Soils. *Journal of Soil Science* 6: 1–31.

Hamblin, Robert L., and Brian L. Pitcher. 1980. The Classic Maya Collapse: Testing Class Conflict Hypothesis. *American Antiquity* 45: 93–112.

Hammond, Norman. 1972. Obsidian Trade Routes in the Mayan Area. *Science* 178: 1092–1093.

———, ed. 1973. *Corozal Project, 1973 Interim Report*. Centre of Latin American Studies, Cambridge University.

———. 1974a. The Distribution of Late Classic Maya Major Ceremonial Centres in the Central Area. In *Mesoamerican Archaeology: New Approaches*, N. Hammond, ed., pp. 313–334. Austin: University of Texas Press.

———. 1974b. Preclassic to Postclassic in Northern Belize. *Antiquity* 48: 177–189.

———, ed. 1976a. *Corozal Project, 1976 Interim Report*. History Faculty, Cambridge University.

———. 1976b. Maya Obsidian Trade in Southern Belize. In *Maya Lithic Studies: Papers from the 1976 Belize Field Symposium*, T. R. Hester and N. Hammond, eds., pp. 71–82. Center for Archaeological Research, Special Report 4. University of Texas at San Antonio.

———. 1977. The Earliest Maya. *Scientific American* 236: 116–133.

———. 1978. The Myth of the Milpa: Agricultural Expansion in the Maya Lowlands. In *Pre-Hispanic Maya Agriculture*, P. D. Harrison and B. L. Turner II, eds., pp. 23–34. Albuquerque: University of New Mexico Press.

———, D. Pring, R. Wilk, S. Donaghey, F. P. Saul, E. S. Wing, A. V. Miller, and L. H. Feldman. 1979. The Earliest Lowland Maya: Definition of the Swasey Phase. *American Antiquity* 44: 92–109.

Harrison, Peter D. 1972. Precolumbian Settlement Distribution and External Relationships in Southern Quintana Roo, Part 1: Architecture. *Atti del XL Congresso Internazionale degli Americanisti*: 479–486. Genoa: Tilgher.

———. 1977. The Rise of the *Bajos* and the Fall of the Maya. In *Social Process in Maya Prehistory: Studies in Memory of Sir Eric Thompson*, N. Hammond, ed., pp. 469–508. London: Academic Press.

———. 1978. *Bajos* Revisited: Visual Evidence for One System of Agriculture. In *Pre-Hispanic Maya Agriculture*, P. D. Harrison and B. L. Turner II, eds., pp. 249–253. Albuquerque: University of New Mexico Press.

———. 1981. Some Aspects of Preconquest Settlement in Southern Quintana Roo, Mexico. In *Lowland Maya Settlement Pattern*, W. Ashmore, ed., pp. 259–286. Albuquerque: University of New Mexico Press.

———. 1982. Subsistence and Society in Eastern Yucatán. In *Maya Subsistence: Studies in Memory of Dennis E. Puleston*, K. Flannery, ed., pp. 119–130. New York: Academic Press.

——— and B. L. Turner II, eds. 1978. *Pre-Hispanic Maya Agriculture*. Albuquerque: University of New Mexico Press.

Harry, Harold W. 1950. Studies in the Nonmarine Mollusca of Yucatán. *Occasional Papers of the Museum of Zoology, University of Michigan* 524: 1–34.

Haviland, William A. 1963. Excavations of Small Structures in the Northeast Quadrant of Tikal, Guatemala. Ph.D. dissertation, University of Pennsylvania. Ann Arbor: University Microfilms.

———. 1969. A New Population Estimate for Tikal, Guatemala. *American Antiquity* 34: 429–433.

———. 1970. Tikal, Guatemala, and Mesoamerican Urbanism. *World Archaeology* 2: 186–197.

———. 1972. Family Size, Prehistoric Population Estimates, and the Ancient Maya. *American Antiquity* 37: 135–139.

Hayden, B., ed. 1979. *Lithic Use-Wear Analysis*. New York: Academic Press.

——— and J. Kamminga. 1979. An Introduction of Use-Wear: The First CLUW. In *Lithic Use-Wear Analysis*, B. Hayden, ed., pp. 1–14. New York: Academic Press.

Healy, Paul F., C. van Waarden, and J. J. Anderson. 1980. Nueva evidencia de antiguas terrazas mayas en Bélice. *América Indígena* 40: 733–796.

Hellmuth, Nicholas. 1977. Cholti-Lacandon (Chiapas) and Petén-Ytza Agriculture, Settlement Pattern, and Population. In *Social Process in Maya Prehistory*, N. Hammond, ed., pp. 421–448. New York: Academic Press.

Hester, Thomas R. 1976. Belize Lithics: Forms and Functions. In *Maya Lithic Studies: Papers from the 1976 Belize Field Symposium*, T. R. Hester and N. Hammond, eds., pp. 11–20. Center for Archaeological Research, Special Report 4. University of Texas at San Antonio.

———, ed. 1979. *The Colha Project, 1979: A Collection of Interim Papers*. Center for Archaeological Research, University of Texas at San Antonio.

———. 1980. 1980 Season at Colha, Belize: An Overview. In *The Colha Project: Second Season, 1980 Interim Report*, T. R. Hester, J. D. Eaton, and H. J. Shafer, eds., pp. 1–14. Center for Archaeological Research, University of Texas at San Antonio, and Centro Studi e Ricerche Ligabue, Venice.

———, Jack D. Eaton, and Harry J. Shafer, eds. 1980. *The Colha Project: Second Season, 1980 Interim Report*. Center for Archaeological Research, University of Texas at San Antonio, and Centro Studi e Ricerche Ligabue, Venice.

———— and Norman Hammond, eds. 1976. *Maya Lithic Studies: Papers from the 1976 Belize Field Symposium.* Center for Archaeological Research, Special Report 4. University of Texas at San Antonio.

————, R. N. Jack, and R. F. Heizer. 1978. The Obsidian of Tres Zapotes, Veracruz, Mexico. In *Archaeological Studies of Mesoamerican Obsidian*, T. R. Hester, ed., pp. 36–99. New Mexico: Ballena Press.

High, L. R., Jr. 1975. Geomorphology and Sedimentology of Holocene Coastal Deposits, Belize. In *Belize Shelf-Carbonate Sediments, Clastic Sediments, and Ecology*, K. F. Wantland and W. C. Pusey, III, eds., pp. 53–96. American Association of Petroleum Geologists Studies in Geology 2. Tulsa.

Hills, Rodney C. 1970. The Determination of the Infiltration Capacity of Field Soils Using the Cylinder Infiltrometer. *Technical Bulletin of the British Geomorphological Research Group* 3.

Hinkley, A. A. 1920. Guatemala Mollusca. *Nautilus* 35: 37–55.

Houbrick, Richard S. 1974. Growth Studies on the Genus *Cerithium* (Gastropoda: Prosobranchia) with Notes on Ecology and Microhabitats. *Nautilus* 88: 14–27.

Hubendick, B. 1958. Factors Conditioning the Habitat of Freshwater Snails. *Bulletin of the World Health Organization* 18: 1072–1080.

————. 1962. Aspects of the Diversity of the Freshwater Fauna. *Oikos* 13: 249–261.

Ingram, William M., and Walter E. Heming. 1942. Food, Eggs and Young of the Carnivorous Snail *Euglandina rosea* (Ferussas). *Zoologica* 27: 81–84.

Instituto Geográfico Nacional. 1970. Geologic Map of the Republic of Guatemala. Guatemala City.

Jensen, H. I. 1911. The Nature and Origin of the Gilgai Country. *Journal of the Proceedings of the Royal Society of New South Wales* 45: 337–385.

Kamminga, J. 1979. The Nature of Use-Polish and Abrasive Smoothing on Stone Tools. In *Lithic Use-Wear Analysis*, B. Hayden, ed., pp. 143–147. New York: Academic Press.

Keeley, L. H. 1977. The Functions of Paleolithic Flint Tools. *Scientific American* 237: 108–126.

Kelly, T., F. Valdez, and T. R. Hester. 1979. Lithic Workshops in the Rockstone Pond Road #2 Area. In *The Colha Project, 1979: A Collection of Interim Papers*, T. R. Hester, ed., pp. 173–175. Center for Archaeological Research, University of Texas at San Antonio.

Kidder, A. V. 1947. *The Artifacts of Uaxactún, Guatemala.* Carnegie Institution of Washington Publication 576. Washington, D.C.

Killingley, John S. 1981. Seasonality of Mollusk Collecting Derived from O–18 Profiles of Midden Shells. *American Antiquity* 46: 152–158.

Kirke, C. M. St. G. 1980. Prehistoric Agriculture in the Belize River Valley. *World Archaeology* 2: 281–287.

Kosakowsky, Laura J. n.d. Formative Ceramic Variability at Cuello, Belize: A Preliminary Summary. Paper presented at the 45th annual meeting of the Society for American Archaeology, Philadelphia, 1980.

Lassen, Hans H. 1975. The Diversity of Freshwater Snails in View of the Equilibrium Theory of Island Biogeography. *Oecologia* 19: 1–8.

Laws, Derby W. 1961. Investigations of Swamp Soils from Tintal and Pinal Associations of Petén, Guatemala. *Wrightia* 2: 127–132.

Lundell, Cyrus L. 1934. Preliminary Sketch of the Phytogeography of the Yucatán Peninsula. In *Contributions to American Archaeology* 12, Carnegie Institution of Washington Publication 436. Washington, D.C.

———. 1937. *The Vegetation of Petén*. Carnegie Institution of Washington Publication 478. Washington, D.C.

———. 1938. Plants Probably Utilized by the Old Empire Maya of Petén and Adjacent Lowlands. *Papers of the Michigan Academy of Science, Arts, and Letters* 24: 37–56.

———. 1940. The 1936 Michigan-Carnegie Botanical Expedition to British Honduras. In *Botany of the Maya Area, Miscellaneous Paper* 14, Carnegie Institution of Washington Publication 522. Washington, D.C.

———. 1945. The Vegetation and Natural Resources of British Honduras. *Verdoorn* 1945: 270–273.

MacDonald, Roy C. 1979. Tower Karst Geomorphology in Belize. *Zeitschrift für Geomorphologie N.F.* 32: 35–45.

Maier, Elizabeth. 1979. *Chinampa tropical: Una primera evaluación*. Mexico City: Centro de Ecodesarrollo.

Malek, Emile A. 1969. Studies on "Tropicorbid" Snails (*Biomphalaria*: Planorbidae) from the Caribbean and Gulf of Mexico Areas, Including the Southern United States. *Malacologia* 7: 183–209.

Martens, Eduard von. 1890–1901. Land and Freshwater Mollusca. *Biologia Centrali-Americana, Zoologia* 9: 1–706.

Martin, P. S., and F. Plog. 1973. *The Archaeology of Arizona*. Garden City, N. Y.: Doubleday.

Martini, J. A. 1977. A Field Method for Soil Test Calibration—Developing Countries. *Soil Science* 123: 165–170.

Matheny, Ray T. 1976. Maya Lowland Hydraulic Systems. *Science* 193: 639–646.

Michels, J. W. 1976. Some Sociological Observations on Obsidian Production at Kaminuljuyu, Guatemala. In *Maya Lithic Studies: Papers from the 1976 Belize Field Symposium*, T. R. Hester and N. Hammond, eds., pp. 109–118. Center for Archaeological Research, Special Report 4. University of Texas at San Antonio.

Miksicek, Charles H., Robert McK. Bird, Barbara Pickersgill, Sara Donaghey, Juliette Cartwright, and Norman Hammond. 1981. Preclassic Lowland Maize from Cuello, Belize. *Nature* 289: 56–59.

Miller, Barry B. 1978. Nonmarine Molluscs in Quaternary Paleoecology. *Malacological Review* 11: 27–38.

Millon, René F. 1955. When Money Grew on Trees: A Study of Cacao in Ancient Mesoamerica. Ph.D. dissertation, Columbia University.

Minnis, Paul, and Steven LeBlanc. 1976. An Efficient, Inexpensive Arid Lands Flotation System. *American Antiquity* 41: 491–493.

Miranda, F. 1959. Estudios acerca de la vegetación. In *Los recursos naturales del sureste y su aprovechamiento,* E. Beltrán, ed., vol. 1, pp. 215–271. Mexico City: Instituto Mexicano de Recursos Naturales Renovables.

Moholy-Nagy, Hattula. 1978. The Utilization of *Pomacea* Snails at Tikal, Guatemala. *American Antiquity* 43: 65–73.

Murray, G. E., and A. E. Weidie, Jr. 1965. Regional Geologic Summary of Yucatán Peninsula. In *Guide Book, Field Trip to Peninsula of Yucatán,* G. E. Murray and A. E. Weidie, Jr., eds. pp. 5–51. New Orleans Geological Society.

National Academy of Sciences. 1975. *Underexploited Tropical Plants with Promising Value.* Washington, D.C.

———. 1976. *Making Aquatic Weeds Useful: Some Perspectives for Developing Countries.* Washington, D.C.

Nations, James D. 1979. Snail Shells and Maize Preparation: A Lacandon Maya Analogy. *American Antiquity* 44: 568–571.

Nemeth, K., K. Mengel, and H. Grimmeh. 1970. The Concentration of K, Ca and Mg in the Saturation Extract in Relation to Exchangeable K, Ca and Mg. *Soil Science* 109: 179–181.

Olson, Gerald W. 1969. Description and Data on Soils of Tikal, El Petén, Guatemala, Central America. Mimeo 69-2, Department of Agronomy, Cornell University.

———. 1970. Examples of Ancient and Modern Use and Abuse of Soils. In *Environmental Geomorphology and Landscape Conservation,* D. R. Coates, ed., vol. 1. Stroudsburg, Pa.: Dowden, Hutchinson, and Ross.

———. 1974. Field Report on Soils Sampled around San Antonio in Northern Belize (British Honduras). Mimeo 74-23, Department of Agronomy, Cornell University.

———. 1975. Study of Soils in the Sustaining Area around San Antonio in Northern Belize (British Honduras). Mimeo 75-1, Department of Agronomy, Cornell University.

———. 1977. Significance of Physical and Chemical Characteristics of Soils at the San Antonio Archaeological Site on the Río Hondo in Northern Belize. *Journal of Belizean Affairs* 5: 22–35.

Orozoco-Segovia, Alma D. L., and Stephen R. Gliessman. n.d. The *Marceño* in Flood-Prone Regions of Tabasco, Mexico. Paper presented at the 43rd International Congress of Americanists, Vancouver, 1979.

Ower, Leslie H. 1927. Features of British Honduras. *Geographical Journal* 70: 372–386.

———. 1928. Geology of British Honduras. *Journal of Geology* 36: 494–509.

———. 1929. *The Geology of British Honduras.* Belize: Clarion.

Pain, T. 1963. The *Pomacea flagellata* Complex in Central America. *Journal of Conchology* 25: 224–230.

Palacio, J. O. 1976. *Archaeology in Belize.* Belize: Cubola Productions.

Palerm, Angel. 1973. *Obras hidráulicas prehispánicas en el sistema lacustre del Valle de México.* Mexico City: Instituto Nacional de Antropología e Historia.

Parmalee, Paul W., and Walter E. Klippel. 1974. Freshwater Mussels as a Prehistoric Food Resource. *American Antiquity* 39: 421–434.

Parodiz, Juan José. 1979. Marine Mollusca Collected in Yucatán. *Pittsburgh Shell Club Bulletin* 1979: 1–20.

Parsons, Jeffrey R. 1976. The Role of Chinampa Agriculture in the Food Supply of Aztec Tenochtitlán. In *Cultural Change and Continuity*, C. E. Cleland, ed., pp. 233–257. New York: Academic Press.

Pasricha, N. S., and F. N. Ponnamperuma. 1977. $Na^+ - (Ca^{2+} + Mg^{2+})$ Exchange Equilibrium under Submerged Soil Conditions. *Soil Science* 123: 220–223.

—— and T. Singh. 1977. Ammonium Exchange Equilibria in the Submerged Soils and Forms of Ammonium Which Are Not Water-Soluble but Are Available to Lowland Paddy. *Soil Science* 124: 90–94.

Pennington, T. D., and José Sarukhan. 1968. *Manual para la identificación de campo de los principales árboles tropicales de México.* Mexico City: Instituto Nacional de Investigaciones Forestales, Secretaría de Agricultura y Ganadería.

Pilsbry, Henry A. 1891. Land and Fresh-Water Mollusks Collected in Yucatán and Mexico. *Proceedings of the Academy of Natural Sciences, Philadelphia* 1891: 310–334.

Portig, W. M. 1976. The Climate of Central America. In *Climates of Central and South America*, W. Schwerdtfeger, ed., pp. 405–478. Amsterdam: Elsevier.

Prescott, J. A. 1931. The Soils of Australia in Relation to Vegetation and Climate. *Australian Bulletin* 52. Canberra.

Price, Barbara J. 1977. Shifts in Production and Organization: A Cluster-Interaction Model. *Current Anthropology* 18: 209–233.

Pring, Duncan C. 1976. *Illustrations for Preclassic Ceramic Complexes, Northern Belize.* Centre of Latin American Studies, Cambridge University.

——. 1977a. The Preclassic Ceramics of Northern Belize. Ph.D. dissertation, Cambridge University.

——. 1977b. Influences or Intrusion? The Protoclassic in the Maya Lowlands. In *Social Process in Maya Prehistory: Studies in Memory of Sir Eric Thompson*, N. Hammond, ed., pp. 135–165. London: Academic Press.

Puleston, Dennis E. 1965. The Chultuns of Tikal. *Expedition* 7: 24–29.

——. 1974. Ancient Maya Settlement Patterns and Environment at Tikal, Guatemala: Implications for Subsistence Models, Ph.D. dissertation, University of Pennsylvania. Ann Arbor: University Microfilms.

——. 1977a. The Art and Archaeology of Hydraulic Agriculture in the Maya Lowlands. In *Social Process in Maya Prehistory: Studies in Memory of Sir Eric Thompson*, N. Hammond, ed., pp. 449–467. London: Academic Press.

——. 1977b. Experiments in Prehistoric Raised Field Agriculture: Learning from the Past. *Journal of Belizean Affairs* 5: 36–43.

——. 1978. Terracing, Raised Fields, and Tree Cropping in the Maya Lowlands: A New Perspective in the Geography of Power. In *Pre-Hispanic*

Maya Agriculture, P. D. Harrison and B. L. Turner II, eds., pp. 225–245. Albuquerque: University of New Mexico Press.

———— and Olga Stavrakis Puleston. 1971. An Ecological Approach to the Origins of Maya Civilization. *Archaeology* 24: 330–337.

Rathje, William L. 1975. The Last Tango in Mayapan: A Tentative Trajectory of Production-Distribution Systems. In *Ancient Civilizations and Trade*, J. A. Sabloff and C. C. Lambert-Karlovsky, eds., pp. 409–443. Albuquerque: University of New Mexico Press.

Record, Samuel J., and Robert W. Hess. 1942–1948. Keys to American Woods. *Tropical Woods* 72: 19–29 (1942), 73: 23–42 (1943), 75: 8–26 (1943), 76: 32–47 (1944), 85: 11–19 (1946), 94: 29–52 (1948).

Reddy, R., and N. H. Patrick, Jr. 1979. Nitrogen Fixation in Flooded Soil. *Soil Science* 128: 80–85.

Rees, W. J. 1965. The Aerial Dispersal of Mollusca. *Proceedings of the Malacological Society of London* 36: 369–382.

Rehder, Harold A. 1966. The Non-Marine Mollusks of Quintana Roo, Mexico, with the Description of a New Species of *Drymaeus* (Pulmonata: Bulimulidae). *Proceedings of the Biological Society of Washington* 79: 273–296.

Richards, Horace G., and H. J. Boekelman. 1937. Shells from Maya Excavations in British Honduras. *American Antiquity* 3: 166–169.

Richards, L. A., ed. 1954. *Diagnosis and Improvement of Saline and Alkali Soils*. United States Department of Agriculture Handbook 60. Washington, D.C.

Ricketson, Oliver G., and E. B. Ricketson. 1937. *Uaxactún, Guatemala: Group E, 1926–1931*. Carnegie Institution of Washington Publication 477. Washington, D.C.

Roemer, Erwin. 1980. Operation 2007: A Preliminary Report on the Excavations of a Late Classic Lithic Workshop. In *The Colha Project: Second Season, 1980 Interim Report*, T. R. Hester, J. D. Eaton, and H. J. Shafer, eds., pp. 87–104. Center for Archaeological Research, University of Texas at San Antonio, and Centro Studi e Ricerche Ligabue, Venice.

Sanchez, P. A., and S. W. Buol. 1975. Soils of the Tropics and the World Food Crisis. *Science* 188: 598–603.

Sanchez, W. A., and J. E. Kutzbach. 1974. Climate of the American Tropics and Subtropics in the 1960s and Possible Comparisons with Climatic Variations of the Last Millennium. *Quaternary Research* 4: 128–135.

Sanders, William T. 1973. The Cultural Ecology of the Lowland Maya: A Re-Evaluation. In *The Classic Maya Collapse*, T. P. Culbert, ed., pp. 325–366. Albuquerque: University of New Mexico Press.

————. 1976. The Agricultural History of the Basin of Mexico. In *The Valley of Mexico*, E. Wolf, ed., pp. 59–67. Albuquerque: University of New Mexico Press.

————. 1977. Environmental Heterogeneity and the Evolution of Lowland Maya Civilization. In *The Origins of Maya Civilization*, R. E. W. Adams, ed., pp. 287–297. Albuquerque: University of New Mexico Press.

————. 1979. The Jolly Green Giant in Tenth Century Yucatán, or Fact and Fancy in Classic Maya Agriculture. *Reviews in Anthropology* 6: 493–506.

————, Jeffrey R. Parsons, and R. S. Stanley. 1979. *The Basin of Mexico: Ecological Processes in the Evolution of a Civilization.* New York: Academic Press.

Sapper, Karl. 1899. Über Gebirgsbau und Boden des nördlichen Mittelamerika. *Petermanns Mitteilung* 27.

Schalie, Henry van der. 1940. Notes on Mollusca from Alta Vera Paz, Guatemala. *Occasional Papers of the Museum of Zoology, University of Michigan* 413: 1–11.

————. 1948. The Land and Freshwater Mollusks of Puerto Rico. *Miscellaneous Publications of the Museum of Zoology, University of Michigan* 70: 1–134.

Semenov, S. 1964. *Prehistoric Technology.* London: Cory Adams and MacKay.

Serpenti, L. M. 1965. *Cultivators in the Swamps: Social Structure and Horticulture in a New Guinea Society.* Assen: Royal van Gorlum.

Shackleton, Nicholas J. 1973. Oxygen Isotope Analysis as a Means of Determining Season of Occupation of Prehistoric Midden Sites. *Archaeometry* 15: 133–141.

Shafer, Harry J. 1973. Lithic Technology at the George C. Davis Site, Cherokee County, Texas. Ph.D. dissertation, University of Texas at Austin. Ann Arbor: University Microfilms.

————. 1976. Belize Lithics: "Orange Peel" Flakes and Adze Manufacture. In *Maya Lithic Studies: Papers from the 1976 Belize Field Symposium,* T. R. Hester and N. Hammond, eds., pp. 21–34. Center for Archaeological Research, Special Report 4. University of Texas at San Antonio.

————. 1979. A Study of Two Maya Lithic Workshops at Colha, Belize. In *The Colha Project, 1979: A Collection of Interim Papers,* T. R. Hester, ed., pp. 28–78. Center for Archaeological Research, University of Texas at San Antonio.

————. n.d. Lithic Artifacts from Petroglyph Cave, Belize. Manuscript on file at the Department of Anthropology, Texas A&M University.

———— and Thomas R. Hester. 1979. Lithic Research at Colha: An Overview. In *The Colha Project, 1979: A Collection of Interim Papers,* T. R. Hester, ed., pp. 18–27. Center for Archaeological Research, University of Texas at San Antonio.

————, Thomas R. Hester, and Thomas Kelly. n.d. An Analysis of Lithic Artifacts from Cuello, Belize. Manuscript on file at the Center for Archaeological Research, University of Texas at San Antonio.

———— and R. G. Holloway. 1979. Organic Residue Analysis in Determining Stone Tool Function. In *Lithic Use-Wear Analysis,* B. Hayden, ed., pp. 385–399. New York: Academic Press.

———— and F. Oglesby. 1980. Test Excavations in a Colha Debitage Mound: Operation 4001. In *The Colha Project: Second Season, 1980 Interim Report,* T. R. Hester, J. D. Eaton, and H. J. Shafer, eds., pp. 195–200.

Center for Archaeological Research, University of Texas at San Antonio, and Centro Studi e Ricerche Ligabue, Venice.

Sheets, Payson D. 1977. The Analysis of Chipped Stone Artifacts in Southern Mesoamerica. *Latin American Research Review* 12: 139–158.

———. 1978. A Model of Mesoamerican Obsidian Technology Based on Workshop Debris in El Salvador. In *Archaeological Studies of Mesoamerican Obsidian*, T. R. Hester, ed., pp. 159–170. New Mexico: Ballena Press.

Sidrys, R. 1980. Supply and Demand among the Classic Maya. *Current Anthropology* 20: 594–597.

——— and J. Kimberlin, n.d. Obsidian Sources and Izapan Influence at Yaxha, Guatemala. Manuscript on file at the Department of Anthropology, Texas A&M University.

Siemens, Alfred H. 1978. Karst and the Pre-Hispanic Maya in the Southern Lowlands. In *Pre-Hispanic Maya Agriculture*, P. D. Harrison and B. L. Turner II, eds., pp. 117–143. Albuquerque: University of New Mexico Press.

———. 1982. Pre-Hispanic Use of Wetlands in the Tropical Lowlands of Mesoamerica. In *Maya Subsistence: Studies in Memory of Dennis E. Puleston*, K. Flannery, ed., pp. 205–225. New York: Academic Press.

——— and Dennis E. Puleston. 1972. Ridged Fields and Associated Features in Southern Campeche: New Perspectives on the Lowland Maya. *American Antiquity* 37: 228–239.

Simmons, C. S., J. M. Tárano, and J. H. Pinto. 1958. *Clasificación de reconocimiento de los suelos de la República de Guatemala*. Guatemala City: Editorial del Ministerio de Educación Pública.

Smith, C. Earle, Jr. 1965. The Archaeological Record of Cultivated Crops of New World Origins. *Economic Botany* 19: 322–334.

Smith, Frank H., and Brian L. Gannon. 1973. Sectioning of Charcoals and Dry Ancient Woods. *American Antiquity* 38: 468–472.

Snyder, Noel F. R., and Helen A. Snyder. 1971. Defenses of the Florida Apple Snail *Pomacea paludosa*. *Behaviour* 40: 174–215.

Solem, Alan. 1956. The Helicoid Cyclophorid Mollusks of Mexico. *Proceedings of the Academy of Natural Sciences, Philadelphia* 108: 41–59.

Sparks, B. W. 1964. Non-Marine Mollusca and Quaternary Ecology. *Journal of Animal Ecology* 33: 87–98.

Standley, P. C., and S. J. Record. 1936. *The Forests and Flora of British Honduras*. Field Museum of Natural History Publication 350. Chicago.

Stephen, I., E. Bellis, and A. Muir. 1956. Gilgai Phenomena in Tropical Black Clays of Kenya. *Journal of Soil Science* 7: 1–9.

Stevens, Rayfred L. 1964. The Soils of Middle America and Their Relation to Indian Peoples and Cultures. In *Handbook of Middle American Indians*, R. C. West, ed., vol. 1, pp. 265–315. Austin: University of Texas Press.

Stross, F. H., Thomas R. Hester, R. F. Heizer, and R. N. Jack. 1976. Chemical and Archaeological Studies of Mesoamerican Obsidians. In *Advances in Obsidian Glass Studies—Archaeological and Geochemical Perspec-*

tives, R. E. Taylor, ed., pp. 240–258. Park Ridge, N.J.: Noyes Press.

Sturrock, R. F. 1974. Ecological Notes on Habitats of the Freshwater Snail *Biomphalaria glabrata*, Intermediate Host of *Schistosoma mansoni* on St. Lucia, West Indies. *Caribbean Journal of Science* 14: 149–160.

Thompson, Fred G. 1967. The Land and Freshwater Snails of Campeche. *Bulletin of the Florida State Museum* 11: 221–256.

Thompson, J. Eric S. 1974. "Canals" of the Río Candelaria Basin, Campeche, Mexico. In *Mesoamerican Archaeology: New Approaches*, N. Hammond, ed., pp. 297–302. Austin: University of Texas Press.

Transportation Research Board. 1976. *State of the Art: Lime Stabilization*. Transportation Research Board Circular 180. Washington, D.C.

Tsirk, Are. 1979. Regarding Fracture Initiation. In *Lithic Use-Wear Analysis*, B. Hayden, ed., pp. 83–96. New York: Academic Press.

Tsukada, Matsuo, and Edward S. Deevey. 1967. Pollen Analyses from Four Lakes in the Southern Maya Area of Guatemala and El Salvador. In *Quaternary Paleoecology*, E. J. Cushing and H. E. Wright, Jr., eds., pp. 303–332. New Haven: Yale University Press.

Turner, B. L., II. 1974a. Prehistoric Intensive Agriculture in the Mayan Lowlands. *Science* 185: 118–124.

———. 1974b. Prehistoric Intensive Agriculture in the Mayan Lowlands: New Evidence from the Río Bec Zone. Ph.D. dissertation, University of Wisconsin-Madison. Ann Arbor: University Microfilms.

———. 1976. Prehistoric Population Density in the Maya Lowlands: New Evidence from Old Approaches. *Geographical Review* 66: 73–82.

———. 1978. Ancient Agricultural Land Use in the Central Maya Lowlands. In *Pre-Hispanic Maya Agriculture*, P. D. Harrison and B. L. Turner II, eds., pp. 163–183. Albuquerque: University of New Mexico Press.

———. 1979. Prehispanic Terracing in the Central Maya Lowlands: Problems of Agricultural Intensification. In *Maya Archaeology and Ethnohistory*, N. Hammond and G. R. Willey, eds., pp. 103–115. Austin: University of Texas Press.

———. 1980. La agricultura intensiva de trabajo en las tierras mayas. *América Indígena* 40: 653–670.

———. n.d.a. Agricultural Change in Prehistory: Subsistence to Non-Subsistence. Paper presented at the annual meeting of the Association of American Geographers, Los Angeles, 1981.

———. n.d.b. Agricultura y desarrollo del estado en las tierras mayas. *Estudios de Cultura Maya* 13 (in press).

———. n.d.c. Comparisons of Agrotechnologies in the Basin of Mexico and the Central Maya Lowlands: Formative to the Collapse of the Classic Maya. In *Interdisciplinary Approaches to the Study of Mesoamerican Highland-Lowland Interactions*, A. Miller, ed. Washington, D.C.: Dumbarton Oaks (in press).

———. n.d.d. Constructional Inputs for Major Agrosystems of the Ancient Maya. In *Drained Fields: History and Potential*, J. P. Darch and R. Smith, eds. British Archaeological Reports, Oxford University, Oxford (in press).

———, Robert Q. Hanham, and Anthony V. Portararo. 1977. Population Pressure and Agricultural Intensity. *Annals of the Association of American Geographers* 67: 384–396.

——— and Peter D. Harrison. 1978. Implications from Agriculture for Maya Prehistory. In *Pre-Hispanic Maya Agriculture*, P. D. Harrison and B. L. Turner II, eds., pp. 337–373. Albuquerque: University of New Mexico Press.

——— and ———. 1979. Comment on William T. Sanders' Review of *Pre-Hispanic Maya Agriculture*. *Reviews in Anthropology* 6: 544–555.

——— and ———. 1981. Prehistoric Raised-Field Agriculture in the Maya Lowlands. *Science* 213: 399–405.

——— and William C. Johnson. 1979. A Maya Dam in the Copán Valley, Honduras. *American Antiquity* 44: 299–305.

——— and Charles H. Miksicek. n.d. Economic Species Associated with Prehistoric Agriculture in the Maya Lowlands. Paper presented at the 13th International Botanical Congress, Sydney, 1981.

United States Commerce Department. *World Weather Records*. Washington, D.C.

United States Department of Agriculture. 1962. *Soil Survey Manual*. Handbook 18. Washington, D.C.

———. Soil Conservation Service. 1975. *Soil Taxonomy: A Basic System of Soil Classification for Making and Interpreting Soil Surveys*. Handbook 436. Washington, D.C.

Vermeij, Geerat J. 1978. *Biogeography and Adaptation*. Cambridge, Mass.: Harvard University Press.

——— and Alan P. Covich. 1978. Coevolution of Freshwater Gastropods and Their Predators. *American Naturalist* 112: 833–843.

Vivó Escoto, Jorge A. 1964. Weather and Climate of Mexico and Central America. In *Handbook of Middle American Indians*, R. C. West, ed., vol. 1, pp. 187–215. Austin: University of Texas Press.

Voorhies, Barbara. 1976. *The Chantulo People: An Archaic Period of the Chiapas Littoral, Mexico*. Papers of the New World Archaeological Foundation 41. Provo, Utah: Brigham Young University Press.

Waddell, Hakon. 1938. Physical-Geological Features of Petén, Guatemala. In *The Inscriptions of Petén*, by S. G. Morley, Carnegie Institution of Washington Publication 437, vol. 4. Washington, D.C.

Wagner, P. L. 1964. Natural Vegetation of Middle America. In *Handbook of Middle American Indians*, R. C. West, ed., vol. 1, pp. 216–264. Austin: University of Texas Press.

Walker, S. H. 1973. Summary of Climatic Records for Belize. Land Resources Division Supplementary Report 3. Surrey: Her Majesty's Stationery Office.

Wallen, C. C. 1955. Some Characteristics of Precipitation in Mexico. *Geografiska Annaler* 37: 51–85.

———. 1956. Fluctuations and Variability in Mexican Rainfall. *American Association for the Advancement of Science Publication* 43: 141–155.

Wefer, G., and J. S. Killingley. 1980. Growth Histories of Strombid Snails from Bermuda Recorded in Their O-18 and C-13 Profiles. *Marine Biology* 60: 129–135.

Wellhausen, E. J., Alejandro Fuentes O., Antonio Hernandez Corzo, and Paul C. Mangelsdorf. 1957. *Races of Maize in Central America*. National Academy of Sciences–National Research Council Publication 511. Washington, D.C.

West, Robert C. 1964. Surface Configuration and Associated Geology of Middle America. In *Handbook of Middle American Indians*, R. C. West, ed., vol. 1, pp. 33–83. Austin: University of Texas Press.

Wilk, Richard. 1978. Microscopic Examination of Chipped Flint and Obsidian. In *Excavations at Seibal, Department of Petén, Guatemala*, G. R. Willey, ed., pp. 139–145. Memoirs of the Peabody Museum 14. Cambridge, Mass.

———, Linda Reynolds, and Hal Wilhite, n.d. The Settlement Area Sampling Program at Cuello. Paper presented at the 45th annual meeting of the Society for American Archaeology, Philadelphia, 1980.

Wilken, Gene C. n.d.a. Mucks, Mucking and Soils of the Chinampas of Mexico. Paper presented at the 43rd International Congress of Americanists, Vancouver, 1979.

———. n.d.b. A Note on the Buoyancy of the "Floating Chinampas of Mexico." Paper presented at the 43rd International Congress of Americanists, Vancouver, 1979.

Willey, Gordon R. 1972. The Artifacts of Altar de Sacrificios. *Papers of the Peabody Museum of Archaeology and Ethnology* 64. Cambridge, Mass.

———, ed. 1978. *Excavations at Seibal, Department of Petén, Guatemala*. Memoirs of the Peabody Museum 14. Cambridge, Mass.

———, William R. Bullard, Jr., John B. Glass, and James C. Gifford. 1965. Prehistoric Maya Settlements in the Belize Valley. *Papers of the Peabody Museum of Archaeology and Ethnology* 54. Cambridge, Mass.

——— and Demitri B. Shimkin. 1973. The Maya Collapse: A Summary Review. In *The Classic Maya Collapse*, T. P. Culbert, ed., pp. 457–501. Albuquerque: University of New Mexico Press.

Wilson, Eugene. n.d. Physical Geography of the Yucatán Peninsula. Manuscript on file at the University of South Alabama, Mobile.

Wiseman, Frederick M. 1972. A Model for Increased Productivity in Lowland Milpa Agriculture. *Journal of the Arizona Academy of Sciences Proceedings* 7: 14.

———. 1978. Agricultural and Historical Ecology of the Maya Lowlands. In *Pre-Hispanic Maya Agriculture*, P. D. Harrison and B. L. Turner II, eds., pp. 63–115. Albuquerque: University of New Mexico Press.

———. n.d.a. Ecological and Archaeological Pollen Analysis at Copán, Honduras. In Habitat and Agriculture in the Río Copán Zone, by B. L. Turner II, W. C. Johnson, G. Mahood, F. M. Wiseman, B. L. Turner, and J. Poole, 1980 report to the Proyecto Arqueológico Copán, C. Baudez, director. On file with F. M. Wiseman, Louisiana State University.

———. n.d.b. Evidence for Preclassic Land Use at Komchen, Yucatán: The Pollen Evidence. In *Komchen*, E. W. Andrews V, ed., Middle American

Research Institute, Miscellaneous Series, Tulane University. New Orleans (in press).

———. n.d.c. Paleoecology and the Prehistoric Maya. M. S. thesis, University of Arizona.

Witthoft, J. 1967. Glazed Polish on Flint Tools. *American Antiquity* 32: 383–388.

Wood, W. R., and D. L. Johnson. 1978. A Survey of Disturbance Processes in Archaeological Site Formation. In *Advances in Archaeological Method and Theory*, M. B. Schiffer, ed., pp. 315–381. London: Academic Press.

Wright, A. C. S., D. H. Romney, R. H. Arbuckle, and V. E. Vial. 1959. *Land Use in British Honduras*. London: Her Majesty's Stationery Office.

Zeitlin, Robert N. 1978. Long-Distance Exchange and the Growth of a Regional Center: An Example from the Southern Isthmus of Tehuantepec, Mexico. In *Prehistoric Coastal Adaptations: The Economy and Ecology of Maritime Middle America*, B. L. Starks and B. Voorhies, eds., pp. 183–210. New York: Academic Press.

Zipser, E., and Geerat J. Vermeij. 1978. Crushing Behavior of Tropical and Temperate Crabs. *Journal of Experimental Biology* 31: 155–172.

Index